The Quality of Thought

The Quality of Thought

DAVID PITT

OXFORD
UNIVERSITY PRESS

Great Clarendon Street, Oxford, OX2 6DP,
United Kingdom

Oxford University Press is a department of the University of Oxford.
It furthers the University's objective of excellence in research, scholarship,
and education by publishing worldwide. Oxford is a registered trade mark of
Oxford University Press in the UK and in certain other countries

© David Pitt 2024

The moral rights of the author have been asserted

All rights reserved. No part of this publication may be reproduced, stored in
a retrieval system, or transmitted, in any form or by any means, without the
prior permission in writing of Oxford University Press, or as expressly permitted
by law, by licence or under terms agreed with the appropriate reprographics
rights organization. Enquiries concerning reproduction outside the scope of the
above should be sent to the Rights Department, Oxford University Press, at the
address above

You must not circulate this work in any other form
and you must impose this same condition on any acquirer

Published in the United States of America by Oxford University Press
198 Madison Avenue, New York, NY 10016, United States of America

British Library Cataloguing in Publication Data
Data available

Library of Congress Control Number: 2023942267

ISBN 978-0-19-878990-1

DOI: 10.1093/oso/9780198789901.001.0001

Printed and bound in the UK by
Clays Ltd, Elcograf S.p.A.

Links to third party websites are provided by Oxford in good faith and
for information only. Oxford disclaims any responsibility for the materials
contained in any third party website referenced in this work.

For Fred

Contents

Acknowledgments xi

Introduction 1
   I.1 Analytic Phenomenology 2
   I.2 A Plea for Agnosticism 7
   I.3 The Plan of the Book 13

1. Phenomenal Intentionality 19
   1.1 Causal-Informational-Teleological Theories of Conceptual Content 19
   1.2 Phenomenal Intentionality of Thought 24
   1.3 Phenomenal Intentionality of Perception 26
   1.4 Content Internalism 29
      1.4.1 Propositional Hallucination 31
      1.4.2 Propositional Illusion 34

2. The Experience of Thinking 37
   2.1 An Epistemological Argument for Propositional Phenomenology 37
   2.2 Knowing What It Is Like and Knowledge by Acquaintance 42
      2.2.1 Mary 44
          2.2.1.1 Retaining Acquaintance Knowledge 45
      2.2.2 Tye on Knowing What It Is Like 46
   2.3 Objections to the Epistemological Argument 48
      2.3.1 Reliable Mechanisms 48
      2.3.2 Extrospectionism 49
      2.3.3 Levine 54
   2.4 A Metaphysical Argument for Propositional Phenomenology 60
   2.5 Phenomenal Contrast Arguments 64
   2.6 Against Conceptual Phenomenology 67
      2.6.1 The Humean Objection (Cognitive Acuity) 67
      2.6.2 Carruthers and Veillet 69
      2.6.3 Tye and Wright 74
   2.7 Internal Worries 76
      2.7.1 The Matching Content Challenge 76
      2.7.2 Phenomenal Compositionality 79
      2.7.3 Complexity and Phenomenal Presence 83

3. Externalism 87
  3.1 Putnam 88
  3.2 Burge 91
    3.2.1 The Structure of the Argument and the Role of the
          Naturalness Intuition 92
    3.2.2 Objections 97
      3.2.2.1 The Principle of Charity 100
      3.2.2.2 Malaprops, Misnomers and Other Miscellaneous Mistakes . 104
    3.2.3 Anti-Individualism without the Principle and the Intuition? . 107
    3.2.4 Perceptual Anti-Individualism 109
    3.2.5 Externalism without Thought Experiments? 110
  3.3 Phenomenal Externalism, the Paraphenomenal Hypothesis 112

4. Indexical Thought 118
  4.1 What Is Thought 121
  4.2 Modality 125
  4.3 Understanding 131
  4.4 Attitude Reports 132
  4.5 Agreement and Disagreement 133
  4.6 Tautology, Contradiction, Analyticity and Antonymy 135
  4.7 Phenomenal Demonstratives 138

5. Thinking with Names 143
  5.1 Metalinguistic Descriptivism 144
    5.1.1 Kripke's Objections 150
      5.1.1.1 Modality 150
      5.1.1.2 Kneale 153
      5.1.1.3 Non-Circularity 154
      5.1.1.4 Ignorance and Error 155
    5.1.2 Back to Frege? 155
  5.2 Direct Reference, Rigidity and Necessity 155
  5.3 Kripke's Puzzles 165
  5.4 Determining Nominal Reference 167
  5.5 The Paratactic Theory of Nominal Concepts 169

6. Unconscious Thought 173
  6.1 Searle 174
  6.2 Strawson 176
  6.3 Horgan and Graham 178
  6.4 Kriegel 179
  6.5 Smithies 180
  6.6 Unconscious Phenomenology? 181
    6.6.1 Intrinsic Unconscious Phenomenology 182
      6.6.1.1 Blindsight 183
      6.6.1.2 Phenomenal Sorites 186
      6.6.1.3 The Mark of the Mental 192
    6.6.2 Unconscious Consciousness 193

6.7 Unconsciousness Contentlessness	195
6.7.1 The Causal Role of Content	199
6.8 Concluding Remarks	201
7. Conceptual Reference	203
Bibliography	213
Index	223

Acknowledgments

I am grateful to the U.S. Department of State, Bureau of Educational and Cultural Affairs, with the cooperation of the Hungarian-American Commission for Educational Exchange in Hungary and the Council for International Exchange of Scholars (CIES) in the United States, for a Fulbright research grant (#2214101) during the academic year 2014–2015, which supported research for this book. Thanks also to the Department of Philosophy and the Institute for Advanced Studies at Central European University, Budapest for their support and hospitality during this period.

I have discussed the issues addressed in this book with many philosophers over many years. The following people have had memorable effects on my thinking (in one way or another), for which I thank them: Adam Arico, Brandon Ashby, Jody Azouni, Kent Bach, Mark Balaguer, Tim Bayne, Ed Becker, Hanoch Ben-Yami, Sara Bernstein, Sharon Berry, Ned Block, Paul Boghossian, Davide Bordini, David Bourget, David Braun, Brit Brogaard, Richard Brown, Emma Bullock, Alex Bundy, Tyler Burge, Alex Byrne, David Chalmers, Phillipe Chuard, Eli Chudnoff, Sam Coleman, Arthur Collins, Tim Crane, Will Davies, Esa Diáz-León, Fred Dretske, Cormac Duffy, Marius Dumitru, Kati Farkas, Jerry Fodor, Rose Fonth, Martina Fürst, Manuel Garcia-Carpintero, Heather Gert, Brie Gertler, Philip Goff, Fred Goldstein, Laura Gow, Delia Graff Fara, David Miguel Gray, Nate Greely, Enrico Grube, Alex Grzankowski, Michael Hatcher, Jeff He, Chris Hill, Terry Horgan, Huo Huoranski, Marta Jorba, Jerry Katz, Amy Kind, Frank Kirkland, Ole Koksvik, Uriah Kriegel, Linda Lázár, Andrew Lee, Joe Levine, Brian Loar, Barry Loewer, Bill Lycan, Farid Masrour, Tom McClelland, Ron McIntyre, Brian McLaughlin, Angela Mendelovici, Michelle Montague, Jacob Naito, Bence Nanay, Lex Newman, Martine Nida-Rümelin, David Papineau, Adam Pautz, Jeffrey Poland, Péter Rauschenberger, Howard Robinson, William Robinson, David Rosenthal, Susanna Schellenberg, Stephen Schiffer, Tobias Schlicht, Anders Schoubye, Eric Schwitzgebel, Susanna Siegel, Charles Siewert, Jonathan Simon, Declan Smithies, Gianfranco Soldati, Maja Spener, Maarten Steenhagen, Galen Strawson, Pär Sundström, Henry Taylor, Amie Thomasson, Mark van Roojen, Adam Vinueza, Douglas Wadle, David Woodruff-Smith and Sara Worley.

I am grateful in particular to Joe Levine, Charles Siewert and Galen Strawson for comments on the Introduction, and to Joe Levine for challenging discussions that convinced me I should write Chapter 7.

Thanks as well to two anonymous referees for Oxford University Press for many penetrating observations, which (I hope) led to improvement of the manuscript, and to Peter Momtchiloff for his friendship, guidance and patience.

I owe special debts of gratitude to Tim Crane and Kati Farkas. It was Tim who convinced me that I could, and should, write this book, and he and Kati have been unwavering in their support and enthusiasm for the project. Kati's early interest in my work was especially encouraging. I am also beyond grateful to her for a magical year in Budapest.

I am deeply indebted as well to Galen Strawson for his warm support and encouragement over the years, especially at a time when my chances in the profession seemed slim, to Dave Chalmers for significantly improving them, and to Mark Balaguer for raising them to one.

My greatest debt, not specifically philosophical, is to my husband, Fred Goldstein, whose love and support for nearly thirty years have made my life possible.

Introduction

The main thesis of this book is that thinking is a kind of experience, characterized by a *sui generis* phenomenology, determinates of which are thought contents. This sort of phenomenology has been called "cognitive phenomenology" (Strawson 1986; Pitt 2004; Bayne and Montague 2011a; Chudnoff 2015b), though I now prefer "conceptual phenomenology" or "propositional phenomenology," since the term has come to be used to include a phenomenology of *belief* and other broadly cognitive states or processes. What I mean (and meant in Pitt 2004) by it is a phenomenology of thought *content*—what Strawson (1994) calls "understanding experience" (and what I think Searle (1992) means by "aspectual shape" (fine-grained intentional content that only conscious states can have)). Such phenomenology is relevant to the characterization of cognitive states and processes only insofar as those states or processes have conceptual content, or involve states that do. As I understand the term, cognitive phenomenology entails nothing about the phenomenology of cognitive *attitudes* or *processes per se*. It is a proprietary phenomenology of pure thought—the mere entertainment, or grasping, of a proposition.

This thesis, which I call the *phenomenal intentionality of thought thesis*, goes very much against the grain of naturalistic theorizing about the nature and determination of conceptual content. Not only is it resolutely internalist; it also grounds conceptual intentional content in qualitative experience, which remains stubbornly resistant to naturalistic explanation. Jerry Fodor went so far as to pronounce commitment to an essential link between intentionality and experience "intellectual suicide."[1] But I think the facts about intentionality that we know from the first-person perspective—which are (like all subjective facts) *phenomenal* facts—are more secure than a commitment to naturalism. And they are, I maintain, the very foundation of conceptual intentionality; so no account of it that leaves them out can be adequate.[2] If phenomenal facts cannot be reductively explained, we should rather set aside naturalist ambitions and pursue an approach to the study of experience in general that I call "Analytic Phenomenology." Moreover, given the persistent failure of both philosophy and science to explain

---

[1] I am not aware of this remark appearing in print. I heard Fodor make it, and Strawson reports it in his 2008.
[2] The book is thus a chapter in what has come to be called the Phenomenal Intentionality Research Program (Kriegel 2013), which maintains that both perceptual and conceptual intentionality are phenomenally constituted.

the relation between experience and physical reality, I think the proper attitude to take toward the mind-body problem is agnosticism.

We can, and should, study experience from the first-person perspective, while remaining noncommittal on the nature of its connection to the non-experiential.

I.1 Analytic Phenomenology

Husserlian Phenomenology sets aside ("brackets") the question of the existence of a mind-independent world and its relation to our experience in order to focus on experience itself, as we have it, from the first-person perspective. Husserl's motivation for doing this was, at least in part, to avoid the vexed epistemological issues that plagued philosophers from Descartes to Kant. What I am calling Analytic Phenomenology sets aside the problematic relation between experience and the brain, in order to study experience independently of the vexed metaphysical issues that have long plagued analytic philosophers of mind. This Phenomenology is *analytic* because it brings the ethos and methodology of analytic philosophy to bear on the study of experience *per se*. It is *Phenomenology* because it is the study of experience from the first-person perspective. (Though its ambitions are far more modest than those of Husserl, Heidegger, Sartre or Merleau-Ponty and their followers. It is not intended to be a foundation for philosophy in general.) It is to be distinguished from the study of Husserl and the extensions of his ideas pursued by such contemporary analytically inclined philosophers as Hubert Dreyfus, Dagfinn Føllesdal, David Woodruff-Smith and Dan Zahavi. It rather finds inspiration in dissatisfaction with the treatment of experience by analytic philosophy of mind, which it sees as having been traditionally too narrowly focused on mind-body metaphysics, for not especially good reasons. And it finds in the work of the Phenomenologists an example of how to pursue a disciplined philosophical study of experience independently of reductivist and naturalist scruples.[3]

While not denying the interest or significance of the mind-body problem, Analytic Phenomenology insists that an explanation of what experience (by which I mean, paradigmatically, episodes of phenomenal consciousness) has to do with the electrochemical activity in the brain that occasions it is not the only, or indeed the most important, profitable, or interesting goal for philosophers of mind to pursue. From the perspective of Analytic Phenomenology, whether or not experience can be naturalistically explained, either by science or philosophy, is a

---

[3] It is thus very much of a piece with Charles Siewert's project of the same name, as described in his "For Analytic Phenomenology" (Siewert 2016). This paper includes an exemplary application of Analytic Phenomenological principles and methods to controversy over the scope and reliability of introspection. Though Siewert's stated motivations are different from those elaborated here, I think we are in agreement with respect to what we mean by 'analytic phenomenology'—what makes it *phenomenology*, and what makes it *analytic*.

question best set aside (at least for the time being). Experience, whatever it is, and whatever its precise relation to neural activity, undeniably exists. We are directly and indubitably aware of its existence in having it. We cannot tell whether it is a physical phenomenon or not from the first-person perspective—though it certainly *seems* to be something radically different from everything else that gets called "physical"; but we do not need to know this in order to investigate it on its own terms. We can come to understand a great deal about it by studying it from the subjective point of view—not in the bare sense of knowing what *kind* of thing it is, but in the richer sense of knowing its varieties, its structures, its scope, etc., and its role in the constitution of human mentality in general.

Analytic Phenomenology sees the assumption that experience *must* be ultimately explicable in naturalistic terms—e.g., those of neuroscience, and, ultimately, present physics, or some conservative extension of it, and the ceding of ultimate ontological and methodological authority in the study of the conscious mind to empirical science, as an impediment to productive research. (In this it perhaps shares another of Husserl's motivations.) Even in the unlikely event that neuroscientists were to figure out how neurochemical activity in the brain brings about conscious experience, it would not be the case that *only then* would we have come to understand it, because only then would we have determined what it *really* is. In an important sense we already know what it really is, independently of anything we know about the brain. And we would not *only then* have validated experience as a respectable phenomenon, worthy, like chemical and biological phenomena, of its own serious, independent field of inquiry.

Indeed, chemistry and biology would be perfectly legitimate sciences even if reality had turned out to be structured in the way the British Emergentists thought it was. Ultimate reducibility to basic physics cannot be *a priori* assumed to be the fundamental principle of ontological legitimacy, or the fundamental condition of adequacy on explanation, of *any* phenomenon (cf. Crane and Mellor 1990). And even if past experience has confirmed this principle, the evidence is only inductive, and the conclusion can be called into question by recalcitrant phenomena. We must, in the first place, take things as we find them. Perhaps one day we will have stopped discovering new things, and everything will have been shown to be reducible to, or to *superdupervene* (Horgan 1993) on, or be grounded in, basic physics as presently understood (or conservatively extended). But we should not assume that this *must* happen, and we should not let such an assumption determine in advance what can count as really real, or what is a genuinely scientific hypothesis, or what kind of methodology is legitimate. We cannot know if physicalism, the view that everything in the universe is unified under one basic kind, the general nature of which physics has already given us a basic grasp of, is true until we finish explaining everything.[4]

---

[4] David Papineau (2002: Appendix) argues that the causal completeness of physics entails that physicalism must be true. But his argument depends upon the premise that there is empirical evidence

I do not think even physicists assume that physicalism in this sense is, or must be, true. Newton made a non-conservative leap when he introduced gravitational force as physically fundamental. Quantum mechanics has shown how far theoretical physicists are prepared to go in order to accommodate evidence. And contemporary cosmology has posited things the existence of which cannot, in principle, be confirmed by any possible observation. No physicist should balk at the possibility that the best explanation for some phenomenon might be in terms of previously "non-physical" objects or properties. And philosophers should adopt this attitude as well. (David Chalmers's Naturalistic Dualism (Chalmers 1996, 2017) does just this, though Chalmers is still focused on the relationship between consciousness and the physical world.) I suspect that philosophers of mind who assume physical explanation as a criterion of adequacy on an account of experience are so impressed (or embarrassed) by the successes of empirical science (e.g., in reducing biology to chemistry, and chemistry to physics, and in effectively explaining and predicting so many observable phenomena) that they think only empirical science can give us substantive knowledge about the mind (or anything else), and, hence, that philosophy should take a back seat to it. Or get off the bus entirely. This might lead someone to insist (à la Fodor 1987: 97), that if experience is something real, it must really be *something else*—in particular, something ultimately physical—just like all the other real phenomena out there; just like science tells us.

But I think this is bad philosophy of science, and that we are better off putting the assumption aside when doing philosophy of mind. We have the phenomenon itself, right above our noses; and we have a basically sound and refinable introspective methodology (see again Siewert 2016). Philosophers should neither wait upon science to explain how experience is just another physical phenomenon nor cleave to its methodology and results in search of legitimacy. What they need to do, Analytic Phenomenology recommends, is to stop obsessing over ontology and worrying about empirical science, and learn to love experience as we have it—*whatever* it turns out to be.

Beyond promoting a narrow focus on the mind-body problem in particular, naturalistic demands, whether explicitly stated or tacitly assumed, can have a limiting influence on the study of experience generally. Like the principle of *psychological* reality in theoretical linguistics, the principle of *physical* reality (i.e., explicability, ultimately, in the terms of physics) as a criterion of adequacy in analytic philosophy of mind unnecessarily narrows the range of available

that everything that needs to be explained has been shown to have a physical explanation. He cites the gradual abandonment of Vitalism (and other views postulating "special (fundamental) forces") as due to accumulating physiological evidence that biological phenomena had explanations in terms of inanimate physical forces. But I think this sort of argument fails in the case of consciousness, since the relevant physiological evidence is simply not there, and it is, moreover, hard to see how there *could be* such evidence.

theoretical options, and creates a climate of intellectual intimidation. Adherence to dogmatic methodological naturalism, with its constant threat of theoretical delegitimization, has led to counterproductivity and stagnation, and encouraged absurd, Procrustean views of mentality (e.g., logical behaviorism and illusionism). And overenthusiasm regarding over advances in neuroscience, brilliant as they are, has brought us a host of what seem to me to be category-mistaken proposals identifying consciousness with various informational states, functions, interfaces, configurations, and the like.

Now, in advocating for a metaphysically detached first-person methodology for the study of experience, I do not mean to suggest that our intimacy with it and certainty of its existence entail either easy omniscience or infallibility with respect to our judgments about it. It might be quite difficult in some cases, due to limitations of memory, attention or conceptual resources, for example, to state precisely what the experiential facts are. Phenomenology is not easy. Those who impugn introspection-based methodology (e.g., Schwitzgebel 2011) seem to be assuming that introspective judgment must be omniscient and infallible if it is to be at all reliable. I suspect the view that it is, which many philosophers once held, is encouraged by the fact that when it comes to experience, appearing is being. If an experience cannot be other than it appears to be, one might hastily conclude that we cannot be wrong about what it is, what its properties are, etc. But this does not follow—any more than it follows from the fact that mathematical truths are necessary that we cannot make mistaken judgments about them. Judgments and the experiences they are about are distinct existences; there are no necessary connections between them (*pace*, e.g., Chalmers 2003). Carelessness, insufficient attention and unrealistic expectations can come between them, and must be guarded against.

Nor do I mean to suggest that Analytic Phenomenology is the only path for a philosopher of mind to take after turning away from mind-body metaphysics, or to deny the relevance or usefulness of empirical methodology to the study of mind in general. Recent work in the philosophy of perception (e.g., Burge 2010, 2022; Chudnoff 2021; Block 2023) is a good example of how philosophers can engage deeply with empirical psychology, which typically does not pronounce on mind-body metaphysics, and is not concerned with explaining consciousness *per se*. Compare Block (2023: 16):

> ...throughout most of this book, I will be concerned with perception rather than conscious perception. The border I am talking about is the border between perception – whether conscious or unconscious – and cognition – whether conscious or unconscious. In part, this focus stems from the perception literature.... Much of the experimental work on perception and cognition does not address the issue of whether the effects are conscious or unconscious.

And Burge (2022: 6):

> This book focuses on representation, not consciousness. I take perceptual representation to be a basic mark of mind and a mark of nature's mind-mindless joint. This view does not compete with the idea that consciousness is also a basic mark of mind. There may be two joints in nature between minds and the mindless.... I focus on the first mark of mind – representation. Vastly more is known about it. The science of consciousness is in its gestation stage. The science of perceptual representation is in its early maturity.

Empirical work obviously contributes to our understanding of certain structural features of conscious experience. And in some cases the methods of such sciences may be the best or most efficient way to answer questions that resist introspective resolution. (Whether or not visual shape constancy is a sensory or conceptual phenomenon (Pitt 2009: 125–7) and whether or not higher-order properties are presented in perceptual phenomenology (Chudnoff 2021) are examples.) Further, empirical psychology can play a role in making introspection more disciplined, insofar as it offers methods that enable us to focus attention in the right places, to filter out extraneous features in specific perceptual situations, to identify and avoid false assumptions and misguided tendencies in the practice of introspective inquiry, and so on. Phenomenology (critical first-person reflection on experience) can do a lot more than it is too often given credit for (Siewert 2016), but, as I said, it is not easy, and there is no shame in getting empirical help when it is available.

Still, introspection is, I would argue, where we begin the study of the mind. Indeed, we only know there is such a thing from the first-person perspective. Analytic Phenomenology insists that empirical study of the brain and central nervous system is neither the starting point nor the *sine qua non* of the study of experience. It is, rather, the other way around. Disciplined introspection sets the tasks for neuroscience and psychology, not vice versa. Empirical work is relevant only insofar as it can help us understand what we already have direct, subjective access to. Neuroscience is not, *per se*, a science of consciousness.[5] And even if there were introspectively unanswerable questions about experience, it would not follow that introspection is a methodologically second-rate, antiquated instrument that should be traded in for shiny new appliances like fMRI machines, PET scanners, and the like. Still less would it follow that what it is supposed to give us access to does not really exist, or is really something else, because it is not directly empirically measurable. If we abandon or demote the first-person perspective we will not come to understand experience, because in doing so we will abandon or demote the very thing we are trying to understand (a point well made by

---

[5] And neither is cognitive science. The "easy" problems of consciousness are not problems of *consciousness*.

Thomas Nagel (Nagel 1974)). The foundational methodology for the study of the conscious mind is disciplined introspection, careful first-person reflection and theory construction—i.e., Phenomenology.

Moreover, and most importantly, there are, I would argue, fundamental facts about conscious experience that are only discoverable *a priori*—for example, the *Phenomenality Principle*, and its corollaries the *Principle of Phenomenal Difference* and the *Principle of Phenomenal Individuation* (defined and applied in Chapter 2), the *Principle of Phenomenal Immiscibility* (defined and applied in Chapter 4) and the *Principle of Phenomenal Purity* (defined and applied in Chapters 4 and 5). The discovery, exploration and application of such facts is the proprietary business of Analytic Phenomenology, to which this book is a contribution.

I.2 A Plea for Agnosticism

The mind-body problem persists, even as philosophers of mind turn their attention to empirically tractable questions about non-conscious perception and cognition, or sign up for Analytic Phenomenology. Physicalist (naturalist, reductionist) ambitions also persist, if sometimes only in the background, in spite of the persistent failure of philosophers to make good on their ambition of solving the puzzle of conscious experience, by providing a reductive explanation of it, ignoring it entirely, or otherwise trying to deproblematize it. Some have tried to identify it with something else—a brain process, a higher- or lower-order functional property, a representational relation to things in the external world, availability for use in reasoning and rational guidance of speech and action (so-called "access consciousness," which is so often wrongly taken to be a kind of *consciousness*, which it was never intended by Block to be), all of which strike me as category mistakes. But these views are really forms of *eliminativism* about experience (cf. Chalmers 2010a: 111). Some have maintained that only *behavioral dispositions* are psychological, or recommended that we simply stop *talking about it*, or diminish its importance by claiming that it does not *do* anything. But ignoring it does not make it go away. Some have even been perverse enough to flatly deny its existence altogether.

And there are those who think that experience only seems puzzling because we do not yet know enough about the human nervous system, especially the brain, and how it works. They argue that once we do, the philosopher's mind-body problem will go the way of the Vitalists' life-body problem, or the Emergentists' chemical-physical problem (see, e.g., Broad 1925: 62–7), which were dissolved by molecular biology and quantum mechanics, respectively. *Prima facie*, this seems a reasonable thing to think. Past experience has shown that bewilderment and intuitions of impossibility can be rooted in ignorance. The magical becomes mundane once we know how the trick is done. But closer examination of what neuroscience has discovered suggests that illumination is not forthcoming. In spite of the overwhelming evidence that experience is occasioned by neural activity, no one has the slightest idea how this is possible, much less an explanation of how it actually happens. We have correlations, but no understanding of what the correlated phenomena could possibly have to do with each other. For all the astonishing achievements of the sciences of the brain, the organs of sensation, and their connections, we are no closer to understanding what any of them have to do with experience, beyond brute correlation. Indeed, the more detail neuroscience reveals, the more ridiculous the whole thing seems.

It is worth taking a short detour to have a look at some of these revelations.

The "language" of the brain is *action potentials*—differences in electrical charge across neuronal membranes that are propagated from one neuron to another, either directly or via the intervention of neurotransmitters (amino acids, peptides and other complex chemicals). This propagation of action potentials is a virtual electrical current. (The current is *virtual* because it does not involve the flow of negatively charged particles along the cell membrane but, rather, successive depolarization and repolarization of adjacent sections of it. Different concentrations of positive and negative ions and proteins inside and outside a resting neuron result in an overall positive charge outside and negative charge inside. Depolarization occurs when ion channels in the membrane open, allowing influx and efflux of charged particles, which results in a reversal of polarity to negative outside and positive inside. Depolarization of one section of membrane causes depolarization of the next, as the first resets to its resting state.)

Our sensory organs respond to external stimuli (photons, compression waves, chemicals, pressure, temperature) by producing action potentials, which are propagated along various neural pathways to different parts of the brain, where further neural activity occasions the different kinds of experience we have.

But neuroscience offers no explanation of why such electrochemical activity in the brain occasions conscious experience at all, or, even more confoundingly, why activity in different parts of the brain occasions the radically different kinds of experiences we have. Differences in neural activity within the brain seem to amount to no more than differences in location, frequency and pattern. Action potentials generated in bipolar cells in the retina are propagated along pathways that end up *here*, from the hair cells in the inner ear *here*, from the mitral and tufted cells in the olfactory bulb *there*, etc. (the various sensory cortices), where they cause further action potentials. But why should *where* the neurons are firing have anything to do with the qualitative differences among visual, auditory, olfactory, etc. experience? The firings are all the same; and any patterns of such firings within the brain are just patterns of occurrence of these electrochemical reactions. How could differences in rate or speed of current flow explain the profound and incommensurable qualitative differences between visual, auditory and olfactory experience? Even if experiences of different kinds could be pegged to, say, different ranges of frequency, with the language of action potentials being some kind of *code*, the question of why an experience of a particular kind, or any experience at all, arises from this or that coded "message" remains. (Neuroscientists often talk about the brain "interpreting" and "deciding" things, but these can only be metaphors.)

Nor can the variety of sensory experiences be explained by appeal to the various kinds of stimuli our sense organs are sensitive to. The receptors in our sensory organs are *transducers*, whose essential function is to respond to different kinds of stimuli by producing the same kind of response: action potentials.[6] The distinguishing characteristic features of external stimuli are eliminated in the process of transduction. No trace of them survives transduction into action potentials, which can differ only with respect to their frequency and velocity. Sensory transduction can get very complicated—as, for example, in the "phototransduction cascade," the formidably complex process whereby the impact of a photon on a molecule in a retinal receptor (a rod or a cone) results in the production of an action potential in a bipolar cell; or the equally baroque (but beautiful!) process by which the impact of lateral compression waves in the air on the eardrum results in the generation of action potentials in the hair cells in the organ of Corti. But action potentials are action potentials—the same for any neuron: momentary changes in electrical potential across cell membranes due to the influx and efflux of ions. Our sensory receptors are like doorbells: they produce the same kind of response no matter who is on the porch.

Nor can we appeal to differences in intrinsic properties of neurotransmitters to account for experiential differences. Differences in chemical composition and structure seem as unrelated to experiential differences as differences in current flow. And distinctive features of different kinds of neurotransmitters suffer the same fate as distinctive features of different kinds of external stimuli. Receptor proteins in post-synaptic neurons are also transducers, responding in the same kinds of ways (promotion and inhibition of action potentials) irrespective of the intrinsic properties of neurotransmitters. More doorbells.

Neuroscience has not provided any information that would help us understand how conscious experience is occasioned by neural activity. And it is very hard to see how more of the same, further details along the same lines (concerning, for example, wave-function collapses in nanotubules), will get us anywhere. (Going small, we ought to have learned from Descartes, does not make metaphysical problems go away.) Nor does zooming out to look at large-scale patterns

---

[6] It is common, at least in nontechnical contexts, to speak of impinging stimuli being "transformed" or "converted" into action potentials. This is, of course, impossible, and so not what really happens. A receptor responds to inputs of one kind by producing outputs of a different kind. Stimuli are no more transformed into action potentials by receptors than cash is transformed into snacks by vending machines.

of neural firing seem promising. How could such patterns *explain* consciousness and all of its splendid varieties?

The best neuroscience can do for consciousness is to determine (and not without the help of disciplined introspection!) its neural correlates. (Though there may be reasons to doubt it can do even this. See Kriegel 2020.) But, obviously, correlation is not explanation. So we should not wait upon advances in neuroscience to solve the puzzle of experience.

Other philosophers have tried to take the problem out of the mind-body problem by showing that our anxiety and puzzlement are born of misguided assumptions about our knowledge of the physical world, and that proper philosophical treatment will resolve our inner conflicts. Galen Strawson, for prominent example, sees the problematization of consciousness as a fundamental mistake, grounded in the belief, allegedly debunked by Russell, that physics has told or can tell us everything there is to know about matter. (See, e.g., Strawson 2015; 2019.) On the contrary, as Russell urged, physics only tells us about extrinsic, relational properties of matter—how bits of it behave and interact with each other in various situations. It says nothing about its intrinsic nature. It does not tell us what it *is*.[7] Hence, it tells us nothing that justifies the conclusion that materiality is radically incompatible with experientiality, or the conviction that the existence of consciousness is surprising or mysterious. Strawson rejects any notion of the material or the physical that conceives of it in this way, and insists that such terms as 'materialism' and 'naturalism' be freed from their twentieth-century scientistic bondage and restored to their rightful employment, as names for the view that everything that exists in space–time, including conscious experience, is material and natural.

However, Strawson's view—his version of panpsychism—still accepts a distinction between the qualitative properties that characterize experience, and which constitute the intrinsic nature of matter (its *creamy center*, as it were), and the relational properties in terms of which physics characterizes it (its *crispy shell*). It is therefore still engaged in the kind of metaphysics that Analytic Phenomenology urges philosophers to drop. It is concerned, fundamentally and primarily, with providing an account of how experience fits into a world that physics can accurately (if only incompletely) describe, and in the end it does not afford relief from metaphysical anxiety. Even if we accept that conscious experience is a wholly and unproblematically material phenomenon, it is still different from the *non-experiential* material phenomena and properties physics tells us about—electromagnetism, mass, gravity, charge, spin, cause and effect, space–time. (Or should we declare that these are unreal? What would justify this? It is not

---

[7] I am not convinced that physics *cannot*, in principle, tell us anything about the intrinsic nature of matter and its properties—that is, that it cannot discover, or postulate, intrinsic non-experiential properties.

like physics tells us *nothing* about reality. And if we insist that these properties are experiential, why think physics tells us nothing about the nature of consciousness?) Strawson thinks the relation between them cannot be explained by either science or philosophy, and that panpsychism is "just the empirically/scientifically most plausible – least-worst – position. It's where the best metaphysical/philosophical discussion stops"; "it can offer nothing in the way of a 'research program'" (personal communication). But then panpsychism just seems to lead us to the same metaphysical dead end. It might take us down a new and more enlightened path, and it may take us farther than other attempts; but it leaves us no closer to an answer to the question with which it begins, viz., how experiential and non-experiential reality are, or even could be, related.

Strawson urges that full understanding and embrace of his ecumenical materialism will deliver us from the illusion that matter and consciousness are deeply incommensurable, and bring us metaphysical peace. We will stop seeing the existence of experience as in any way problematic if only we meditate upon proper principles. But accepting that experience is a thoroughly material phenomenon—i.e., that it has a natural home in the natural world—does not make it seem any less puzzling that it lives in the house that physics built (or, conversely, that physics lives in the house that experience built—though this still leaves the cohabitation unexplained).

Bewilderment about consciousness does not arise from the study of physics or chemistry or neuroscience. It arises from the simple, untutored recognition of the difference between experience/experiencing things and non-experience/non-experiencing things—between, as it might be, oneself and a stick, or one's pain and the cracking of a stone. Why can sticks and stones not *hurt*? To be informed, and to accept, that these things are at bottom all of the same kind, made of the same stuff, is not to understand how it is possible. Nor does it help to be told that certain configurations of matter are conscious like us, while others are not. Why should it be that *this* configuration of matter is conscious, while *that* one is not? Strawson's materialism recasts the mind-body problem as the equally vexing experiential/non-experiential problem, which, admittedly, it does not solve.

Strawson suggests that we meditate our way into seeing that this is not a *problem*. Perhaps we should simply accept it with natural piety. So, while I advocate agnosticism, he seems to advocate quietism. Either way, however, one might still wonder what, if anything, is left for philosophers of mind to do.

Neither science nor philosophy has shown us how experience could be, or depend upon, non-experiential reality. But neither, on the other hand, has philosophy succeeded in establishing that experience is *not* a physical phenomenon. Philosophers from Descartes to Chalmers have argued that consciousness cannot be physical because consciousness without bodies like ours, or bodies like ours without consciousness, are conceivable, and, hence, possible. But I think these arguments are haunted by the possibility that the conceivability of such states of affairs is due to our ignorance, and that the gap between consciousness and material reality is epistemic, or explanatory, not ontological (Levine 1983)—even if it remains unbridgeable by us. Once upon a time, physically identical beings with and without life were conceivable, but it turned out that this was only due to our limited knowledge, and an impoverished conceptual repertoire. Now, physically identical beings one of which is alive and one of which is dead are inconceivable.

And there is the further nagging problem of understanding how consciousness, if it is not physical, could influence and be influenced by physical states of our bodies. If conscious experiences are not physical phenomena, how could physical phenomena be responsible for their occurrence? And how could they be responsible for the occurrence of physical phenomena? Postulating brute connections between the two domains leads to overcrowding and other apparent violations of the rules governing the occurrence of events in the spatiotemporal world. So, it seems, we are driven to the conclusion that experiential phenomena *must be* physical.

So we have at once good reason to think that conscious experience could not be physical (i.e., its manifest subjective and qualitative nature), and good reason to think that it must be (its intimate relation to physical phenomena). How should we respond to this antinomy? It seems to me that the counsel of wisdom is agnosticism. Just as the failure of reason to establish either theism or atheism might motivate agnosticism toward the question of the existence of God. In leaving the mind-body problem behind, we should, I think, be noncommittal on its resolution.

We do not know whether consciousness is a physical phenomenon or not. It certainly *seems* like it is not; but how could it not be? A true agnostic must allow for the possibility that though it seems incomprehensible, experiential reality does after all have a complete explanation in terms of non-experiential reality. Perhaps there are undreamt-of properties of matter the discovery of which will cause the scales to fall from our eyes. On the other hand, perhaps there are more kinds of phenomena in the universe than can be dreamt of by science. *Who knows* what the non-experiential world is *really* like; and who knows whether its nature is graspable by the likes of us?[8]

The mind-body problem persists. Trying to understand how conscious experience could arise from neural activity is for us like trying to understand that there is an explanation of color in terms of sound, or of multiplication and division in terms of gravity and the weak nuclear force. Mind-body metaphysics is, at least for the foreseeable future, a mug's game. What we are left with, it seems to me, is the koan that there is overwhelming empirical evidence that electrochemical activity in the brain is responsible for experience, which is impossible.

---

[8] I thus distinguish agnosticism from Mysterianism, about which I am also agnostic.

I.3 The Plan of the Book

What has come to be called the "Phenomenal Intentionality Research Program" (Kriegel 2013), or "phenomenal intentionality" (Horgan and Tienson 2002; Loar 2003), is a part of the business of Analytic Phenomenology. It seeks to provide an account of the intentionality of perception and cognition in experiential terms. It is motivated in part by intuitions like the following. There is *something it is like* to perceive—to be presented with a world of things, properties and events, ..., and to think—to reason, speculate, conceive, imagine, reflect, daydream, ... That is, perceiving and thinking are kinds of experience. As such, they are distinguished and individuated by their various proprietary kinds of phenomenology. But, furthermore, if it is in the nature of perception and thought to be *of* or *about* things, and if it is in addition apparent to us in the very having of these experiences that they have this feature, then this feature, the *intentionality* of perception and thought, must be determined by the phenomenal properties peculiar to them. Only such properties are immediately apparent to us in experience.[9]

The Phenomenal Intentionality Research Program has two main branches, corresponding to these two modes of experiential intentionality, sensory and conceptual. It is traditional to distinguish sensitive and cognitive aspects of human mentality (*sentience* and *sapience*), and the analytic tradition has proceeded on the assumption that these are metaphysically distinct. Sensation (sensory experience) is essentially phenomenal and non-intentional, whereas cognition is essentially intentional and non-phenomenal. (This is the *separatism* of Horgan and Tienson 2002.) Many have seen the latter as a lucky break, since while we have (from Dretske) a really good start on, and (from, especially, Ruth Millikan and Karen Neander) a really good development of a naturalistic theory of conceptual intentionality, phenomenality remains stubbornly resistant to naturalistic treatment.

The exclusive disjoining of these two aspects of mind in this way is denied by proponents of the Phenomenal Intentionality Research Program. They claim that sensational properties *per se* have intentionality (Brian Loar's (2003) mental "paint that purports to point"), that purely sensory intentionality is essential for perception (Montague 2016), and that conceptual intentionality is constituted by a *sui generis* kind of experience. The phenomenal intentionalist insists that neither kind of intentionality can be adequately explained in non-phenomenal terms, however inconvenient this might be for the naturalist.[10]

---

[9] It is also motivated by the apparent failure of non-phenomenal theories to provide adequate explanations of all of the facts about perceptual and conceptual intentionality, to be discussed in detail in Chapter 1.

[10] A kind of separatism does persist on this view, viz., a separatism between sensory and conceptual phenomenology. But this seems no more problematic than separatism among the various sensory phenomenologies.

This book is an extended defense and development of the phenomenal intentionality of thought thesis. I see it as an essay in Analytic Phenomenology because it takes facts about experience to be primary to the study of the mind, and disciplined introspection to be the proper way to study them, and as a chapter of the Phenomenal Intentionality Research Program because it pursues a phenomenal account of conceptual and propositional content.

In Chapter 1, "Phenomenal Intentionality," I present a series of problems for Dretske-inspired causal-informational-teleological theories of conceptual intentionality, which I take to be the best hope for the naturalization of intentionality. I argue that these problems arise from the exclusion of the subjective aspects of intentionality, and that the phenomenal-intentionalist approach avoids them. This approach is resolutely internalist, and as such is very much against the grain of recent mainstream analytic philosophy of mind (and language). I then present two arguments for internalism about thought content, one based on the possibility of propositional hallucination, and one based on the impossibility of propositional illusion. (Though I stop short of identifying thought content with a kind of experience here.)

Chapter 2, "The Experience of Thinking," offers a precise characterization of, and two arguments for, the thesis that there is a proprietary, distinctive and individuative experience of thinking that constitutes the content of concepts and thoughts. One of these arguments is epistemological, the other metaphysical. The epistemological argument claims that we have a capacity for a kind of first-person knowledge of the contents of conscious occurrent thoughts that we would not have if there were no such phenomenology. I develop the position further by arguing that such knowledge is based on direct acquaintance, which itself constitutes a kind of knowledge—knowledge of *what it is like*. I distinguish what I call "acquaintance-knowledge," which is not propositional, from knowledge *by* acquaintance, which is propositional, where the latter is based upon the former. I defend this construal against Michael Tye's argument that acquaintance cannot constitute knowing what it is like. The metaphysical argument claims that since all *non*-conceptual kinds of conscious states, as well as differences within them and the identities of their tokens, are individuated phenomenally, the same should be true for conscious conceptual states.

I defend the epistemological argument against three proposed alternative explanations of conscious, non-inferential knowledge of occurrent conscious thought content, one that appeals to the notion of a reliable belief-forming mechanism to account for such knowledge, one that argues that such knowledge is not introspective, and one that argues that self-knowledge of content does not require experience of it.

I then provide a brief critique of the popular "phenomenal contrast" strategy before addressing three arguments against the existence of conceptual phenomenology, what I call the "Humean Objection" (one finds no such thing as conceptual phenomenology upon introspection), the alleged absence of an explanatory gap for conceptual experience, and the alleged impossibility of thought appearing in the stream of consciousness (because it does not "unfold"). I end the chapter by addressing some internal worries for the thesis, viz., the possibility of shared intentional content between perceptual and conceptual states, phenomenal compositionality and context effects, and the immediate availability of complex conceptual contents. Other, more serious challenges for the view receive their own chapters.

In Chapter 3, "Externalism," I defend conceptual internalism in general by critiquing Hilary Putnam's and Tyler Burge's classic arguments for (linguistic and psychological, natural and social) externalism. I maintain that the classic arguments were never sufficient to motivate externalism in the first place. I also present a critique of phenomenal externalism.

Chapter 4, "Indexical Thought," addresses another central source of externalist intuitions regarding the individuation of intentional content, viz., David Kaplan's theory of indexicals. I argue that the intuitions Kaplan appeals to concerning "what is said" (which are easily extended to what is *thought*), and on which he bases his elegant semantics for indexicals, are not inevitable. I develop an account of indexical concepts and thought consistent with the phenomenal intentionality of thought thesis. In the second part of the chapter I offer a critique of "phenomenal concepts"—especially *demonstrative* ones—as these are understood by defenders of physicalism against Jackson's famous Mary thought experiment. I argue that since conceptual contents are experiential, they cannot be individuated by things that are not experiences, and since they are *conceptual*-experiential, they cannot be individuated by non-conceptual experiences. I propose a general thesis, which I call the Principle of Phenomenal Immiscibility, according to which an experience of one kind (visual, auditory, cognitive, etc.) cannot have an experience of another kind as a constituent. A *sound*, for example, cannot have a *color* as a constituent. Likewise a *concept*. Since conceptual contents are conceptual-experiential and, hence, intrinsic, they cannot contain (à la Balog 1999; 2012; and Papineau 2002) such things as color percepts or images, or be individuated by their referents or (à la Tye and Sainsbury 2011) historical origins. The knowledge Mary gains when she leaves the black-and-white room does not involve acquisition of special concepts that she could not possess in captivity. It is, rather, acquaintance-knowledge.

In Chapter 5, "Thinking with Names," I take up the challenge to the phenomenal intentionality of thought thesis posed by Saul Kripke's widely accepted Millian account of the meaning of proper names (and, by extension, the contents of nominal concepts). According to Kripke, names are directly referential, having their referents as their meanings, and are, hence, rigid designators.

The idea that the meaning of a term (a concept) is a non-experiential thing is *prima facie* at odds with the thesis defended in this book. Names (and nominal concepts) must, on this thesis, have *thinkable* contents—i.e., *conceptual* contents. I develop a new version of the metalinguistic description theory of the meaning of names (Bach 1994; Katz 1994; Fara 2015a and 2015b; Schoubye 2017), defend it against Kripke's objections, and show how to accommodate (or revise) Kripkean intuitions about naming and necessity, without rigidity. Supposing (as I do throughout the book) that linguistic meaning (in the *sense* sense) is conceptual content, these results might seem to be readily transferable to nominal concepts.

Things are not so easy, however. If it is inconsistent with the phenomenal intentionality of thought thesis that the meaning (conceptual content) of a term is some non-experiential thing, then it is equally at odds with this thesis to hold that the meaning of a term *contains* a non-experiential thing—such as a *name* (whether a type or a token). (This is what I call the Principle of Phenomenal Purity.) In experience, names are presented as visual or auditory images. Hence, to propose that they are part of the content of a thought, as standard metalinguistic description theories imply, is (also) to violate the Principle of Phenomenal Immiscibility. (The problem obviously transfers back to purists about sense (like Frege) who maintain that senses are composed of senses, and cannot include things like Alps—or names.) In response to this I offer what I call the "paratactic theory of nominal concepts," on which names are not thought constituents but, rather, are (mentally or physically) *displayed* in the course of thinking about a thing using its name, as the referents of tokens of the nominal concept A BEARER OF THIS NAME.[11] We use names to think about their bearers in part by thinking about the names.

Chapter 6, "Unconscious Thought," addresses what I see as an especially serious challenge to the phenomenal intentionality of thought thesis. If thought content is experiential, then if there are unconscious thoughts, there must be unconscious experience. But the claim that there could be unconscious phenomenology is at best highly contentious (some think it is a contradiction in terms, though I do not). If there is no unconscious phenomenology, it seems one is forced to conclude either that there are no unconscious thoughts or that the phenomenal intentionality of thought thesis is false. I consider and reject several compromise positions, due to Searle, Strawson, Horgan and Graham, Kriegel, and Smithies, which appeal to "derived," "as-if," or "by-courtesy" intentional content. I argue that there is no such thing, since there is no such thing as derived, as-if or by-courtesy experience. (A thought could no more be merely as-if that *p* than a sensation could be merely as-if pleasurable.) I then consider two arguments for the existence of unconscious phenomenology—one from blindsight and one from phenomenal sorites. Though these phenomena are suggestive, in the end I think the arguments are inconclusive. Finally, I try out another argument, for (what

---

[11] I use expressions in small capitals to refer to concepts and thoughts composed of them.

I call) "unconscious consciousness," according to which all phenomenal states are conscious, but there can be mental states conscious (and phenomenal) in themselves, and which are in a robust sense "mine," but of which I am not directly consciously aware. But this argument too seems inconclusive. It is highly speculative; and it may be a straightforwardly empirical matter whether or not such states exist.

In light of the inconclusiveness of the arguments for unconscious qualia, I consider the plausibility of the claim that unconscious states with the fine-grained intentional contents conscious thoughts have are explanatorily unnecessary (and, hence, that we need not believe in them). I suggest that purely formal computational processes can function as content-respecting transitions between contentful conscious states. Genuine conceptual content exists, as Strawson and Descartes insist, only in the conscious moment. Unconscious neural-computational states can no more be thoughts than states of one's hard drive are photographs. And transitions among such states need no more be governed by processes explicitly representing logical principles than the planets need explicitly represent Kepler's laws of planetary motion as they orbit the sun (Fodor 1987). The unconscious, contentless brain may be "programmed," by evolution or by the conscious mind, in such a way that some of its processes occur in accordance with rational principles defined over intentional contents, both of which can only be grasped in conscious thought.

Chapter 7, "Conceptual Reference," takes up the phenomena of conceptual reference and extension in an uncompromisingly internalist context. Causal-informational-teleological theories of conceptual content have the notable advantage that the very relations that establish content also establish extension and reference. Since the phenomenal intentionality of thought thesis severs this connection, it incurs some responsibility to provide something in its place, if it is to be a general theory of intentionality (including referential aboutness).

In this chapter I develop a Fregean view, on which concepts have in their extensions the objects that have the properties the concepts represent. The causal theorist understands such representation as grounded in causal correlation. The Fregean, on the other hand, understands it in descriptive terms: concepts denote properties by describing them. The challenge for the phenomenal intentionality of thought theorist is to explain how cognitive phenomenal properties describe the properties they denote. The short answer is that the relation between a conceptual phenomenal property and the property it describes is *primitive*. This is just what conceptual phenomenology does, by its nature. Chapter 7 offers a slightly longer answer, and shows that this assertion of primitiveness is not *ad hoc*.

* * *

The thesis that conceptual/propositional content is experiential is, in relation to traditional analytic philosophy of mind and language, pretty radical (some might say heretical). I do not think it has been widely appreciated, even among those who endorse it, just how radical the thesis is, how far-ranging its consequences are, and how uncompromising its development must be. Many "standard" doctrines in philosophy of mind and language must be thoroughly revised, or discarded entirely, if it is true. I hope this book shows both that these doctrines are not inevitable, and that there are satisfying and sturdy alternatives to them.

1
Phenomenal Intentionality

1.1 Causal-Informational-Teleological Theories of Conceptual Content

Fred Dretske was almost the Darwin of intentionality. His insight that causal relations, insofar as they carry *information* about the occurrence of the events they relate, establish a kind of proto-intentionality is simple and profound. Though not yet what we have, this proto-intentionality is sufficiently like it to get us a conceptual foot in what seemed to be the unopenable door between this feature of the mind and our physical constitution. Dretske's idea promised to show how it is possible that a highly sophisticated and puzzling aspect of our mentality could arise from simple, natural beginnings, by entirely natural processes.[1] It had a significant impact on the philosophy of mind. Jerry Fodor even claimed that "Turing and Dretske have between them solved the mind/body problem" (Fodor 1994: 56). Turing showed how a physical thing could reason, and Dretske showed how a physical thing could represent. There was still the problem of conscious qualitative experience, which causal relations *per se* do not seem qualified to explain, of which Fodor in particular was always keenly aware. (Qualia freaks would have to await their own Darwin.) But, provided phenomenality could be kept safely quarantined, the philosophical problem of intentionality was thought by many to have been solved.

Theories of this kind have the added benefit of building a connection between thought and its objects into the very nature of representational content. Concepts are individuated by the objects or property instantiations whose presence is lawfully causally correlated with their tokening, and thus acquire their contents and their extensions simultaneously.

Nonetheless, in spite of their promise, causal-informational theories have from the start faced serious internal difficulties. For example, they do not seem to be well suited to explain the contents of mathematical, logical and other concepts whose referents are abstract, causally inert objects, or the contents of concepts of

---

[1] Dretske 1981; 1988; 1995. This would make Dennis Stampe (Stampe 1977) the almost Alfred Russel Wallace of intentionality. (Dretske also cites Grice (1957) and Enç (1982) as essential influences.) C. B. Martin had a different (but also inspired) idea when he noticed that the relation between dispositions and their manifestations can be seen as a kind of proto-intentionality: dispositional states are directed at, indicate, or point to, their manifestations. (See C. B. Martin 2008. Armstrong also advocates this idea (e.g., Armstrong 1981).)

non-existent objects, which have no referents at all. These problems might be addressed by attempting to construct such concepts out of concepts of concrete, existent objects. But even if this could be done, there is still a fundamental problem that besets the causal-informational approach as applied to concepts of concrete objects—what I call the *Proliferation Problem*.

If the content of a mental representation is determined by the information it carries, and the information it carries is bestowed by causal interactions, then it looks like there can be no misrepresentation, and no failure of representation—since there can be no mis-causation. An event, such as the tokening of a concept, cannot fail to be caused by whatever causes it; so no concept can fail to carry information about, and hence represent, whatever causes it. But we do not think that concepts represent *anything* (any property instantiation) that causes them to be tokened. Representational content is, as Fodor often put it, *robust*: states that have it maintain it against a proliferation of pretenders—properties instantiations of which cause them, but do not determine their contents. However, it is not clear that this resistance to unwanted causes can be delivered by causal-informational approaches. And if it cannot, it seems inevitable that these theories will assign either indeterminate or wildly disjunctive contents to concepts whose contents are clearly determinate and non-disjunctive.

Here I discuss three versions of the Proliferation Problem: Quine's Problem, which arises out of *causal superimposition*; the Disjunction Problem, which arises out of *causal spread*; and the Stopping Problem, which arises out of *causal depth*. In all of these cases, there are multiple candidates for content determiner/extension, and no obvious way to choose among them derivable from the basic machinery of causal-informational theories.

The kinds of examples W. V. O. Quine (1960) used to argue for the indeterminacy of radical translation can be used to show that for any property that is a candidate for determining the content of a concept (the meaning of a term), there are indefinitely many other simultaneously instantiated—*superimposed*—nomologically or otherwise necessarily, that cannot be teased apart causally. Any instantiation of *rabbithood*, for example, is also, necessarily, an instantiation of *undetached-rabbit-parts-hood*, *rabbit-stage-hood*, and indefinitely many other properties. If these properties are distinct, they ought to determine distinct contents for the concept (mental representation) RABBIT (and the expression 'rabbit'). But since they are necessarily co-instantiated, there can be no causal relations between mental states and *one* of them that are not also causal relations between mental states and *all* of them. Hence, a causal-informational theory cannot, at least *prima facie*, assign one of them as the content of RABBIT, as against the others. There is by the theory's lights no fact of the matter about which of these properties determines (or is) the content of the concept RABBIT (or the term 'rabbit').

These examples could also be viewed as entailing massive disjunctiveness of content. On this construal, the content of RABBIT would be *rabbithood or undetached-rabbit-parts-hood* or *rabbit-stage-hood* or.... In this case there would be a fact of the matter about what the content of a given concept is, but it would be, counterintuitively, disjunctive (perhaps open-endedly). This is problematic because, intuitively, the content of RABBIT is not disjunctive. Moreover, as Fodor often pointed out (e.g., Fodor 1987), there ought to be psychological generalizations that apply to mental states in virtue of their content. However, in keeping with the naturalistic project, such generalizations should be causal (or otherwise nomological). But natural laws are typically not formulated in terms of disjunctive properties, which do not in general constitute natural kinds.

Dretske himself (1981) recognized this problem (dubbed the "Disjunction Problem" by Fodor (1984)) as it arises in cases where there are causal correlations between the occurrence of mental representations and the presence of a wide range of distinct things (property instantiations) that are, intuitively, not in the extensions of those representations. Thus, though there may be law-like relations between the occurrence of horses (instantiations of *horsehood*) and occurrences of the concept HORSE, such relations *also* hold between HORSE occurrences and indefinitely many other things: donkeys in the dark, zebras in the mist, ripples in horse-infested waters (Fodor 1990b), etc.—anything that might cause one to think, correctly or incorrectly, (e.g.) LO, A HORSE! Thus, for HORSE (or any empirical concept), there is a *spread* of different property instantiations (by distinct objects) sufficient for its tokening, and, hence, by the theory's lights, sufficient for determining its content. But HORSE does not disjunctively mean all of these indefinitely many things. The reasons for resisting a disjunctive content are the same here as they were in the causal superimposition cases.

Indeed, though this is not frequently remarked upon, one could just as well construe the Disjunction Problem as a problem of indeterminacy: there is, consistent with the resources of the theory, no fact of the matter about which one of the indefinitely many causally correlated property instantiations determines a concept's content.

The third problem (called the "Stopping Problem" by Strawson (2008), and the "horizontal disjunction problem" by Pierre Jacob (1997)[2]), arises because the causal relations between mental states and property instances that are supposed to establish content are *mediated*. Thus, causal relations to cows—instantiations of *cowhood*—are supposed to constitute a mental representation of the concept COW. But there are also causal relations between occurrences of COW and indefinitely many links in the causal chain between cows and COWS. These include links to things *within* the perceptual system, such as bovine retinal irradiations, bovine

---

[2] Though in the kinds of cases used to generate the Disjunction Problem we want "wild" tokenings (Fodor's term) to be *mis*representations of their causes, in Stopping-Problem cases (as well as Quine's-Problem cases) what we want is *non*-representation. We do not want COW tokenings to *mis*represent bovine retinal irradiations or cow-stages as cows; we want them not to represent them at all.

olfactory bulb activity, bovine visual or olfactory cortical activation patterns, etc. (as pointed out in Adams and Aizawa 1997, Antony and Levine 1991, Fodor 1990b and Sterelny 1990), as well as links between retinal images (or other sensory-transducer representations) and cows—such as cow reflections, cow shadows, cow breezes, ... There are also less obvious candidates, like photons reflected from a cow, the cow's parents, distant ancestor bovine species, . . . , the Big Bang. All of these can lay equal claim to inclusion in a causal chain leading to tokenings of COW, though, obviously, the vast majority of them are not plausible candidates for determining (or being) the content or extension of the concept COW.

The causal chains connecting concept tokenings to what are supposed to be their content-conferring property instantiations are *dense*, involving indefinitely many property instantiations (events) as links, and they extend well beyond those instantiations. And while we may find it impossible to take seriously candidates such as objects or events in the distant past, or property instantiations undetectable by us, if all we have at our disposal is causal relations—that is, if the theory says that conceptual contents are individuated by their causes—it is not obvious what principled reasons there could be for excluding any of them. And if there is no way to prune away the unwanted causes, then we are faced, as in the other problematic cases, with the invidious choice between indeterminacy and untamable disjunctiveness.

Causal-informational theorists have expended considerable effort and ingenuity in responding to these problems. The most influential response appeals to the evolved function of a given mental representation type (or the system deploying it). According to these *teleological* theories (Dretske 1986, 1988, 1995; Millikan 1984, 1989, 2000, 2017; Neander 1995, 2017; Papineau 1998; Shea 2018), the content of a concept is determined by the objects and properties it (or the system it functions in) was selected, by evolution or some other natural process (such as learning), to indicate. Hence, since the concept COW does not have the evolved function of indicating bovine retinal irradiations, cow shadows, the Big Bang, etc., it does not mean any of these things. But, while this kind of approach might eliminate some of the unwanted contents, it does not eliminate them all. Indeterminacy/disjunction problems persist, since selection *qua* causal process cannot distinguish nomologically necessarily co-instantiated properties, and it is unclear that the theory can offer principled reasons for assigning one content over another on the basis of evolved function. For example (Fodor 1990b), these theories do not seem to give us reason to assign the representation that figures in the operation of a frog's snapping mechanism the content *fly*, as opposed to *little black dot, buzzing thing, bee-bee*, or any other property (or disjunction of properties) the instantiation of which would have gotten the frog fed in the environment in which the snapping mechanism evolved.

Fodor's own suggestion (Fodor 1990b) is that the unwanted contents can be excluded according to a principle of asymmetric dependency (Neander (2012; 2017) offers a similar account). HORSE means *horse*, for example, and not *zebra-in-the-mist*, because zebras in the mist would not activate mental horse detectors if horses did not, though the converse is not true. (More picturesquely, the nomologically possible worlds in which horses and zebras in the mist cause HORSE tokens are closer than those in which only zebras in the mist do.) But this seems only to change the question to an equally difficult one: *Why* is it that zebras in the mist would not cause false alarms unless horses caused real alarms? (Why are *these* worlds closer than *those*?) Intuitively, it is because 'horse' means *horse*, and not *zebra-in-the-mist*; but of course this gets us nowhere.

Another way of dealing with these problems is to appeal to internal content-determining causal relations—conceptual or inferential or functional roles—among mental representations (Block 1986; Field 1977; Harman 1973, 1987; Loar 1981). These relations may be taken to be entirely constitutive of conceptual content (they are naturalistic if the relevant roles are causal). But they may also be combined with external relations in such a way as to eliminate unwanted contents. On such "two-factor" (McGinn 1982) theories, intra-conceptual relations determine "narrow" contents, which themselves determine "wide" (or "broad") contents in combination with mind-world relations. Wide contents are world-involving and partly determined by causal-informational relations. The wide content of the concept WATER, for example, is determined by which substance, H_2O or XYZ, say, one is causally related to in one's environment. Narrow contents can set limits on which substances can determine such wide contents. The narrow content of WATER could be something (like *watery stuff*) that limits, in a given environment, which substance determines its wide content. So, for example, a cow might cause one's water concept to be tokened, but the narrow content of the concept determines that this is a mis-tokening, and thereby prevents the wide content of one's concept from being *cow* (or *cow-or-water*, etc.). Cows are not watery stuff.

But conceptual-role theories have their own technical difficulties, arising from their *prima facie* commitment to meaning holism (see, e.g., Fodor and Lepore 1992). Moreover, an intuitive objection to such views (which I find especially compelling) is that inferential relations among concepts are determined by their contents, and not vice versa.

These problems may, of course, be treated as challenges to be met within the naturalist, causal-informational-teleological program. And I think it would be rash to say that theories of content of this kind are defunct. (Philosophical theories are rarely, if ever, definitively defunct. What usually happens is that people get bored with them and move on to something else. Eventually, a discarded theory may come back into fashion.) And maybe, as brilliant as Dretske's idea was, causation is not after all the right phenomenon in terms of which to analyze conceptual intentionality. Perhaps some other natural property or relation would fare better. But I think the problems I have detailed are general enough and stubborn enough to motivate a different approach toward conceptual intentionality. Moreover, given the central and obvious role sensory phenomenology plays in constituting perceptual states, phenomenology seems a natural place to look.

1.2 Phenomenal Intentionality of Thought

There have all along been dissenters from causal-informational theories, who have insisted that they fail because they ignore the essential role of experience in constituting intentionality. John Searle has defended a "connection principle" (Searle 1992), according to which a mental state cannot have fine-grained intentional content (what he calls "aspectual shape") unless it is either conscious or potentially conscious. Since consciousness and its "aspectual shape" properties are internally determined, no external-relationist theory can on its own provide an adequate explanation of our kind of intentionality. (Searle (1980) also objected to the idea that Turing solved the naturalization problem for reasoning, arguing that rule-governed symbol-manipulation without understanding (for Searle, a form of experience) is not thinking.) And Strawson (1994) and Siewert (1998) have taken seriously the idea that mentality in general (and conceptual intentionality in particular), is essentially experiential. (Not to mention Husserl and the Phenomenologists.) On this point of view, reductionist theories of intentionality, insofar as they leave out experience, are bound to encounter the problems that plague them; and taking experience into account provides a way to avoid them.

Causal-informational theorists, unsurprisingly, resist this claim. If true, it would short-circuit their naturalistic explanation of intentionality, since no one has any idea how to give such an explanation of conscious experience, and, as *per* Fodor, amount to intellectual suicide.

But it is only intellectual suicide given a narrow focus on reductionist metaphysics of mind. From the perspective of Analytic Phenomenology, blind faith in natural science and an overweening ambition to solve the problem of human intentionality *now* are the true paths to intellectual ruin. The phenomenophobia engendered by these commitments is at the root of what seems to me one of the cardinal sins of twentieth-century analytic philosophy: the attempt to constitute mentality (as well as many other phenomena) out of its causes and effects. (Another is confusing models of things with the things they model.) Intentionality is a phenomenon we first encounter in our own experience. That conscious perceptual and conceptual states are *of* things is immediately apparent from the first-person perspective, as an intrinsic feature of certain subjective states (as has been pointed out by authors from Brentano (1874/1973) to Mendelovici (2018)). And it is only through reflection upon our experience that we come to have a concept of intentionality in the first place: the very idea of intentionality is the idea of an experiential phenomenon. To abandon this perspective is to lose sight of what it is we are trying to explain.

Moreover, including experience in the explanation of intentionality confers immunity to Indeterministic Disjunctivitis. Searle (1987) and Graham, Horgan, and Tienson (2007, 2009) respond to Quinean indeterminacy; and Strawson (2008) addresses the Stopping Problem. It has also been argued that phenomenology can solve the Disjunction Problem (Horgan and Graham 2012; Pitt 2009). (Given that disjunctiveness and indeterminacy have the same source, any prescription against one ought to be a prescription against the other.) The shared idea is that what our concepts are *of* is what we *take them to be of*, where *taking* is a manner of *experiencing*. What HORSE means is what *we* mean by it; and what we mean by it is experiential, and introspectively available to us. We know, first-personally, that the extension of HORSE is horses, and not horse-part-fusions or zebras in the mist or equine retinal arrays,.... And we know this in this way because conceptual contents (and thought contents) are experiential in nature. (Thus, one reason causal-informational theories of content have the problems they do is that we do not have first-person access to the causal relations that are supposed to establish content.) Indeed, as has often been pointed out, if we could make no such distinctions as those between the contents *rabbit* and *rabbit-stage* (for example), indeterminacy and disjunction would not appear to us to be *problems* at all. Of course, Quine famously denied that, after all, there is a difference between *rabbit* and *rabbit-stage* for the radical translator—or any other speaker of English. But, as Searle (1987) has argued, this strains credibility (to say the least). It seems more plausible to see Quinean indeterminacy as a *reductio* of verificationist semantics.

Kripke's (1982) *plus/quus* problem, which is meant to raise the question whether one can know what one means (or has meant) by 'plus' (i.e., whether there is a fact of the matter about what one means), is obviously related to Quine's Problem. And it has an analogous solution. If PLUS and QUUS are different concepts (which they must be if the problem is to have any traction), and concepts (their contents) are experience types, then it will be possible to know by introspection which of them one is entertaining in a given case. (See Goff 2012; Graham, Horgan, and Tienson 2007, 2009; Strawson 2010: Appendix.)

Not everyone who accepts that there is a proprietary phenomenology of thought agrees. Some (e.g., Siewert 1998) maintain that conceptual phenomenology does not determine intentional content at all, while others (Horgan and Kriegel 2008; Strawson 2008) hold that conceptual phenomenal content is not the only kind of intentional content, which can be either *narrow* or *wide*. Angela Mendelovici (2018) argues that the cognitive-phenomenal content of occurrent conscious thoughts is relatively impoverished, and in general only dispositionally (derivatively) has the full, "cashed-out" propositional content of the language one might use to express them.

In spite of these differences, I think it can be said that there is a shared commitment to the idea that genuine conceptual intentionality of the kind we enjoy is essentially an experiential phenomenon. Without experience (which for most philosophers means without *consciousness*) there can be no mental representation with the fineness of grain or selectivity that our thoughts and concepts display.

But the view I defend in this book is steadfastly and exclusively internalist about conceptual-propositional content. Such content is entirely fixed by (because identical to) internally instantiated experiential properties of the proprietarily conceptual kind. The bifurcation of content into internally and externally determined varieties is an unnecessary capitulation to an unmotivated externalism about intentionality. (Good old-fashioned sense and reference are enough for a theory of mental content and its relation to the world.) And there can be no deferred or derivative content of conscious occurrent thought, since there can be no deferred or derivative *experience* (of *any* kind; I return to this issue in Chapter 6).

1.3 Phenomenal Intentionality of Perception

Though my primary aim in the book is to develop and defend the phenomenal intentionality of thought thesis, I would like to say a few things about perceptual intentionality, since it is the companion explanandum of the Phenomenal Intentionality Research Program, and because there are overlapping issues and challenges.

In their various modalities, perceptual states also represent to us the world around us, providing information about the existence and condition of the things with which we interact. And they can be more or less accurate; veridical or not. What is the role of consciousness in the intentionality of perception? Obviously, conscious perceptual experiences must be conscious. But what role do the phenomenal properties apparent in conscious perception play in determining the intentional content of a perceptual state—what it is a perception *of*? On what we can call the "Pure Causal View," they play no role whatever. A conscious perceptual state is a perception of an object or property (instantiation) if and only if it is caused by that object or property. Whatever phenomenal character the experience may have is irrelevant to its being a perception of what caused it. Opposed to this is what Michelle Montague (2016) calls the "Matching View," according to which there is a (probably vague) limit to how badly the phenomenal properties characterizing a perceptual experience can misrepresent its cause before it ceases to be a perception of it. Perceptual states whose phenomenal character completely misrepresents their causes are not perceptions of them at all.

It seems clear that a causal relation between token perceptual states and specific objects or properties is *necessary* for perception. No state not caused by an elephant is a perception of an elephant. The role of causation with respect to perceptual states is thus different from its role with respect to conceptual states. In the latter case, even if causal relations featured in the determination of the content of conceptual state *types*, we want to allow that *token* concepts can be of things that are not their token causes. A token concept ELEPHANT should be a concept *of* elephants (have elephants in its extension) no matter what causes it, and whether or not it was caused by any external thing or property instantiation. But a token perceptual state cannot be a perception of an elephant unless it is caused by an elephant. Because of this difference, the Disjunction Problem does not arise for perceptual states. Perceptions *of elephants* cannot be caused by hippos-in-the-mist or large gray rocks, or by nothing at all.

Quine's problem also does not arise for perceptual states, since (e.g.) a perceptual state caused by an elephant is also caused by an elephant-stage and a sum of undetached elephant parts, etc. The *conceptual* distinctions do not seem to be relevant to what is being perceived in the way they are relevant to what is being thought about. A perception of an elephant is simultaneously (and unproblematically, it seems to me) a perception of a collection of undetached elephant parts, an elephant stage, etc.

But the Stopping Problem does arise. Any state caused by an F is also caused by other links in the causal chain leading to the occurrence of the state. A visual perception of an elephant is caused by the elephant; but it is also caused by whatever caused the elephant, the photons reflected from the elephant, the firing of cells in the retina, the lateral geniculate nuclei and the primary visual cortex, etc.—none of which we would want to say the experience is a perception of.

Montague's Matching View offers a solution to the Stopping Problem: the visual experience one has upon looking at an elephant is not an experience of any of these other causes because it does not *resemble* them. And its resemblance or not to its causes is determined by its visual phenomenal character. Experiences of elephants are introspectively distinguishable from experiences of retinal cells: what it is like to see an elephant is different from what it is like to see retinal cells; elephants and photoreceptors do not look anything alike. A conscious perceptual state "must represent a sufficient number of [an] object's properties correctly in order for it to be true that one [perceives] it" (Montague 2016: 156). Thus, an experience that in no way resembles an elephant—an experience whose phenomenal character conveys no information about the elephant's distinctive features—cannot, according to Montague, be a perception of the elephant that caused it. Causation is not sufficient for perception.

(The Matching View owes us a more complete explanation of what matching, i.e., *correct* representation or *resemblance,* consists in, which is no simple task. Beyond a naive, intuitive gloss (e.g., if the elephant is gray and one's elephant experience is pink, the experience does not resemble the elephant and does not correctly represent it), however, one might say (roughly, and as a first approximation) that an experience of a thing does not resemble the thing if it is not *phenomenally typical*, where being phenomenally typical is a matter of how the thing typically affects typical perceivers in typical circumstances. If typical perceivers have phenomenally gray experiences in response to gray elephants in ordinary circumstances, then anyone who has a phenomenally pink experience in response to a gray elephant is not representing it correctly.[3] The naive conception, on which the elephant and one's experience of it can both be gray, will do for present purposes.)

This perceptual phenomenal solution is analogous to the conceptual phenomenal solution to the Stopping Problem for conceptual representations—the concepts RABBIT and RABBIT-STAGE, HORSE and COW-IN-THE-MIST, etc., are introspectively distinguishable, phenomenally different, conceptual experiences. What it is like to think that something is a rabbit is different from what it is like to think that it is a rabbit-stage.

I think the intuitions on both sides are respectable, and that the correct account of the role phenomenology plays in the fixing of perceptual content lies between the extremes of the Pure Causal View and the Matching View. On the one hand, it does seem reasonable to say that an experience caused by an F is a perception of that F no matter how unlike its cause it is—just as it seems reasonable to say that a photograph is of a particular F if it was photons bouncing off the F that were responsible for its production (cf. Evans 1982: 78), no matter how little it resembles its cause; and that a portrait is a portrait of a particular F if the artist intended it to be a portrait of that F, no matter how little it might resemble the (or an) F (e.g., Man Ray's *Self Portrait (Invention)*). They may be *bad* photographs or portraits of the F; but they are photographs or portraits of it nonetheless. Moreover, what makes an experience as of an F a *hallucination* of an F, and hence *not* a perception of it, is just the absence of a causal connection between the experience and an F. So it does seem that being caused by an F is sufficient for perception of it, and that phenomenal character has a role only in determining how accurate or inaccurate the perception is.

On the other hand, if we consider things from the perspective of the representation itself, it seems reasonable to say that resemblance *is* required. No one shown a picture of an elephant would take it to be a picture of a refrigerator, or vice versa. And no one would take a completely blank image to be a photograph of either an elephant or a refrigerator. Moreover, it seems entirely natural to say that an image with the appropriate properties is an image of an elephant, whether or not it resulted from causal interaction with one, and somewhat perverse to say that such an image is not an image of an elephant because it was not caused by one.

---

[3] See Chalmers 2010b, especially 404–7 and 430–41, for a rich discussion of a view along these lines, and the surrounding issues.

These intuitions are not inconsistent. There is a perfectly good sense of 'a perception *of* an *F*' on which it means *a perception caused by an F*, and an equally good sense on which it means *a perception resembling an F*. The latter sense is commonly marked out with the phrase 'perception *as of* an *F*' (or *of an F as an F*). A perception *of* an *F* (like a photograph or painting of an *F*) may or may not also be a perception *as of* an *F*. Being caused by an *F* does not entail, and is not entailed by, resembling an *F*. A perceptual state caused by an elephant could resemble virtually anything, or nothing at all; and a state resembling an elephant could be caused by virtually anything, or nothing at all. Additionally, the former sense may be used in reference to a perception (or photograph or painting) of a *particular F*, the latter in reference to a perception (or photograph or painting) of a *typical F*, though none in particular. An experience can be of a particular elephant without being a typical-elephant experience.

However, if the issue is the intentionality of perceptual *experience* itself, then it is arguable that resemblance, perception *as of*, plays as essential a role in perception as causal connection to represented things. For the content of perceptual experience *as one has it* is constituted by its phenomenal character. Perceivers do not have perceptual access to external causal relations between objects and their perceptions of them. Moreover, given that the *function* of perception is to inform perceivers of the existence and states of external objects, total (or sufficiently severe) misrepresentation of its external cause would render a perceptual experience (more or less) *useless* to the perceiver.

I think the correct thing to say is that an experience *of* (caused by) an *F* that is in no way *as of* (resembles) an *F*, is still a perception of what caused it (in the minimal, causal sense). It is not a hallucination, but, rather, a *total illusion*. However, since such an experience is not suited to play the kinds of roles perceptual states are supposed to play (it does not facilitate interaction between the perceiver and the object), it has a radically degraded status: it is a *failed* perception. For practical purposes, the fact that it is a perception in the causal sense is irrelevant.

1.4 Content Internalism

I have been assuming, with Montague, that the qualities apparent to perceivers in perception are features of their perceptual representations. (This is what makes her project part of the Phenomenal Intentionality Research Program.) Given that the same is true (*mutatis mutandis*) of the qualities apparent to thinkers in thought, the phenomenal intentionalist is committed to a thoroughgoing internalism about mental content, in opposition to the content externalism that has been so widely accepted.

Dretske and others (e.g., Dretske 1995; Harman 1990; Lycan 1996; Tye 2000) have proposed extensions of the causal-informational theory of conceptual content to give a naturalistic account of the qualitative properties apparent in perceptual experience. Such "reductive representationalist" views (see Chalmers 2004 for terminological clarification[4]) attempt to explain the phenomenology of perception in terms of causal-informational representation of objectively instantiated qualitative properties. The yellowness one might mention in describing what it is like to see a ripe banana, for instance, is a property of the banana, not one's experience of it. And it is easy to see how this account could be used to solve the Stopping Problem for perception: a perceptual state represents the thing whose qualitative properties are apparent to the perceiver. However, this "qualia externalism" (Byrne and Tye 2006; Tye 2015) faces insurmountable problems in accounting for dreams, illusions and hallucinations, which I detail in Chapter 3.[5]

The experiential nature of intentionality, both perceptual and conceptual, is a *given* in Husserlian Phenomenology. Philosophers working in this tradition find the suggestion that one needs to argue for a phenomenology of thought bewildering—even shocking. Traditional analytic philosophers of mind, on the other hand, find it completely unbelievable—bordering on absurd—that there should proprietarily be something it is like *to think*. And many also strongly resist the idea that unconceptualized sensory states could be *about* anything. Philosophers who advocate for phenomenal intentionality accept the need for arguments for their internalist position, given the history of analytic philosophy of mind.

In the next chapter I present two arguments for the existence of a *sui generis*, content-constituting phenomenology of thought, what I am calling the phenomenal intentionality of thought thesis, as an alternative to causal-informational-teleological theories. These theories are externalist—though not deliberately so. Dretskean psychosemantics was not introduced in order to accommodate anti-individualist intuitions, or to establish that the contents of general concepts are externally determined. Rather, it *turned out that* the causal theorist's way of naturalizing mental content individuates it externally.

And the same is true of theories of singular thought and concepts that take their cue from Kripke's and Kaplan's semantics for singular terms. *It turned out that* the direct reference theorist's way of accommodating our intuitions about our use of names, indexicals and sentences containing them entails that their contents are individuated extensionally. We could characterize these externalisms as *de facto*. The externalism of Putnam[6] and Burge, in contrast, is *deliberate*. Their classic thought experiments were specifically designed to evoke anti-individualist

---

[4] *Non*-reductive representationalists, such as Loar (2003), hold that phenomenal properties *per se* are intentional.
[5] Moreover, it is not easy to see how externalist theories of this kind could solve the indeterminacy problems for conceptual states. See Byrne 2008, 2011, Pitt 2011, and Section 2.2.2 below.
[6] As tutored by McGinn (1977) and Burge (1979a).

intuitions, and to support an explicit argument for externalistic individuation of conceptual contents.

In Chapter 3 I critique Putnam–Burge externalism, and in Chapters 4 and 5, respectively, I present alternatives to Kaplanian and Kripkean semantics for indexical and nominal concepts that are consistent with the phenomenal-internalist view I defend.

Meanwhile, to close this chapter I offer two arguments in favor of the view that conceptual content is wholly determined by properties internal to the thinker. (In the next chapter I argue that conceptual content is wholly determined by properties intrinsic to *concepts*, construed as experientially constituted.) These arguments are not meant to support the phenomenal intentionality of thought thesis in particular but, rather, content internalism in general. The first argument is from the possibility of propositional hallucination; the second is from the impossibility of propositional illusion.

1.4.1 Propositional Hallucination

From a naive perspective, perception is direct—that is, what we are aware of when we are awake, our sensory systems are working properly, and conditions are right, is the world around us. From within this perspective we do not notice our perceptual experiences, as such. We naively assume (if only implicitly) that the world is all there is to notice when we perceive. Reflection on phenomena like dreams, hallucinations, illusions and distortions (e.g., blurred vision), however, draws our attention to our perceptual experience, as such. It reveals that, in addition to the world that we are perceptually aware of, there is our experience of the world—the way it appears to us; the way we represent it to be—which we are also aware of. These phenomena show that our experience can change in certain ways under conditions in which we are not prepared to say that the world has changed, and that they can occur when we are not in the immediate presence of the extramental things they appear to present to us. And this leads, inevitably in my view, to the conclusion that our initial naive perspective is mistaken.[7] What we are *directly* aware of in perception is not a world external to our minds but, rather, our experience of it. If we are aware of an objective world in perception, it is only indirectly.

This does not entail that we perceive our perceptions—a conclusion that tempts a fatal regress. To perceive something is to have an experience caused by it. But we do not have experience caused by our experience; we are directly aware of it. Nor does it amount to some kind of indictment or delegitimization of perceptual experience, as Tye (2000: 46) has argued:

---

[7] See Pitt 2017 (included herein as Section 3.3) for a refutation of phenomenal externalism.

[t]o suppose that the qualities of which perceivers are directly aware in undergoing ordinary, everyday visual experiences are really qualities of the experiences [representations] would be to convict such experiences of massive error. That is just not credible. It seems totally implausible to hold that visual experience is systematically misleading in this way.

On the contrary, if it were not misleading in this way—if it did not present itself as something it is not (external reality)—it would be useless to us (even *dangerous*). Apparent experiential transparency is an illusion made necessary by the fact that what perceptual experience is supposed to represent is external and non-mental, while experience itself is internal and mental. Perceptual experience cannot present itself to us as what it *is* if it is to be a naively believable guide to what it is *not*. Moreover, it would not follow from the fact that we are only indirectly aware of the world in perception that our experiences are *massively* erroneous. Apart from their apparent transparency (which is illusory), the world could be exactly as it appears to us to be—at least most of the time. The naive realist belief that objects have the properties they seem to us to have does not entail that they (the objects) are perceived directly.

What I want to focus on here, however, is just the fact that reflection on the phenomena of misrepresentation and non-representation draws our attention to the existence of contentful mind-internal, mind-dependent representations of various kinds. We recognize that there are situations in which such representations can exist and persist, and have the apparent contents they do, in the absence of what we naively take them to *be*, or (more sophisticatedly) take them to be *of*. And the mere possibility that a representation could occur in the absence of what it seems to be a representation of is sufficient to show this as well.

Could a situation analogous to hallucination arise for conscious *thought*? This would be a situation in which a token propositional representation does not represent anything external to the mind: it would be *as if* we were representing a proposition p, when in fact there is no such thing as the proposition p. (This would be analogous to hallucinating a non-existent thing (like a Klingon), as opposed to an existent thing that is absent.) This certainly seems possible. Indeed, for a certain kind of nominalist, it is actual. In any case, the non-existence of abstract, mind-independent propositions would not entail that no one ever thinks anything, that no one has contentful conceptual representations. It does not follow from the mere fact that we can think, that there are mind-independent propositions. (This is different from the perceptual case, in that the complete absence of an external world *would* entail that no one ever perceives anything.)

If the possibility that it can appear to us that we are perceptually representing an object o when there is no such thing should lead us to believe in internal perceptual representations, then the possibility that it can appear to us that we are conceptually representing the proposition that p though there is no such thing should lead us to believe in internal conceptual representations. Furthermore, since perceiver-internal properties determine the content of hallucinatory perceptual representations—that is, that make them *as of* what they are as of—we ought to conclude that thinker-internal properties determine the content of a hallucinatory conceptual representation. Perceiver-internal properties make it the case that one is having, say, a *Klingon* hallucination (an hallucination *as of* a Klingon), as opposed to a Ferengi hallucination. And since (*pace* disjunctivists; see Section 3.3 for argument) there can be hallucinations that differ from veridical experiences *only* in the absence of an external cause, it follows that the content of a hallucination—that which makes it the hallucination it is, what it is a hallucination *of*—is not determined by anything external to the perceiver. And the internally determined properties that make a hallucination as of what it is of are also what make a veridical experience the experience it is. The fact that veridical perceptual experiences have referents does not change their contents any more than the fact that the existence of something could make a false (or truth-valueless) sentence true changes its meaning. Suppose you are hallucinating a baboon in a party hat, and while you blink a real, qualitatively indistinguishable baboon in a party hat pops into existence in the very place your hallucinated one appeared to be, and causes the very same neural activity in your visual system that was producing the hallucination. Except in the token sense, you are not having a new experience. You are having the old experience again, except now it is veridical, whereas before it was not. (Likewise, if you are subject to the delusion that aliens have landed in your back yard, and voice your concerns to your neighbor. Were such beings to land in your back yard on your way home, what you said to your neighbor would become true. But the meaning of your utterance would not change.)

Analogously, it is thinker-internal properties that make the representation as of a non-existent proposition p a p-representation, and not a q- or r-representation. Suppose you, a hardcore nominalist, think that there are no such things as propositions, and, hence, in particular, that there is no such thing as the proposition *the history of the world is written by sociopaths*. Suppose further that your thought is true. If God were suddenly to realize that he had forgotten to make propositions, and straightaway remedied his oversight, your thought would become false. But it would remain the thought THERE IS NO PROPOSITION THE HISTORY OF THE WORLD IS WRITTEN BY SOCIOPATHS.

Hence, the possibility of propositional hallucination shows that propositional content (like perceptual content—in both cases as opposed to reference or extension) is determined by features internal to thinkers.

It may be objected that, at best, this shows only that *narrow* content is internally determined, and that *wide* contents of perceptual and conceptual (and linguistic) representations are determined by referential relations. But, as I argue in Chapter 3, the narrow–wide distinction is unmotivated (because the founding externalist thought experiments are unconvincing). (In Chapters 4 and 5 I argue that Kaplan- and Kripke-style intuitions do not motivate a bifurcation of conceptual content either.) There is no good reason to accept that there are two kinds of content, in addition to extension (or reference), one of which is internally determined and the other externally determined. We are not justified in assigning conceptual representations a kind of content that can change with their external relations, or that they lack if they have none.

1.4.2 Propositional Illusion

Perceptual illusion is another kind of misrepresentation. Hallucinations represent absent (or non-existent) things as present. Illusions, on the other hand, represent present things as being ways they are not—as having properties they do not have. They are *mis*perceptions (and, hence perceptions), whereas hallucinations are not perceptions at all.

It is a necessary condition on illusion that a perceiver bear some relation to the misrepresented thing that is independent of the way it is represented. (Typically, this is causal; but if there are other ways of establishing an independent connection they would do as well.) An experience cannot attribute to some particular thing a property it does not have unless it is an experience of that thing; and what makes it an experience of that particular thing cannot be solely a matter of the *way* it represents. An experience as of a wet road cannot be an illusory experience of a dry road unless it is an experience caused by a dry road. This is what makes it a misrepresentation of that road, as opposed to an accurate representation of some other road (or a hallucination). In the absence of any experience-independent connection establishing that a perceptual experience is of some particular thing, illusion is impossible: illusions misattribute properties to things we are in fact perceiving. Hence, a *total* illusion—an experience of a thing that misrepresents *all* of its properties—is not a hallucination, since there is still the connection between the experience and the thing that is necessary for it to be a misrepresentation of that particular thing. (There are other ways for an experience to be illusion-proof. For example, its experience-independent connection to its cause may be of the wrong *kind*—you have an experience as of an elephant because it stepped on you, or because its tail hit you in the eye; or the properties it manifests are not experienced as properties *of its cause*—an auditory experience caused by a punch in the nose is not an illusory experience of the fist.)

If a wet-road experience is not illusory because there is no experience-independent connection to a dry road that would establish correctness conditions for it, then its content—its being the kind of experience it is—is not determined by the relevant non-experiential properties of the road, or, *perforce*, a causal connection to it. Its content—what makes it an experience as of a wet road, and not of a dry road, or a refrigerator—is constituted by its intrinsic phenomenal properties.

In general, if there is no connection between a representation and something external to it that is independent of the way it represents, then there is no basis for attributing inaccuracy to it. And if there is no basis for attributing inaccuracy to it, it is not possible for it to be illusory. It cannot misrepresent a thing if it is not *of* that thing independently of the way it represents. In such a case, extra-representational facts cannot figure in the determination of the content of the representation: the *way* it represents *is* its content. Further, if a *kind* of representation is not subject to illusion for this reason, then the contents of representations of that kind cannot be determined by extra-representational facts. They are the representations they are independently of any connections to anything they may purport to represent.

Now, without assuming that thoughts are experiences, we may observe that conceptual illusion is impossible. For what would such a thing be? It would be a case in which what one seemed to be thinking (where, again, this is not assumed to be some kind of conscious appearance) was not in fact what one was thinking. It would be a case in which what one was representing—a *proposition*, some kind of mind-independent thing—did not have the properties one represented it as having: the object of one's thought is, say, the proposition that cats are finicky, whereas one's mental representation is as of the proposition that cats are feline. One's thought misattributes to the proposition that cats are finicky the property of predicating felinity of cats. But this cannot happen. How *could* it happen? In the case of perceptual illusion, misattribution of properties to objects is only possible because there is a relatedness to those objects that is independent of how they are represented. But there is no analogous relation to a thought content (a proposition) independently of how one represents it to ground the possibility of propositional illusion. It makes no sense to say that I am mis-grasping a proposition if there is no relation to it independent of how I represent it that makes it the case that it is *that* proposition that I am (mis)representing. Propositions (at least as most commonly construed) do not *cause* our representations of them. Nor is there any other sort of representation-independent connection we might have to them that would underwrite the possibility of conceptual illusion. So, there is no mind-independent basis for a standard of comparison between a propositional mental representation and what it represents that would allow for mis-grasping. But if there is no such thing as mis-grasping, then the content of the thought that we apprehend must be a mind-internal property of our representation.

I am not suggesting that it is impossible for thinkers to be wrong about what they think—that is, to make false judgments about what their occurrent thoughts are. We certainly can make mistakes in identifying what we are thinking, or what we have thought. Since such judgments involve the formation of second-order thoughts (beliefs), there is room for confusion, distraction, and other forms of interference that can result in a false belief about what one's thoughts are or were. An externalist might object that one can believe that one is thinking that, e.g., water is wet when in fact one is thinking that twater is wet, thereby misrepresenting the proposition that is the content of one's thought. But this would also be a case of thinker misidentification of an occurrent thought, and so is not what I am drawing attention to here. What I am arguing is, rather, that thoughts themselves—mental representations of propositions—cannot misrepresent their contents: they cannot misrepresent the propositions that are their contents, in the way perceptual experiences can misrepresent the objects they are of. It cannot be that what is presented to a thinker in first-order thought is not what the thinker is thinking, because the true object of the thought—its true content—is not as the thought presents it to be.

Nor do I think it can be concluded just from this that there are propositional *appearances* in the same sense as there are perceptual appearances—that is, that there are propositional experiences (and propositional phenomenology). For one might insist that some other kind of mind-internal properties determine conceptual content (conceptual/inferential roles, for example). The thesis that there is propositional experiential appearance requires further argument, which I offer in the next chapter. But I do think that the impossibility of propositional illusion, like the possibility of propositional hallucination, shows that conceptual content is internally determined.

2
The Experience of Thinking

In the previous chapter I argued that propositional intentional content is *internally* determined, but stopped short of claiming that it is *phenomenally* determined. In this chapter I provide two arguments for this additional thesis. I think these arguments support a very strong version of the thesis, on which conceptual phenomenology is *identical to* conceptual intentional content, and conceptual states *instantiate* rather than *express* their contents. On this view there is no need for a bifurcation of content (i.e., that feature of concepts and thoughts expressed by 'that'-clauses and their constituents) into intrinsically determined narrow and externally determined wide components—a move that I take to be independently unmotivated. What I am advocating for is, to adapt a phrase from Kati Farkas, phenomenal conceptual intentionality without compromise (Farkas 2008b).

2.1 An Epistemological Argument for Propositional Phenomenology

In Pitt 2004 ("The Phenomenology of Cognition, Or, *What Is It Like to Think That P?*", hereinafter *PC*) I argued that there is a phenomenology of *pure thought*— a cognitive, conceptual or propositional phenomenology, as different from the more familiar sorts (visual, auditory, etc.) as they are from each other[1]—which distinguishes thought experience from other kinds of experiences (I called it "proprietary"), distinguishes conscious thoughts one from another (I called it "distinctive"), and determines the representational content of thoughts (I called it "individuative"). What I meant by "representational content" was the feature of a thought in virtue of which it expresses the proposition it does, where a proposition is a mind- and language-independent abstract particular. I was assuming in *PC* that intentional content itself is not in the mind, but, rather, is expressed by what is in the mind.

Though I failed to recognize it sufficiently at the time, the argument of *PC* actually entails the stronger claim, which I developed in Pitt 2009, that the

---

[1] Compare Woodworth (1906): "In addition to sensorial elements, thought contains elements which are wholly irreducible to sensory terms. Each such element is *sui generis*, being nothing else than the particular feeling of the thought in question.... There is a specific and unanalyzable conscious quale for every individual and general notion, for every judgment and supposition. An image may call up a meaning, and a meaning may equally well call up an image. The two classes of mental contents differ in quality as red differs from cold, or anger from middle C." (Thanks to Galen Strawson for this wonderful quotation.)

propositional phenomenology of a thought *is* its propositional content. On this view, propositions (at least insofar as they are thought contents) are mind- and language-independent abstract *universals* (propositional-phenomenal *types*), and occurrent thoughts are their tokens.

I did not see this clearly enough at the time, because my point of departure was theories of content that held that causal/referential relations in themselves are insufficient to account for the fine-grained conceptual contents our thoughts can have, and advocated for some kind of internal ("narrow") component that would. A standard move was to appeal to functional, conceptual or inferential roles holding among internal representations. I found this unsatisfactory, since, as I said in the previous chapter, these approaches seem to get things backwards: content determines role, not vice versa. So I approached the problem as one of identifying some *other* internal feature of a mental state that could, perhaps together with its environmental relations, determine which proposition it expressed, what its wide content is. It struck me that phenomenology was a candidate, and I set out to find reasons to believe there might be such a thing as an experience of thinking. Though the idea that there is such a thing was heretical at the time among analytic philosophers, it occurred to me that since it is possible to know *what* one is occurrently consciously thinking in a very direct, non-inferential, introspective way, there must be some kind of introspectively accessible features of thoughts in virtue of which this is possible. One can, it seemed to me, know one's thoughts in the same way one can know one's experiences in general. I did not think this entailed omniscience or infallibility, or that it was the *only* way one could come to know what one is thinking. But it is a way in which, sometimes at least, I came to know the contents of my conscious occurrent thoughts. And it struck me that I would not be able to do this unless the contents of my thoughts were presented *as such* in my conscious experience—phenomenally "manifest," to use Uriah Kriegel's term (Kriegel 2006).

It further seemed to me that the general mode of existence in consciousness is phenomenal. If a state is conscious, then, necessarily, it has phenomenal character; and any change in consciousness is a change in such character. This was, and remains, an unargued but very strong intuition for me. A state can no more be conscious without having phenomenal properties than a physical object could fail to have a shape. Phenomenal properties are *ways* of being conscious; and it is not possible to be conscious without being conscious in some way or other. (I call this the *Phenomenality Principle*, and identify it as one of the basic laws of experience.) It follows that if a mental state is conscious, it has phenomenal properties. This intuition yielded the following simple argument:

(P3) If a mental state is conscious, then it has phenomenal properties.

(P2) Conscious thoughts are conscious mental states.

Therefore,

(P1) Conscious thoughts have phenomenal properties.

Some (e.g., Levine 2011) have challenged the second premise, claiming that perhaps thoughts are *never* conscious; but this seems a desperate move. (I respond to Levine's challenge below.)

This argument, if sound, establishes that there must be a phenomenology of conscious occurrent thought; but it does not, without further ado, establish that this phenomenology must be proprietarily propositional. It is consistent with a view on which the way thoughts are manifested in consciousness is in virtue of some other, more familiar kind of phenomenology (such as hearing or seeing words in one's head; see, e.g., Prinz 2011). But the main argument of *PC*, which is epistemological, is supposed to do this. The idea is that conscious occurrent thoughts can be consciously identified and individuated by thinkers introspectively and non-inferentially. Given that thoughts are individuated by their contents, it follows that conscious occurrent thought contents can be consciously identified and individuated by thinkers introspectively and non-inferentially. But, in order for this to be possible, those contents must be manifest in consciousness in the way that all things are manifest in consciousness—*phenomenally*. And they must be manifest in such a way that they are distinguishable from things that are not thoughts, and from thoughts that are not them. The main argument of the paper is, thus, the following:

(K1) It is possible to identify and individuate one's occurrent conscious thoughts introspectively and non-inferentially. But

(K2) It would not be possible to identify one's conscious thoughts in this way unless each type of conscious thought had a proprietary, distinctive, individuative phenomenology.

Therefore,

(P) Each type of conscious thought (each state of consciously thinking that p, for all thinkable contents p) has a proprietary, distinctive, individuative phenomenology.

This argument does not, and was never intended to, show that there is a proprietary phenomenology of *belief*, or any other propositional attitude. (It might be insisted that merely entertaining a thought, its bare occurrence in consciousness, counts as adopting an attitude toward it. I think this is false; but in the end it does not matter what term we use, so long as we recognize the difference between simply grasping a proposition and taking a stance with respect to its truth.) I am not sure that there is such a thing as a phenomenology of belief. There is surely a phenomenology of consciously *affirming* a proposition. But if (as I tend to think) belief is a functional state, the proof of which is in one's behavior, then it is possible (because actual) that what one affirms is not in fact what one believes. One may consciously affirm what one believes; but affirming and believing are different things. And while it may be possible to experience a thought playing the belief-role with respect to one's behavior, I do not think this would count as a proprietary experience of believing. It would be a complex experience composed of the experience of the thought and the affirmation, together with the formation of an intention and perhaps a perception of the movement of one's body.

The phenomenology of *thinking* is the phenomenology of simply *entertaining*, or *grasping* a propositional content (a proposition). To grasp a proposition, a propositional-phenomenal type, is to token it. I used the term 'grasping' differently in *PC*, to denote knowledge *by* acquaintance. I now think it is better to think of grasping a propositional content in analogy to hearing a sound, smelling a smell, tasting a taste, etc. These states are different from knowing that one is hearing a sound (or knowing what sound it is), etc., which involve the application of concepts to one's experiences. The phenomenal properties of conscious occurrent states constitute the evidence for one's beliefs about them.

In *PC* I followed the standard procedure of assuming that thought contents are mind- and language-independent propositions of some recognized sort (sets of possible worlds, functions from worlds to truth values, structured n-tuples of objects or properties, *sui generis* singular abstract objects, etc.). The argument concludes that which proposition is the content of a given thought is determined by the thought's maximally determinate proprietary propositional phenomenology.

As I said above, I originally intended this argument to show that the relation between propositional phenomenology and propositional content (i.e., propositions) is *representation*. But in fact it shows that the relation has to be something much closer than this, since content itself is introspectively knowable, whereas neither the relations establishing a connection to a proposition nor propositions themselves (as ordinarily construed) are. If it is to account for the possibility of this kind of knowledge, propositional phenomenology must be *identical* to propositional content. The various phenomenologies of different thoughts *constitute* their contents in the way that the phenomenology of any kind of experience does. (Cf. Loar 1987: 89.) The phenomenology of inner speech and reading cannot do this, since one may auralize or visualize sentences one does not understand. Thinking what a sentence expresses requires understanding what it means; so there must also be an experience of its meaning (Strawson's (1994) "meaning experience").

What differentiates conscious visual, auditory, etc., experiences from one another as kinds of experience is their proprietary experiential phenomenologies (visual, auditory, etc.). And what differentiates experiences within each of these proprietary modalities are maximally determinate phenomenologies of the determinable phenomenology that constitutes their proprietary kind (e.g., the sound of middle C, the sound of A above middle C, etc.). Such experiences, and their contents, are distinguishable and introspectively identifiable on the basis of their proprietary and distinctive phenomenological characters. Hence, these characters must be what makes them the experiences they are. (How else could we know which experiences they are simply on the basis of experiencing them?) They are not the experiences they are because they *represent* something non-experiential, but because of their intrinsic phenomenal properties. Likewise, thoughts are not neuro-syntactic sentences that represent non-experiential propositional meanings: they are tokens of those meanings.

This view of thought contents is therefore—entirely appropriately, it seems to me—*psychologistic*. (Cf. Crane 2014.) Propositions, insofar as they are the intentional contents of thoughts, are psychological objects. I may be reminded that Frege (1884) showed that psychologism in logic and mathematics is untenable, since it subjectivizes what is objective, and relativizes such things as consistency, truth and proof in logic and mathematics to the peculiarities and vagaries of individual human psychologies. Logic is the theory of how one *should* think, not how one *does* think. Nor can thoughts be token experiences in the minds of individuals, since then they would be unshareable and unrepeatable.

But none of the virtues of objectivity need be sacrificed by a psychologistic theory, since such a theory can identify propositions with psychological (propositional-experiential) *types*. (They are *psychological* types because they, like all experiential types, can only be tokened by minds.) If a proposition is a *token* thought experience, then it is only accessible to the thinker to whom it occurs, it cannot occur to any other thinker, it cannot occur to the same thinker more than once, and the laws governing its relations to other propositions (the laws of logic) are the idiosyncratic laws governing its co-occurrence with other thoughts in a single thinker (which are more likely to be associational than rational). But if a proposition is a thought experience *type*, and occurrent conscious thoughts tokens of these types, then thoughts are objective, shareable and repeatable—just like any other kinds of experiences; and their formal properties and relations need not include any or all properties and relations of their tokens.

In supposing that *species* are types, one is not committed to saying that contingent physical relations among their members are formal relations among the species themselves. For example, the fact that members (tokens) of the species (types) *cat* and *dog* are mutually antagonistic does not entail that a relation of mutual antagonism holds between the types. (Indeed, this seems absurd.) Likewise, in supposing that thought contents are propositional-experiential types, one is not committed to saying that any and all contingent relations among their tokens in particular minds/brains at particular times are logical relations among the content-types themselves. The thought that I am in my sixties may render me stunned and amazed; but it does not follow that there are corresponding formal relations among the types (the thought-type *I am in my* sixties and the emotional type *stunned amazement*) of which these states are tokens. Relations among tokens cannot in general *be* formal relations among types, since the former are (typically) contingent while the latter are (always) necessary, and they relate entities of different ontological categories. This is, of course, part of Frege's point; but I am emphasizing that its truth does not militate against *type*-psychologism.

Moreover, one and the same phenomenal type can be tokened by more than one thinker, and by a single thinker more than once. Hence, indefinitely many distinct thought tokens can have exactly the same content, and one and the same thought can be shared by indefinitely many thinkers. (Even if there are infinitely many thought contents that are too long or complex to be tokened by any finite thinker. The logical space of thought may be as vast as that of natural language sentences. Cf. Langendoen and Postal 1984. See Pitt 2009 for a fuller discussion of these and other issues pertaining to type-psychologism.) The relation between an occurrent conscious thought and its propositional content is not representation, but tokening.

2.2 Knowing What It Is Like and Knowledge by Acquaintance

Non-inferential introspective knowledge of conscious thought content is, I maintain, knowledge by acquaintance. Knowing that one is occurrently consciously thinking that p (as well as one's knowledge that one is *thinking*, as opposed to seeing or hearing, etc.) is grounded in and justified by one's conscious experience of, one's acquaintance with, a tokening of the propositional-phenomenal content *that p*. One *recognizes* the experience one is having, and on that basis comes to *believe* that one is having that experience (grasping that propositional content) by applying the relevant concepts to it. Hence, introspective knowledge that one is thinking that p is grounded in knowing *what it is like* to think that p.

Knowing what it is like is not propositional knowledge. Knowing what an experience is like does not, in general, require the deployment of concepts of it. Of course, the conscious occurrence of *thoughts* requires the occurrence of the concepts they comprise. But it does not require the occurrence of higher-order concepts of those concepts. The first-order concepts are themselves experiences, and, as is the case with all experiences (as I shall now argue), simply to have them is to know what they are like. Knowing what it is like to have an experience—knowing what the experience is like—is not knowing that one is having it. Nor is it knowing that *this* is what it is like to have it, or knowledge *what* the experience is, in the sense of, for example, knowing what time it is or what the positive square root of 169 is, which is also conceptual (knowing that it is 3:00 a.m., or that the positive square root of 169 is 13). And it is not some kind of know-*how*. It is simple acquaintance with, being familiar with, experiencing, a phenomenal property.

In general, to know what a particular kind of experience is like is to be acquainted with the phenomenal property or properties that characterize it; and to be acquainted with such properties is simply to experience conscious tokens of them. To experience them, in turn, is just for them to be instantiated in one's conscious experience. Acquaintance is the fundamental mode of knowledge of phenomenal properties. It *is* knowing what it is like. I call this kind of knowledge, knowledge of what it is like, "acquaintance-knowledge."[2]

Acquaintance-knowledge is not the same as, and cannot be explained in terms of, knowledge *by* acquaintance. Perhaps acquaintance-knowledge is what Russell (1911; 1912) meant by 'knowledge by acquaintance'. But there is an important distinction to be made between propositional knowledge *based on* acquaintance and the acquaintance it is based on. The former involves thought and the deployment of concepts of experience, whereas the latter consists merely in the occurrence of the experience. As I use the phrase, knowledge *by* acquaintance with a phenomenal property Q has the general form of knowing that Q *is like this* (or that *this is what Q is like*), where the demonstrative refers to an instance of Q with which one is acquainted.

Knowledge by acquaintance that *this is what Q is like* must in turn be distinguished from *non*-acquaintance-based knowledge that *this is what Q is like*. Thoughts about phenomenal qualities one is not acquainted with can have the form *this is what Q is like*, but such thoughts cannot ground knowledge by acquaintance. Since one cannot be acquainted with the experiences of others, one cannot gain knowledge by acquaintance of phenomenal properties their experiences instantiate. One may succeed in referring to an instance of Q in experience not one's own, and one's thought that Q *is like this* may be true. It may even count as knowledge. But it will not be knowledge *by acquaintance*, since acquaintance is lacking. Indeed, supposing there could be unconscious experience, and, hence, that there could be phenomenal properties instantiated in one's *own* experience with which one is unacquainted, one could think such a thought truly about one's own experience. And such a thought might count as knowledge. But, again, it would not count as knowledge by *acquaintance*, since acquaintance requires conscious experience.

Knowing *what Q is like* is not knowing by acquaintance that Q *is like this*, since it does not involve conceptualization or propositional thought at all. To know what shirako tastes like, for example, is just to experience the taste of shirako. The most obvious way to do this is to taste some shirako, though there are other ways (e.g., tasting something that is not shirako but tastes just like it). Not knowing

---

[2] This view of knowing what it is like was (as far as I know) first proposed, as a response to Jackson's Mary thought experiment, by Earl Conee (1994). Conee calls it "phenomenal knowledge."

what shirako tastes like requires never having experienced the taste of shirako, or having experienced it but being unable to remember it. But one can know what shirako tastes like without knowing it is shirako that tastes like that—that is, without knowing by acquaintance the proposition *this is what shirako tastes like*. *This* kind of knowledge requires having the concept SHIRAKO; but one need not have that concept (or indeed any concepts at all) in order to taste shirako and, thereby, to know what it tastes like. Hence, knowing what shirako tastes like is not knowledge by acquaintance that *shirako tastes like this*.

Nor is knowing what shirako tastes like knowing-what, in the sense of knowing what the positive square root of 169 is. To know the latter is to know that the positive square root of 169 is 13, and that requires understanding and deployment of the concept THIRTEEN. But there is no *conceptual* knowledge of what shirako tastes like. (Just try to *tell* someone who has never tasted anything what it is like.) The concept THE TASTE OF SHIRAKO is not like the concept THIRTEEN: grasping it does not enable one to know the full nature of its referent.

Nor, finally, is knowing what shirako tastes like know-how. Though knowledge of what it tastes like—the experience of the taste of shirako—may *enable* certain capacities to recognize, imagine and remember, it is obviously not the same thing. Experiences are not abilities.

2.2.1 Mary

This way of thinking of knowledge of phenomenal properties has (as Conee (1994) recognized) obvious consequences for Frank Jackson's Mary argument. When Mary leaves the black-and-white room and sees red for the first time, she knows what red looks like simply in virtue of visually experiencing it. She experiences something she had not experienced before; and this experience counts as knowledge all by itself. She does not gain propositional knowledge by acquaintance. What she comes to know does not depend upon her coming to be able to think THIS IS WHAT RED LOOKS LIKE, or RED LOOKS LIKE THIS. These are thoughts she was able to think (albeit not truly) in her drab captivity. It does not require that she *think* anything at all. She can know what red looks like without knowing that it is *red* that looks like that—as she might if she were, like Martine Nida-Rümelin's (1995) Mariana, released into a colorful antechamber (the Technicolor Vestibule) containing no identifiable objects. She can know this without having the concept RED at all. Nor is Mary's new knowledge knowledge *what*, in the sense identified above, since there are no concepts the grasp of which enables Mary to know what she knows when she sees red. And, though she becomes able to do things she could not do before her release, the knowledge she gains cannot be identified with any form of knowledge-how. Thus, the only way to substantiate the intuitively correct claim that Mary gains new knowledge is to recognize that acquaintance *per se*, conscious experience, is its own kind of knowledge, knowing what it is like.

2.2.1.1 Retaining Acquaintance-Knowledge

When Mary leaves the room, she gains acquaintance-knowledge of chromatic colors—even if she cannot apply her color concepts to them or identify them by name. Visually experiencing them counts as knowing, in the only way in which it is possible to know the nature of phenomenal properties—to know what they are like. At the instant Mary sees a color, she knows what it is like to see it (what it is like). And as long as she is looking at it, she retains this knowledge. When she is not experiencing a color (perceptually or imaginatively), I claim, she does *not* know what it looks like. If she is not seeing it or imagining it, she does not acquaintance-know it (and, hence, she does not *by*-acquaintance know it). Retention of the capacity to imagine or recognize a phenomenal property is not retention of knowledge of what the property is like. It is retention of the capacity to know what it is like. The capacity to know is not knowing, any more than the capacity to dance is dancing. We may *say* that Mary continues to know what red looks like while she is not experiencing it, just as we say that someone continues to believe that $5 + 7 = 12$, or to be a good dancer, while asleep. But it is not literally true. (I develop this point further, in application to conscious belief, in Pitt 2016.)

Suppose Mary, still in the room, has never tried to imagine red, but could in fact do so if she tried. If she tries, she will come to know what red looks like. But before she imagines it, she does not know what it looks like, because she has never been acquainted with it. Hence, having the capacity to imagine red is not knowledge of what it looks like. Moreover, having the capacity to (imaginatively) *remember* what red looks like does not count as knowing what it is like either. For this is just the capacity to imagine it. Having the capacity to memorially experience a phenomenal property does not count as knowing what it is like any more than having the capacity to non-memorially imagine it. Again, the capacity to know what it is like—the capacity to experience it—is not the same as experiencing it. If Mary is asked if she knows what red looks like, she will not be able to give a truthful positive answer unless she can re-experience it. She may *think* she does, because she *thinks* she can; but if she cannot, then she does not know. If she tries and fails, she must admit that though she once knew what red looks like, she no longer does. She would have to remind herself what it looks like by looking at a sample of it. Acquaintance-knowledge of phenomenal properties exists only *in the conscious moment* (to borrow a phrase from Strawson 1994). If you know what red looks like, it is not because you can imagine it. You know what red looks like when you imagine it (or see it). If you *can* imagine it, then you *can* know it. But 'can' does not imply 'is'. Being able to know what it is like does not imply that you do know it what it is like.

2.2.2 Tye on Knowing What It Is Like

Michael Tye has argued (Tye 2011) that being acquainted with a phenomenal property (which I assume is what he means by "know[ing] the phenomenal or subjective character of an experience" (2011: 300)) cannot be the same as knowing what the property (the experience) is like, because of the logic of knowledge-*wh* statements. For example, according to Tye the following argument is invalid:

1. Mary knows the phenomenal character of the experience of seeing red.
2. The phenomenal character of the experience of seeing red is what it is like to see red.

Therefore,

3. Mary knows what it is like to see red.

It is invalid because it has the same form as the following obviously invalid arguments:

1a. Samantha knows the color red.
1b. The color red is what my favorite color is.

Therefore,

1c. Samantha knows what my favorite color is.
2a. Paul knows Ann.
2b. Ann is whom Sebastian loves.

Therefore,

2c. Paul knows whom Sebastian loves.

His explanation of the invalidity of these arguments is that it is in general not true that *wh*-expressions can be replaced with co-referring expressions in intensional contexts, *salva veritate*. I do not think this is correct. These arguments are invalid because they equivocate, not because *wh*-expressions cannot be replaced with co-referring expressions within the scope of an intensional verb. The word 'know' is being used in different senses in their first premises and their conclusions. In the premise-sense, to 'know' is *to be acquainted with* (to bear a certain relation to a property); in the predicate-sense, to 'know' is *to know that* (to bear a certain relation to a proposition). It is easy to see why these arguments are invalid if we disambiguate:

1a.′ Samantha is acquainted with the color red.
1b. The color red is what my favorite color is.

Therefore,

1c.* Samantha knows what my favorite color is.

(That is, Samantha knows that my favorite color is red.)

2a.' Paul is acquainted with Ann.

2b. Ann is whom Sebastian loves.

Therefore,

2c.* Paul knows whom Sebastian loves.

(That is, Paul knows that Sebastian loves Ann.)

If we read 'know' in the conclusion in the acquaintance-sense, the arguments are valid:

1a.' Samantha is acquainted with the color red.

1b. The color red is what my favorite color is.

Therefore,

1c.' Samantha is acquainted with what my favorite color is.

2a.' Paul is acquainted with Ann.

2b. Ann is whom Sebastian loves.

Therefore,

2c.' Paul is acquainted with whom Sebastian loves.

These arguments are valid because 'acquaintance' contexts are *extensional*.

If 1c' and 2c' sound a bit awkward, it is because 1b and 2b sound a bit awkward. They are awkward ways of saying, respectively, that red is my favorite color and that Ann is the person Sebastian loves. (Perhaps they are best thought of as employing *focus* or *topicalization*.) If we adopt the less awkward phrasing, it is even clearer that the arguments are valid:

1a.' Samantha is acquainted with the color red.

1b.' Red is my favorite color.

1c.' Samantha is acquainted with my favorite color.

2a.' Paul is acquainted with Ann.

2b.' Ann is the person Sebastian loves.

2c.' Paul is acquainted with the person Sebastian loves.

Of course, 'acquainted with' *can* be used to describe a relation one stands in to propositions, as in "I am acquainted with the continuum hypothesis" (I know what it is; I know that it is the hypothesis that there are no numbers between $\aleph_0$

and $2^{\aleph_0}$) or "You are acquainted with my opinion of the human species" (you know what it is; you know that I think the human species is an evolutionary dead end). But to interpret the conclusions in this way is to equivocate on the two senses of this phrase, for surely it is not being used in *this* sense in the first premises. It does not follow from 1a′ and 1b′ that Samantha is acquainted with the fact that my favorite color is red, or from 2a′ and 2b′ that Paul is acquainted with the fact that Sebastian loves Ann.

I conclude that there is no logical reason not to identify knowing what it is like with acquaintance-knowing.

2.3 Objections to the Epistemological Argument

The argument in *PC* is transcendental. It is meant to be an inference to the only explanation of a capacity we have. One way to challenge it is, therefore, to argue that there is an alternative, non-phenomenal explanation of the capacity that works just as well. In this section I consider, and reject, what seem to me to be the best available candidates.

2.3.1 Reliable Mechanisms

One alternative involves application of an account on which self-knowledge is explained in terms of a reliable cognitive mechanism that generates second-order beliefs about one's occurrent conscious states. Thus, to *know* that one is tired, or hungry, is to be informed of such a fact by an internal messaging system whose texts are composed of non-phenomenal mental representations. One *knows* that one is tired or hungry in virtue of being caused to *believe* that one is tired or hungry, by a messaging system that typically gets things right. In this way, the belief counts as knowledge. Likewise for knowledge about one's occurrent cognitive states. Phenomenology is playing no epistemic role.

Aside from the fact that this is obviously *not* the only way one can come to know whether one is tired or hungry (which everyone's ordinary experience bears out), it does not explain how it is that the reliable tokening of a higher-order belief about an occurrent thought that *p* could constitute Immediate conscious knowledge that one is thinking that *p*. If the higher-order belief itself is unconscious, then one's knowledge of one's occurrent state is unconscious. But, by hypothesis, one is *consciously* aware of what state one is in. In this case, the belief itself would have to be conscious. But its being conscious can only explain Immediate conscious knowledge, for the subject, if the content of the belief is itself Immediately consciously apparent to the subject. But if the consciousness of the higher-order belief is not in itself sufficient for the subject to have Immediate conscious knowledge of what *its* content is, then a still-higher-order belief specifying that content would be required, and an infinite regress would ensue.

By hypothesis, the first-order state is conscious. What has to be explained is not the consciousness of that state but, rather, the Immediate conscious knowledge of its content. (Even if it were a higher-order thought about the state that made it conscious, a *further* higher-order belief would be required for knowledge of that state.) In order for the knowledge to be conscious and Immediate, the higher-order belief about it must also be conscious, and its content Immediately knowable.

To block the regress, we have to say that *some* state's being conscious is itself sufficient to ground Immediate conscious knowledge of its content. Some state must wear its content on its conscious sleeve. If it is a first-order thought, then its consciousness is sufficient to ground propositional knowledge of its content. If it is a second-order thought, then *its* consciousness is sufficient to ground propositional knowledge of *its* content. Either way, the consciousness of a thought (i.e., its being conscious) is sufficient to justify beliefs about its content. But this could only be the case if the content of the thought were manifest in consciousness. As argued above, however, the only way for a state to be consciously manifest is for it to have phenomenal properties. It follows that conscious thoughts must have phenomenal properties.

2.3.2 Extrospectionism

Another way to challenge the epistemic argument does not appeal to a reliable belief-forming mechanism. It claims that knowledge of what one is thinking, or believing, desiring or wondering, is obtained not by directing one's attention inward, but by directing it outward.

Extrospectionist theorizing about self-knowledge of propositional attitudes takes its cue from Gareth Evans, who (interpreting a remark of Wittgenstein's) writes (1982: 225):

> [I]n making a self-ascription of belief, one's eyes are, so to speak, or occasionally literally, directed outward – upon the world. If someone asks me "Do you think there is going to be a third world war?," I must attend, in answering him, to precisely the same outward phenomena I would attend to if I were answering the question "Will there be a third world war?"

Evans's view has recently been developed by Richard Moran, in his book *Authority and Estrangement* (2001).[3] Moran generalizes Evans's claim, and couches it in terms of *transparency*:

---

[3] I am indebted here to Alex Byrne's discussion of Moran's views in Byrne 2005.

> With respect to the attitude of belief, the claim of transparency tells us that the first-person question "Do I believe P?" is "transparent" to, answered in the same way as, the outward-directed question as to the truth of P itself.
>
> (Moran 2001: 66)

Here, as qualia externalists claim in the case of perceptual experience, one determines the contents of one's mental states by looking *outward*. If you want to know if you believe that justice is a virtue, do not look into your mind, but consider *justice* and its relation to *virtue*.

This account has the same problem as the reliabilist account: How is it that we know what the result of our attending to outward phenomena is? How do we know the answer to the question we pose to the external world? Presumably it is apparent to us what the answer is, without asking any further questions (which would lead to a regress). But this is the kind of Immediate knowledge of content I have argued requires a proprietary, distinctive and individuative phenomenology of thought.

The view has internal problems as well.

Byrne (2005) argues persuasively that Evans–Moran-style views, on which self-knowledge of belief is achieved by a process akin to decision-making, cannot be the complete story. (Michael Martin (2000) has objected along similar lines. See also Gertler 2015. Byrne further develops his views about transparency and self-knowledge in Byrne 2018.) As Byrne points out, there are many cases in which, when asked what one believes, one *already knows* the answer and, therefore, does not have to *figure it out*:

> Consider the question "Do I live in Cambridge, Massachusetts?" or "Do I believe that Moran is the author of *Authority and Estrangement*?" These questions can be answered transparently, by considering the relevant facts of location and authorship, but I do not need to make up my mind. On the contrary, it is already made up. (2005: 85)

Byrne concludes that transparency, *per se*, "does not show that knowledge of one's beliefs is in general a matter of making up one's mind" (2005). He then goes on to develop an extrospectionist account of self-knowledge which, he claims, avoids the Evans–Moran limitation and explains both privileged and peculiar access to one's own intentional states. (Beliefs about one's own mental states are *privileged* in that they are more likely to yield knowledge than beliefs about the mental states of others, and *peculiar* in that they are acquired in a distinctive way that one could not acquire beliefs about the mental states of others.)

On Byrne's view, one comes to know what one believes by applying to oneself (or at least attempting to apply to oneself) the transparent epistemic rule BEL (2005: 95):

(BEL)   If p, believe that you believe that p.

In order to establish the truth of the antecedent, one considers whether or not p, where p is, typically, not a proposition about oneself or one's mental state. One looks outward to determine the status of p, and recognizing it to be true, applies the rule and believes that one believes that p.

But how is it that considering whether or not it is the case that p, where p concerns facts not about oneself but about a mind-independent world, can support attributions of mental states to oneself? This is the "puzzle of transparency." As Byrne puts it (2005), it seems that "surely [BEL] is a *bad* rule: that p is the case does not even make it *likely* that one believes that it is the case." Here one seems to be in the same situation with respect to oneself as one is with respect to others. BEL, it would seem, is just as bad as BEL-3 (2005: 96):

(BEL-3)   If p, believe that Fred believes that p.

Determining the truth value of p will not help at all in coming to know what Fred believes.

Byrne claims that the solution to the puzzle of transparency lies in the fact that "[o]ne is only in a position to follow BEL... when one has recognized that p. And recognizing that p is (inter alia) coming to *believe* that p" (2005: 96). Simply entertaining the proposition that p is not sufficient, since one can think that p without believing it. That is, the only conditions under which BEL can be applied to yield self-knowledge are those in which the that-clause of its consequent is true: one must *recognize that* p, where recognizing that p entails *believing* that p. Hence, BEL is self-verifying. p may be a mind-independent fact, but that one recognizes that p is not; it is a psychological fact about oneself, and as such justifies a psychological conclusion. In making cognitive contact with the fact that p, one licenses the inference to an explicit self-attribution of a psychological state—in a way that making cognitive contact with p would not license attribution of a psychological state to someone else. Given that one is in the proper circumstances—the circumstances of recognizing that p—one is justified in applying the rule and inferring (the that-clause of) its consequent.

But now it seems BEL is no longer *transparent*. For, in order to apply it, you have to know that you are in the proper circumstances. It is one thing to *be* in the proper circumstances—for there to be a justification for the application of BEL; but if you do not know that you are—if you do not know that you have such justification, then you have no reason, no motivation, for applying the rule. Byrne likens application of BEL when one recognizes that p to application of the rule of necessitation ($p \rightarrow \Box p$) "whenever one is in circumstances in which the rule applies—whenever, that is, one is confronted with a proof whose initial premises are axioms" (2005: 95). But just as you would have no reason to infer $\Box p$ from p

unless you knew that p was occurring in a proof whose initial premises are axioms (why not infer $\neg q$, as you would if p appeared in a proof below a line on which $\neg p$ appeared, under assumption of q?), you would have no reason to infer that you believe that p from the recognition that p unless you knew that you recognized that p. In the absence of such knowledge, you would have no more reason to apply BEL to yourself than you would have to apply BEL-3 to Fred.

Moreover, given that recognizing that p is, as Byrne notes, *inter alia*, believing that p, knowing that one is in a position to apply BEL is *already* knowing that one believes that p. But that is what is supposed to be achieved by the application of BEL. Byrne claims that "the puzzle of transparency is solved by noting that BEL is self-verifying" (2005: 96). But the puzzle is not solved, since one is not really looking outward after all. Additionally, the explanatory value of the theory is lost, since application of BEL presupposes the knowledge it is supposed to generate: the theory is viciously circular.

Though I have focused on Byrne's account, I think these problems arise for any theory that relies on transparency. The general problem is that external facts are only relevant when they are cognized, and one must know the *way* in which they are cognized in order to draw any inference about one's psychological state. But knowledge of the way in which they are cognized is what the inference is supposed to yield.

It might be objected that one need not recognize that one is in proper circumstances for application of BEL in order to apply it and come to know what one believes, because its application is *automatic*: whenever you are in the circumstances of recognizing that p, some mechanism that implements BEL is activated, and forthwith you believe that you believe that p. Simply being in the proper circumstances is sufficient to trigger the relevant mechanism; it is not necessary that you consciously recognize that you are, or self-consciously apply BEL, in order for application of BEL to yield self-knowledge. My challenge relies on an internalist conception of justification, which is not inevitable.

But the sorts of cases Byrne is trying to explain are not automatic. He is concerned with a process in which one *considers* how things are, *applies* BEL, and *concludes* that one believes that p—a conscious, voluntary process of coming to know what one believes. (Note that the consequent of BEL is an imperative—an instruction to *do* something, and that this is something one may *try* to do and *succeed in* doing.) Surely this is one way to come to know what one believes. Whether or not there is a mechanism of the other kind, its operation cannot explain such a process.

Moreover, mechanizing the inference does not avoid the transparency and circularity problems. Given that the mechanism needs as input not just the content that p, which could be believed, doubted, hoped, etc., but, again, the *mode* in which it is cognized, the rule it implements would have to have the form of (something like) AUTO-BEL,

(AUTO-BEL) If that p is recognized, place a token of 'I believe that p' into the belief box,

the antecedent of which is not about the world—the fact that p—but about the psychological state of recognizing that p. Hence, even if the inference is automatic (and/or unconscious), the implemented rule is not transparent: its antecedent refers to a psychological state.

Further, whether the inference is voluntary or automatic, the conditions under which the rule is applicable must be represented somewhere in the system. If there are a number of such mechanisms, each putting out a different kind of attitude with potentially the same content (belief that p, fear that p, hope that p,...), they will each require information about the mode in which the content is cognized—whether it is built into the rule explicitly, as in AUTO-BEL, or encoded somewhere "upstream" in some kind of input sorting mechanism, or otherwise represented. Without this information, the system will not "know" which routine to run, any more than a conscious, voluntary user of the rule. So the automated account is just as circular as the voluntary one: it requires that in order to come to know what you believe, you must already know (be in possession of information concerning) what you believe.

It might be countered that the "knowing" of the subpersonal system and the knowing of the believer are sufficiently different to render the account non-circular. The state the automaton is in is not a psychological state—it is *not* the very state the believer comes to be in when the routine is run. But whether or not the state is properly called psychological, it must carry information in some form about content and attitude if it is to play a role in the causation of the second-order belief. And this is sufficient to render the account circular.

The same sorts of problems would confront an effort to apply this approach to self-knowledge that one was merely *thinking*—as opposed to believing, desiring, etc.—that p. Suppose I ask you what you are thinking, and you answer, "I am thinking about inner-sense and Byrne-style extrospectionist accounts of self-knowledge of belief." How is it that you knew what you were doing—i.e., that you were *thinking* about something? Should we say that you applied the transparent epistemic rule TNK?

(TNK) If p, believe that you are thinking that p.

But there is no more reason to suppose that TNK can be transparently and non-circularly applied than BEL. In order to *be in a position to* apply TNK, you must be thinking (merely entertaining the proposition) that p; but in order to have *reason* to apply TNK (to do what its consequent tells you to do), you must know that you are in that position. Hence, you must know that you are thinking that p in order to conclude that you are thinking that p.

Comparison of BEL and TNK is telling. Given that their antecedents are identical, it is imperative that one know what *kind* of cognitive contact one has made with the content of the antecedent. Otherwise, one would not know which rule to apply, and which consequent to detach.

Further, TNK lacks a feature that gave BEL whatever initial plausibility it may have had. For if one takes BEL's antecedent to record the result of an act of looking outward to determine the way (non-mental) things are, there would seem to be a fairly direct route to the conclusion that what the antecedent records is something one believes. One's answer to the self-posed question "How is it with the world?" expresses how one takes the world to be; and how one takes the world to be is what one believes. BEL formalizes this connection between answers to world-directed questions and knowledge of what one believes; so if you believe BEL, you can apply it to yourself and come to know what you believe. What is doing the work here is the close connection between how one takes things to *be*—what one takes to be true— and what one believes. But it is hard to see what features of the extra-mental world, and, hence, of one's stance with respect to it, could be used to ground knowledge that one is (merely) thinking something. Mere thinking is a *neutral*. In either case, in merely entertaining a thought, there is no question of the truth or falsity of what one thinks, no way in which one is taking the world to be. There is no *stance* to correlate with properties of extramental reality; there is no objective correlate (the way things *are*, the way they *ought to be*, the way they are *not*) of a propositional attitude (belief, desire, disbelief) for the extrospectionist to exploit here.

The extrospectionist theory of self-knowledge of propositional attitudes does not succeed in explaining how it is that one can know *that* one is believing, desiring or thinking, or *what* one is believing, desiring or thinking. Hence, neither this theory nor the reliable belief-formation theory provides a viable alternative to the explanation of self-knowledge of the contents of one's occurrent conscious thoughts in terms of one's acquaintance with their proprietary, distinctive and individuative propositional phenomenologies.

2.3.3 Levine

In "On the Phenomenology of Thought" (Levine 2011), Joe Levine maintains that the argument from self-knowledge in *PC* does not establish that there is a proprietary phenomenology of thinking, since the kinds of self-knowledge it is introduced to explain can be explained without it. Levine begins his critique by making a distinction between *implicit* and *explicit* self-knowledge of thought. Implicit self-knowledge

> is not the result of any explicit formulation or reflection. Rather, it's the knowledge that seems to come with the very thinking of the thought itself.... All that's

required is that one thinks in one's language of thought, mentalese. To implicitly know what one is thinking is just to think with understanding.

(Levine 2011: 108–9)

Explicit self-knowledge, in contrast,

is what we have when we explicitly formulate a meta-cognitive thought, such as "I believe that San Francisco is a beautiful city," (2011: 108)

and is explicable in terms of

the reliability of the relevant process yielding the higher-order sentence expressing the fact that one is thinking a certain content. (2011: 107)

He maintains that implicit and explicit self-knowledge, so construed, are all we need to explain self-knowledge of thought, and that neither requires a special phenomenology of cognition.

I think the distinction between implicit and explicit self-knowledge is very useful (it is similar to my distinction between acquaintance-knowledge and knowledge by acquaintance); but I do not think it can explain self-knowledge of thought content if it is understood in Levine's terms.

For one thing, Levine's account runs into a dilemma. If representational content is *extrinsic* (i.e., determined by a representation's relational properties), then one cannot have implicit knowledge of it simply by tokening a representation—any more than one could have knowledge of the meaning of a sentence simply by inscribing it. Presumably it is the tokening of a representation in one's mind/brain that puts one in a relationship to it that is intimate enough to engender implicit knowledge of it. But if the content of the representation is not tokened with it—if it is not intrinsic to the representation—then there can be no such intimate relationship with content. Hence, it would seem, in order for tokening to constitute implicit knowledge of content, content must be an intrinsic feature of representations. But this does not sit well with the sort of computational picture Levine is appealing to, on which contents are, typically, taken to be extrinsic—i.e., either extra-personal (externalism) or extra-representational (conceptual role theories).

On the other hand, if understanding a representation is knowing what its content is, then supposing that content is extrinsic leads to regress, for it entails that all knowledge of content is explicit, and explicit knowledge, on Levine's account, requires tokening of further representations. Knowledge of the extrinsic content of a representation would be achieved through the tokening of a second-order representation that explicitly attributes content to it. But (as I argued above in Section 2.2.1) if one does not know, at least implicitly, what the content of the second-order representation is, then one will not know the content of the first-order representation. One will not know what one has thought about it. However, *ex hypothesi*, content is extrinsic, and, hence, knowledge of it must be explicit. So knowing the content of the second-order representation requires tokening a third-order representation that explicitly attributes content to *it, etc.* It seems the only way to avoid such a regress would land Levine back in the intrinsicalist soup. He would owe us some sort of theory of intrinsic contents, which would be *prima facie* in tension with his computationalist outlook. And, given Levine's rejection of syntax and semantic phenomenology as candidate implicit *content* discriminators, it is hard to see what sorts of intrinsic properties he might enlist for the job.

Moreover, I do not think Levine's account can explain *conscious* implicit knowledge of thought content, since such knowledge requires the instantiation of properties sufficient to individuate content in consciousness; but, since (as argued above) conscious states are individuated by their phenomenal properties, such knowledge requires a distinctive phenomenology of content.

Mere occurrence of a mental state could not constitute conscious implicit self-knowledge of its content unless the occurrence is itself conscious, and consciousness entails phenomenology. Even if there were some sense in which mere tokening of a mental representation whose content is that p counts as implicit knowledge that one is thinking that p—i.e., that the computational system "knows" which representations are being tokened—this in itself does not explain how *I* can implicitly know what *I am* consciously thinking. You cannot have implicit conscious knowledge of what you are thinking in virtue of tokening an unconscious mental representation. Levine's account does not seem to allow for there to be an *epistemic* difference between conscious and unconscious thinking. Any occurrence, conscious or not, of a mental representation counts as implicit knowledge of its content, and an occurrence of a relevant meta-representation of it counts as explicit knowledge of its content. So it seems that consciousness makes no difference to what I can know about what I am thinking (unless Levine is advocating a higher-order theory of consciousness, on which thinking about a thought *makes it* conscious, which I do not think is the case). But it does make a difference. There is a perfectly good sense in which I *do not* know what I am thinking, believing, fearing, desiring, etc. if these states are unconscious, and I *do* come to know when they become conscious.

In addition, without characteristic phenomenal differences among occurrent conscious states, implicit self-knowledge could not be discriminative—that is, one could not be implicitly consciously aware *that* one is thinking, or of *what* one is thinking. Implicit knowledge of conscious experience requires implicit individuation of experiences, which, in consciousness, is purely phenomenal. One cannot consciously implicitly know what one is experiencing unless the experience is implicitly discriminated in consciousness from all others. Hence, there must be a proprietary, distinctive and individuative phenomenology of conscious thoughts if one is to have implicit conscious knowledge of them.

Levine seems to maintain that we simply *do not have* conscious implicit knowledge of the contents of our thoughts. Indeed, he seems to concede that such knowledge would require a distinctive phenomenology of content, and, hence, that to suppose that we have it begs the question against opponents of propositional phenomenology. And he suggests that all we have implicit conscious knowledge of is the *vehicles* of thought—sentences of mentalese.

But I do not think the claim that we are acquainted with the contents of our conscious thoughts begs the question. And discrimination of the vehicles of thoughts, as such, is not sufficient for distinguishing the thoughts themselves, given that thoughts are individuated by their contents.

In *PC* I characterized self-knowledge of content as direct, non-inferential conscious knowledge of what we are consciously thinking. This does not, *per se*, presuppose phenomenology. It does need an explanation, however, and I provided an argument that the only available one requires a proprietary phenomenology of content. Though some have tried to show that consciousness, and, presumably, conscious acquaintance, does not require phenomenology, I think this position is untenable (see *PC*, 23–4). And I considered what I thought was the most promising non-phenomenal account, based on a reliabilist-computationalist theory of knowledge and belief (of the kind Levine appears to favor), and argued (as I did above) that such theories cannot explain direct access to conscious conceptual contents.

Claiming that it is question-begging to affirm direct introspective knowledge of what we are consciously thinking *because* it turns out that the only explanation for it appeals to propositional phenomenology is like claiming that it is question-begging to affirm direct introspective knowledge of what we are consciously feeling because it turns out that the only explanation for it appeals to somatosensory phenomenology. It is plausible only given a prior commitment to the nonexistence of the phenomenology in question. It is not question-begging to maintain the existence of what is required in order to explain a capacity we have. And it does seem to me to be non-tendentiously, obviously true that we can have non-inferential conscious knowledge of the contents of our occurrent conscious thoughts—of what we are occurrently consciously thinking—and, hence, that providing an alternative explanation for it is a far better (though in the end doomed) strategy for resisting propositional phenomenology than denying its existence. The connection between conscious acquaintance and phenomenology is very close. But this does not make it question-begging to assert it. It only makes it curious that it is been overlooked in the case of conscious thought.

Levine claims that all the phenomenal contrast that is required for such discrimination is a contrast between non-semantic features of mental representations. Phenomenal contrast in the case of entertaining different interpretations of an ambiguous natural-language sentence is just the contrast between tokening distinct sentences in mentalese which represent (unambiguously) the two readings. We tell our thoughts apart by distinguishing non-semantic features of their vehicles that *track*, but are not *identical to*, their contents. The mentalese vehicles of our thoughts are individuated in experience, but not their contents. There is a phenomenology of cognition, but it is not conceptual; it is a kind of linguistic phenomenology, where the relevant language is the language of thought.

It seems implausible to affirm that mentalese tokens have distinctive phenomenal properties, since they are supposedly subpersonal, computational entities. But, in any case, I do not see that Levine's account can explain knowledge of what we are thinking: we have direct conscious access to (unambiguous) mental representations of contents, which are individuated in consciousness by their phenomenal features. But these features are not the contents themselves; nor are they sufficient for determining what the contents are. So direct acquaintance with them cannot explain first-person non-inferential knowledge of what one is consciously occurrently thinking.

Taking into account the distinction between acquaintance-knowledge and knowledge by acquaintance, my argument from self-knowledge is this: Immediate knowledge *by* acquaintance of conscious thought requires acquaintance-knowledge of it, and acquaintance-knowledge requires distinctive phenomenology. Acquaintance-knowledge of the content of a thought (knowledge of *what it is like* to entertain that content) consists in simply the conscious occurrence of the thought. (In *PC*, following Dretske, I called this kind of knowledge of one's experience "simple" (i.e., non-epistemic) introspection. I now think it *is* epistemic in the sense that it constitutes a kind of knowledge. It is just not conceptual or doxastic, in the sense elaborated above. It is knowledge of one's experience (what it is like) that consists simply in the having of it.) Hence, my view is not committed to the regress Levine charges it with (2011: 108–9). One has implicit knowledge of the second-order thoughts whose occurrence constitutes explicit knowledge of the contents of first-order thoughts. I do not, as Levine suggests, "assimilate these two forms of self-knowledge" (2011: 109)—though in *PC* I did not think of implicit occurrence as a kind of self-*knowledge*. Knowledge by acquaintance consists in beliefs about one's mental states formed on the basis of their conscious occurrence. One recognizes what one is thinking—just as one recognizes what one is hearing or smelling or seeing—and applies the relevant concepts and forms the relevant beliefs. The recognition is neither conceptual nor inferential, and the formation of the relevant beliefs, while of course conceptual, is not inferential either.

No doubt Levine would still consider all of this question-begging, since he maintains that we can be "as it were, magically" (2011: 108) aware of our occurrent conscious thoughts (i.e., I guess, we are privy to the results of a computational process, but not to the process itself), without invoking "phenomenal appearance, as we have with sensory experience" (2011: 108). A conscious thought occurs; a mechanism that can register which thought it is causes me to believe that it is that thought (tokens a mentalese sentence that expresses the fact that one is thinking it), and if the mechanism is reliable, the belief will count as knowledge. There is no work here for a proprietarily propositional phenomenology to do.

But it is not the case that we *always* "as it were, magically" know what we are thinking or feeling—that the belief about our experience just pops into our heads. We often recognize what we are thinking or feeling, identify it on the basis of its recognizable properties, and self-ascribe it. We make voluntary judgments about the contents of our consciousness on the basis of recognition of their distinctive phenomenologies. We are consciously aware, not just *that* we are in a particular conscious state but *of* the state itself. Sometimes I come to have a belief about what I am experiencing on the basis of attending to it and recognizing what it is. This is the kind of self-knowledge the argument in *PC* is concerned to explain. Maybe there is a reflex "I am in pain!" that pops into my head when something hurts me. But I can also, so to speak, browse around in my conscious mind (selectively attend to the contents of my consciousness) and attend to things that are there (the song that has been in my head all day, the ringing in my ears, the thought that I am condemned to be free). I may or may not form the thought that I am in any of these states; but if I do, it seems that I can do it voluntarily. The seemingly automatic belief-forming mechanism story cannot explain this.

The issue between me and Levine here is not whether or not there are conscious experiences, or whether or not we can have introspective knowledge of their occurrence and nature. Our difference concerns, rather, *how* beliefs about experience are formed. Levine seems to be claiming that they are *always* formed by a reliable, automatic belief-forming mechanism. My claim is that, whether or not there are beliefs about experience formed in this way, we can *also* voluntarily form beliefs about our conscious experiences on the basis of active introspection, and that this presupposes that we have some way of identifying and distinguishing them from each other, *qua* conscious. But the only properties of conscious experiences that can serve to distinguish them *qua* conscious are phenomenal properties (because these are the only intrinsic properties that conscious experiences as such can have). So, given that it is possible to gain self-knowledge of thought in this way, there must be a distinctive phenomenology of thought contents—a propositional phenomenology. The activity of an automatic belief-forming mechanism cannot, *qua* automatic, explain this sort of self-knowledge. (It would be odd to suppose that all of our knowledge of our conscious occurrent *sensory* states is automatic, since this would render the phenomenology of such states irrelevant to our knowledge of them—we would come to know that, for example, we are hearing the dinner bell in the absence of conscious auditory phenomenology.

It seems much more plausible that one consciously recognizes the sound of the dinner bell, and on that basis comes to believe that the dinner bell has rung.)

Levine suggests that I rely on an (in the context) unduly "rich"—i.e., phenomenal, hence question-begging—conception of consciousness in the argument in PC. But the alternative is to suppose either that thoughts are never conscious at all, or that they are only ever *access*-conscious. I consider the first disjunct to be a nonstarter. On the second, for a thought to be conscious is just for it to be available for use in control of reasoning and behavior. But it is difficult to see how a thought could actually be used in conscious control of reasoning and behavior without the user being conscious of its content in a *non*-access sense (i.e., without being consciously acquainted with it). And I cannot see how that could be explained if all cognitive consciousness were access-consciousness. Non-inferential introspective acquaintance with and knowledge of the contents of conscious states requires phenomenology.

2.4 A Metaphysical Argument for Propositional Phenomenology

For all *non*-conceptual kinds of mental states, sameness and difference *within* consciousness are entirely phenomenally constituted. The various modes of conscious sensory experience, for example, are, *qua* conscious (that is, *as manifested in consciousness*, as opposed to as, e.g., caused by, or realized in, different sorts of brain states; this qualification should be understood throughout this section), constituted and individuated by their proprietary kinds of phenomenology. Conscious *visual* experiences share a particular kind of phenomenology that makes them *visual*, and distinguishes them from conscious experiences in all of the other modes. What it is like to have a conscious experience of yellow is the same, *qua visual*, as what it is like to have a conscious experience of green (or of any other visible property), *qua* visual, and it is the visual kind of phenomenology that makes them both visual experiences. To be a conscious visual experience is to be conscious in the visual way—to have conscious visual phenomenology. Any conscious experience that has this kind of phenomenology is, necessarily, a conscious visual experience, and no conscious experience that lacked it could be a conscious visual experience. There is a proprietary visual mode of conscious experience, and it is phenomenally constituted.

Likewise, there is a proprietary kind of conscious *auditory* experience, and it is also phenomenally constituted. A conscious experience of the sound of thunder is of the same general kind as a conscious experience of the sound of a C-minor triad; and their sameness *qua* conscious auditory experiences is due to their shared auditory phenomenology. (I intend the definite descriptions used here in characterizing experiences to designate particular kinds of experience, regardless of their causes. 'The sound of thunder' in 'an experience of the sound of thunder', for example, designates a particular kind of auditory experience—the sound that thunder makes—whether or not it is caused by the relevant atmospheric phenomenon.) Any conscious experience that has this kind of phenomenology is, necessarily, a conscious auditory experience, and no conscious experience that lacked it could be a conscious auditory experience. There is a proprietary auditory mode of conscious experience, and it is phenomenally constituted.

The same is true of all the other kinds of conscious sensory experience (olfactory, gustatory, tactual,...) we are capable of. Each is, *qua* conscious, constituted by its own general kind of phenomenology (olfactory, gustatory, tactual), and differs from all the others in virtue of its phenomenal kind. A conscious experience of the sound of thunder is fundamentally different from a conscious experience of the smell of burning hair because of the intrinsic differences between auditory and olfactory phenomenology.

Further, differences within the various modes of conscious sensory experience are also phenomenal differences. A conscious experience of the smell of burning hair is of a kind different from a conscious experience of the smell of fresh basil, in virtue of their differing olfactory phenomenologies: what it is like to smell burning hair is different from what it is like to smell fresh basil. They differ as kinds of conscious olfactory experiences because of their distinctive olfactory phenomenologies. A conscious experience of the taste of sugar is different from a conscious experience of the taste of salt in virtue of the difference in their distinctive gustatory phenomenal properties. It is the difference between sweet and salty phenomenologies that makes them different types of gustatory experiences.

In general, then, there can be no differences, or changes, in consciousness without differences or changes in phenomenology. We can call this the *Principle of Phenomenal Difference*. It is a corollary to the Phenomenality Principle: if there can be no consciousness without phenomenology, there can be no difference in consciousness without difference in phenomenology.

Finally, the phenomenology of a conscious experience makes it the kind of conscious experience it is. Differences in kinds of phenomenology between and within the various modes of conscious sensory experience make them different kinds of conscious experiences; but what individuates a conscious experience, *qua* conscious, is also its particular phenomenal character. A conscious experience of the feel of an unshaved chin is different from a conscious experience of the feel of polished marble in virtue of their differing tactual phenomenologies. But it is also the case that a conscious experience of the feel of an unshaved chin is the particular kind of experience it is because of its phenomenal character. Nothing that felt like *that* could be a conscious experience of the feel of polished marble, and, necessarily, any conscious experience that feels like that is a conscious experience of the feel of an unshaved chin (whether or not it is caused by an unshaved chin). No conscious experience that lacked thundery auditory phenomenology could be a conscious experience of the sound of thunder (the sound that thunder makes), and any experience that has it is, necessarily, an experience of the sound of thunder. Likewise for the visual experience of green, the olfactory experience of the smell of burned hair, the gustatory experience of the taste of salt, etc.

Similar considerations could be adduced with respect to all of the further determinates of these determinable sensory experiences, as well as all of the other familiar kinds of conscious experience—e.g., somatic, proprioceptive, emotional, etc. They are all, *qua* conscious experiences, individuated and identified by their proprietary, distinctive and individuative phenomenologies. To *be*, in consciousness, is to be *phenomenal*. A conscious experience cannot occur unless some phenomenal property is instantiated, and *which* phenomenal property is instantiated determines which kind of conscious experience (up to maximal determinateness) has occurred. In short, in all of these cases consciousness *supervenes on* phenomenology: difference in consciousness entails phenomenal difference, and sameness in phenomenology entails sameness in consciousness. (Which is not to say that phenomenality entails consciousness. Given that phenomenality without consciousness is conceivable (as I believe it is; see Chapter 6), to say that sameness of phenomenology entails sameness in consciousness is to say that *if* two experiences are phenomenally identical, then *if* they are conscious they are type-identical conscious experiences.) We can call this the *Principle of Phenomenal Individuation*: conscious states are the states they are in virtue of their phenomenology.

Now, that these principles of phenomenal individuation should be applicable to all kinds of conscious states *except* conscious thoughts is, at the very least, improbable. Given that they apply across such a wide range of so radically different kinds of states of consciousness, surely the burden of proof falls on anyone who claims that conscious thinking is exempt. Why should it be so different?

Furthermore, if conscious thoughts do not have proprietary, distinctive and individuative phenomenal characters, then they would have to be conscious in some way *other than* phenomenally. But what could that be? How could a state be conscious—i.e., be *manifest* in, or *appear* in, consciousness—without being conscious (or appearing) in some way or other? And what could such ways be if not phenomenal properties? Again, the burden of proof is on anyone who would claim that there can be consciousness without phenomenality.

The only attempt I know of to make such a case is Lormand 1996; but I think Lormand's efforts are unsuccessful. (My reasons for thinking so are given in *PC*: 23–4.) Moreover, claiming that conscious thoughts are "access" conscious without being "phenomenally" conscious will not help here, since to be available for conscious use is not *per se* to be *in* consciousness. And to say that something is *in* consciousness is not *per se* to say that it is phenomenal. Even if it is necessarily the case that conscious states have phenomenal properties, it is *not* the case that consciousness and phenomenality are *identical* (or that 'conscious' and 'phenomenal' have the same *meaning*.) They are not the same property. If they were, then phenomenality without consciousness would be inconceivable (which it is not), and Lormand's claim that some conscious states lack phenomenality would be *prima facie* incoherent, which it is not. (It is incorrect, and necessarily so; but it is not conceptually incoherent.) Further, since consciousness is a *unitary* (non-determinable) property, if phenomenality were identical to it, then all conscious states would be phenomenally identical. But they are not: phenomenality is a *determinable*.[4]) So it cannot be the same property as consciousness. Phenomenality is necessary, but not sufficient, for consciousness. Hence, the claim that some thoughts are conscious is not, in this context, trivially question-begging. It is not *trivially* (conceptually) true that conscious thoughts have phenomenal properties, since it is not trivially true that conscious states in general have phenomenal properties. It is a substantive necessary truth. (Cf. *PC*: n. 4.) And the claim that some thoughts are conscious is not just the claim that some thoughts are phenomenal in thin lexical disguise.

Thus, if conscious propositional states (thoughts) constitute their own general kind—if they differ from all other kinds of conscious mental states—then they must enjoy their own proprietary sort of phenomenology. Pains are not tastes, sounds are not smells, visual experiences are not moods, in virtue of having different proprietary phenomenologies. Hence, if thoughts are not pains or tastes or sounds or smells or visual experiences or moods, etc., then they must have a proprietary mode of conscious existence—a proprietarily propositional (conceptual) phenomenology. If they *are* different sorts of conscious states, then, *qua* conscious, they must be *phenomenally* different.

But conscious thoughts cannot be identified with any other sort of conscious states (the most plausible candidate being conscious verbal imagery), since it is possible for any such to occur in the absence of thought. Thinking is *not* the same as producing internal sentence tokens, since it is possible to auralize or visualize a sentence one does not understand without thinking what it means, and monolingual speakers of different languages can think the same thing though they auralize or visualize different sentences. Thoughts are mental states of a different kind from all others. Hence, they must have a proprietary phenomenology—a

---

[4] I do not think phenomenal properties are determinates of consciousness, since I think phenomenality without consciousness is conceivable. Consciousness and phenomenology are not related in the way that, e.g., extension and shape are: if something has a shape, it is not conceivable that it does not take up space. Phenomenal properties are ways of being conscious, just as shapes are ways of being extended. But their occurrence does not entail consciousness. Their relation to consciousness is like the relation of making sounds of a certain volume to singing. One cannot sing without making sounds of a certain volume—these are ways of singing (softly, loudly); but making sounds of a certain volume does not entail that one is singing. It is conceivable that one is making sounds of a certain volume without singing. Thanks to Declan Smithies for helping me to get clear on this.

proprietarily *conceptual* way of appearing; a phenomenology that makes a state conceptual, as opposed to visual, auditory, olfactory, somatic, proprioceptive, etc.

And if there are different types of conscious thoughts, then each distinct type must have its own unique mode of conscious existence. Thus, the phenomenal properties of distinct thought-types must be sufficient to differentiate them from each other (as well as from all other kinds of conscious states), just as the phenomenal properties of different smells or sounds or color experiences must be sufficient to differentiate them. If a conscious occurrent thought t is to *be* a different thought from a conscious occurrent thought t', then t and t' must have distinctive propositional-phenomenal characters.

Finally, since in general conscious states are the states they are in virtue of their proprietary and distinctive phenomenologies, the conceptual phenomenology of a conscious thought must be individuative as well. A conscious occurrent thought is a thought, and the thought that it is, in virtue of its distinctive propositional phenomenology. Moreover, if thought-types are individuated by their contents, then thought contents are propositional phenomenal properties. Each thought that $p, q, r, \ldots$, where $p, q, r, \ldots$ are different contents, has a proprietary, distinctive and individuative phenomenal character that constitutes—is identical to—its propositional content. None of this is because this is the only way we can *know* what they are and discriminate them one from another in conscious introspection. Rather, it is because, *qua* conscious, this is the only way for them to *be* what they are, and to be different from one another and all other kinds of conscious states.

2.5 Phenomenal Contrast Arguments

A common form of argument that there is a *sui generis* experience of conscious thinking is from *phenomenal contrast*. In one kind of case, we are invited to compare the experience of hearing discourse in a language that is understood to the experience of discourse in a language that is not understood (Strawson 1994: 5–6). In another, we are invited to consider *changes* in our own conscious occurrent thought (Siewert 1998: 275–8). In yet another, we are to imagine an individual who lacks all sensory, emotional, algedonic, etc., experience, yet who can still *think*, and consider what it is like for this individual to reason mathematically (Kriegel 2015: 56–62). In all cases it is argued that there is a phenomenal difference—a difference in what it is like for the thinker—and, further, that this is not a difference in familiar kinds of phenomenology, such as that of verbal or auditory imagery, emotional tone, etc. It is then concluded that there is an irreducible, distinctively conceptual kind of experience that accompanies (or constitutes) thinking, differences in which account for the experiential contrasts. (Other proponents of this kind of argument include Horgan and Graham (2012), Horgan and Tienson (2002), Moore (1962), Peacocke (1998) and Siewert

(1998; 2011). The abstract published with *PC* characterizes section 3, "Getting Acquainted with Cognitive Phenomenology," as presenting an argument for conceptual phenomenology. This is incorrect. (Who *wrote* that thing?) I did not intend the discussion there to constitute an argument. Having presented the argument in the first parts of the paper that there *must be* a phenomenology of thought, I intended the examples in that section to acquaint the skeptical reader with some examples of it.

Phenomenal contrast arguments are in my view too vulnerable to competing claims about what the contrast between experiences with and without understanding actually consists in to be definitive in establishing the existence of a proprietary phenomenology of thought. What proponents attribute to a difference in conceptual phenomenology, critics maintain is a difference in auditory, visual, emotional, or some other more familiar kind of phenomenology. Such positions are bolstered by claims of a lack of introspective evidence in the objector's own experience for the existence of such *sui generis* conceptual phenomenology. (See, e.g., Carruthers and Veillet 2011, Chudnoff 2015a, Jorba and Vicente 2020, Koksvik 2015, Levine 2011, Pautz 2013, Prinz 2011 and Tye and Wright 2011.) Moreover, disputes over what is phenomenally manifest to introspection are notoriously difficult (though I think not impossible) to adjudicate. They can too easily devolve into a blunt conflict between introspective reports.

Indeed, it was just this sort of conflict with respect to the existence of thought phenomenology that precipitated the demise of introspectionist psychology. Oswald Külpe insisted that there was introspective evidence for "imageless thought," whereas others (including Wilhelm Wundt and Edward Titchener) maintained that Külpe's work was methodologically unsound, and that subjects' introspective reports could be explained as awareness of fleeting imagery or bodily sensations. (See Nigel Thomas, *Mental Imagery*, section 3.2, "The Imageless Thought Controversy," in *Stanford Encyclopedia of Philosophy* online.)

Hence, though I think that phenomenal contrast argument cases do in fact show that there is conceptual phenomenology, I also think that in such a controversial context a stronger argument is preferable. (This is why I did not use them in making the case for conceptual phenomenology in *PC*.)

Elisabetta Sacchi (2016) has proposed combining the phenomenal contrast strategy with a phenomenal *similarity* strategy. Though she presents the combined strategy only as a way of establishing the irreducibility of conceptual phenomenology to sensory phenomenology, and not its existence, I think it is worth considering whether or not the similarity strategy might be employed to establish the latter.

Contrast arguments typically appeal to situations in which linguistic sensory phenomenology is shared by two individuals but understanding is not. So, we may imagine two monolingual speakers, Jack and Ákos, of, respectively, English and Hungarian, and compare the experiences they have of spoken Hungarian. They would, it seems fair to say, be very different. For one thing, aside from the presence or absence of bewilderment or anxiety, Ákos would understand what he hears, while Jack would not. Proponents of the phenomenal contrast strategy argue that the understanding itself makes a constitutive contribution to the phenomenology of Ákos's overall experience, and that this is, at least in part, why Jack's experience, which lacks it, is different.

Sacchi does not think contrast arguments show that understanding makes a constitutive, as opposed to merely causal, contribution to the experience of speech. She does, however, think that similarity cases, in which understanding is shared but phenomenology is not, can show this. She concludes that in combination these strategies show that sensory and conceptual phenomenology are different kinds of phenomenology, and that the former is not reducible to the latter (though, again, she does not argue that in combination these two strategies can establish the existence of the former).

Sacchi imagines a bilingual individual, let us call him Celestino, who hears utterances of sentences with the same meaning in both languages he speaks (or entertains a thought in inner speech in the two languages he speaks)—for example (Sacchi's), 'A cat is on the mat' and 'Un gatto è sul tappeto'. Since he is fluent in both English and Italian, Celestino will understand utterances of both sentences (whether outwardly or inwardly uttered), and in the same way. Furthermore, he will be introspectively aware of the meanings of the sentences, and of their sameness. So he will recognize that his experiences of the sentences, though auditorily distinct, share a common core—the experience of understanding them, of grasping the propositions they express.

What is nice about Sacchi's strategy is that it makes an explanation of sameness of content in terms of sameness of sensory phenomenology unavailable. Celestino's auditory experiences of 'A cat is on the mat' and 'Un gatto è sul tappeto' are quite different. So it seems one is forced to recognize that what the experiences share is some non-sensory phenomenology.

I personally find this as convincing as arguments based on phenomenal contrast—and not just for the irreducibility of conceptual phenomenology to sensory phenomenology, but also for its existence. But I think the strategy is vulnerable to resistance of the same general kind as the contrast strategy. It is not enough to show that the experiences share non-sensory phenomenology, since the sensory-conceptual distinction is not exhaustive. An opponent could insist that what the experiences have in common is not an experience of meaning but (for example) a generalized feeling of understanding—a sense that one knows what the sentences mean, and even that they mean the same thing, without a distinctive experience of their shared meaning; something analogous to the "Aha!"-experience appealed to to explain intrasubjective changes in understanding. Or perhaps what is shared is the *absence* of a feeling of bewilderment.

Though I do not find such alternative explanations in the least compelling, given that phenomenal similarity arguments rely on the same kinds of introspective judgments as phenomenal contrast arguments, they are equally difficult to argue against, and just as likely to end in stalemate. It seems there will always be some non-conceptual kind of experience a determined opponent could, however implausibly, appeal to and insist upon.

2.6 Against Conceptual Phenomenology

2.6.1 The Humean Objection (Cognitive Acuity)

I have found that even among those sympathetic to the idea of a proprietary phenomenology of thought—including those persuaded by my arguments, there can be difficulty discerning it introspectively. Outright opponents of the idea often object that they never stumble on any such phenomenology in their own case, even when they enter most intimately into their conscious minds. They claim they never observe any experiential properties but the familiar and (relatively) uncontroversial ones—proprioceptive, visual, emotional, auditory, etc. I have always thought this the most ingenuous objection to the thesis, and in some respects the most troubling.

Supposing that my arguments in this chapter are successful, and there really *must be* such a thing as propositional phenomenology, it would be useful to have some kind of explanation for why it is so easy to miss. In this section I offer some suggestions.

The elusiveness of conceptual phenomenology might be due to the fact that it is not as vivid as other sorts of phenomenology (cf. Strawson's (1994) claim that it is "diaphanous"), and so typically escapes one's notice—like the humming of the air conditioner in a noisy office, or a subtle component in the taste of a complex wine. And it may sometimes be drowned out entirely. In particular, given that, for most of us, conscious thought is always accompanied by inner speech, we may always be distracted from it by our auditory and visual linguistic experience. If we are constantly chattering at ourselves when we think, the subtler phenomenology of thought itself can escape our attention.

Indeed, it may be that conceptual phenomenology is, in us, somewhat like, say, visual phenomenology in a flatworm. If there is such a thing, it seems very likely that it is significantly less vivid, varied and articulated—less "pugilistic" (to use a technical term coined by me and Charles Siewert)—than our own. We stand, on the phylogenetic scale of visual experience, far higher than the lowly flatworm—and, presumably, many other creatures we have reason to believe have visual experience (moles, Gila monsters, murder hornets). In any case, it is easy to imagine creatures (including human beings) whose visual experience is quite impoverished compared to that of visually typical people. And if we further imagine that such a creature might nonetheless enjoy other sorts of phenomenology of much greater vividness and articulation, it does not seem at all improbable that it might in general miss the visual aspects of its experience.

For all our vaunted brilliance and intellectual superiority to everything else on the planet, we might nonetheless be, in the grand scheme of things, really not all that great at thinking. Our conceptual experience is not all that clear, vivid or articulated compared to what is possible. We (most of us, anyway) need spoken and written language to help us think, reason, calculate, remember, etc. If this were true, it might explain why it is so difficult for us to think clearly and precisely (especially about philosophical, mathematical and theoretical matters); how we (again, most of us) have to be *trained* how to think precisely and consistently; why philosophy, in particular, is so *hard,* and takes *so long* to do. We are, in contrast, very good at seeing. Visual experience is overwhelming. It presents itself *as the world*, its phenomenology is extremely rich and varied, and it carries a large amount of information about the world, which we are very good at processing very quickly. But the conceptual-experiential aspect of mind may be a relative newcomer on the terrestrial mental scene, and our cognitive acuity correspondingly primitive compared to what it might be in other creatures—just as our olfactory experience is relatively primitive compared to that of dogs.

A further consideration is that in general it takes philosophical reflection to overcome the "natural attitude" toward experience, particularly visual perceptual experience—viz., naive realism. We naturally take what we are directly visually aware of when awake and alert to be external objects, and not our experience of them. Indeed, we generally do not notice our visual experience, as such, at all. But attention to the phenomena of illusions, hallucinations and dreams reveals the distinction between how things seem to us and the way they are, and focuses our attention on the seeming itself. It would not be surprising if we begin with the same sort of naive realism with respect to thoughts. We are directly aware of the contents of our thoughts—*what* we are thinking—i.e., propositions—and not any *experience* of them. And this might lead us to ignore such experience, and even to conclude that there is no such thing, even upon reflection. There is just our mind-independent thought contents, which we directly apprehend.

Moreover, it might be argued in support of this that there *could be* no appearance–reality distinction with respect to thought; and so nothing to appeal to in attempting to dislodge the natural attitude. While there may be such a thing as, e.g., seeming to see a Klingon while not actually seeing a Klingon (misperceiving a human, hallucinating or dreaming a Klingon), there is no such thing as seeming to think that p while not actually thinking that p (mis-grasping, hallucinating or dreaming that p). Thinking is more like being in pain than seeing a Klingon: there is no such thing as seeming to be in pain while not being in pain.

However, while it may be correct that one cannot seem to be thinking that p without actually thinking that p, and that this is analogous to the pain case, it is not analogous to visual hallucination. It may be tempting to think so, because 'seeming to think that p without thinking that p' is, superficially, just like 'seeming to see a Klingon while not seeing a Klingon'. But understanding hallucination in this way would rule it out for perceptual experience: there can be no seeming to see, hear, smell or touch a Klingon while not actually having Klingonesque visual, auditory, olfactory or tactile experiences. The comparison should rather be to cases in which a putatively represented external object does not exist, though one is having a perceptual experience representing its existence. To visually hallucinate a Klingon is to have visual perceptive experience of a Klingon, though there are none. In the case of thought, the putatively represented external object would be a *proposition*, and the hallucinatory case would be one in which the proposition one is putatively representing does not exist. (Because, perhaps, there are no such things as propositions.) To cognitively hallucinate the proposition that p is to cognitively represent the proposition that p though there is no proposition that p. And that, as I argued at the end of the previous chapter, certainly seems possible. So we ought to be able to think our way out of the natural attitude with respect to propositional experience.

Yet another feature of thought that might make its phenomenology hard to detect is its *speed*. Thoughts are short-lived. They are not like experiences of sounds or smells or pains, which may last arbitrarily long. They are more punctate—momentary flashes, so to speak (though, as I argue below, in Section 2.6.3, they do have duration). One way to approximate having a thought for a more extended period of time is to repeat it. (This is something I find I do almost constantly.)

Finally, introspective searches are typically conducted in cognitive mode (*"Now, where is that experience they keep telling me about? Is this it? What about this?"*). One is thus using the very thing one is searching for to search for it (like searching for your glasses with your glasses on, or using your flashlight to try to find your flashlight).

Taking all of these considerations together—thought experience is relatively weak, transparent, brief, constantly conjoined with linguistic experience, and typically used to search for itself—it is not hard to see why our introspective attention might be consistently deflected from it. Conceptual phenomenology is a thing for connoisseurs.

2.6.2 Carruthers and Veillet

Peter Carruthers and Bénédicte Veillet (Carruthers and Veillet 2011: 44) argue that conceptual content cannot be phenomenal because phenomenal content is *ineffable*: one cannot *say*, for example, what the taste of pineapple is (what it is like to taste pineapple), whereas conceptual content is not. We can perfectly well say what "the conceptual content of our experience" (2011: 44) is. For example, a concept may be "*of* red, or *of* a rose, or *of* coffee" (2011: 44).

The objection equivocates. What it is like to think that *p* is, on the phenomenal intentionality of thought thesis, just as ineffable as what it is like to taste shirako. Moreover, just as one can say what one's concept is *of*, one can say what one's non-conceptual experience is *of* (red, a rose, coffee). Carruthers and Veillet are conflating two senses of 'content' (and 'of')—the sense in which one's experience or concept may be *of* or *about* something that does not exist, and the sense in which it may be *of* or *refer to* some existent thing that causes it. (It seems to me that this equivocation infects their whole discussion.)

Their main objection to conceptual phenomenology is that since conscious thought does not contribute to the "hard problem" of consciousness—because it does not induce an explanatory gap—it cannot be phenomenally constituted. (Carruthers and Veillet reaffirm their commitment to this strategy in their 2017.) They argue that a property is phenomenal only if it induces an explanatory gap, and that a property induces an explanatory gap only if we have inferentially isolated concepts of it. Having inferentially isolated concepts is, they claim, a necessary condition for the conceivability of the scenarios (inversion, zombie and achromatic-Mary thought experiments) that are taken to reveal an explanatory gap between the physical and the phenomenal. If there were *a priori* inferential (conceptual) connections between physical/functional and phenomenal concepts of an experiential property, such scenarios would not be conceivable. However (they continue), since there are no inferentially isolated concepts of conceptual properties (concepts), conceptual properties do not induce an explanatory gap. Hence, conceptual properties are not phenomenal.

Inferentially isolated concepts that can give rise to explanatory gaps must bear an especially intimate and immediate relation to the properties they are concepts of. It is not sufficient simply to have distinct, inferentially isolated concepts, since inferential isolation on its own does not guarantee an explanatory gap. For example, though (supposing that IRONY is Kierkegaard's favorite concept) the concepts KIERKEGAARD'S FAVORITE CONCEPT and IRONY are inferentially isolated (there is no *a priori* connection between them), no explanatory gap is generated from their application. The isolated concepts must each reveal something of the nature of their referents. On some accounts, concepts of sensory properties (so-called "phenomenal concepts") contain samples of the properties they are concepts of (Papineau 2002; Balog 1999; 2012). Carruthers and Veillet maintain that the requisite intimacy between a concept and a concept of that concept can only be achieved by *including* the former in the latter. The required revelatory relationship does hold between the concepts THE CONCEPT OF IRONY and IRONY. Obviously, however, such containment precludes inferential isolation. And with no inferential isolation, gap-supporting scenarios should not be conceivable.

I do not believe that the standard gap-inducing scenarios depend upon the presence of inferentially isolated concepts. It seems to me that explanatory gaps arise not from our *conceptions* of phenomenal properties, but from our *direct experience* of them. Moreover, gap-inducing scenarios *are* conceivable in the conceptual case, in spite of the lack of inferential isolation between concepts and concepts of them (though one must be careful in formulating them).

Consider first Mary. Achromatic Mary knows all the physical facts about color vision, but has never experienced chromatic colors. When she is released from the room, the argument goes, she learns something new—what color experiences are like. Hence, what it is like to experience color is not reducible to physical facts. In the cognitive case, we would imagine that Mary knows all the physical facts about cognition, but has never experienced it, and argue that she learns something new—what cognitive experiences are like—when she does. Hence, there is an explanatory gap between the physical and phenomenal facts about cognition. (Alvin Goldman (1993) argues that a Jackson-style argument can be mounted for a phenomenology of propositional attitudes.)

This seems perfectly conceivable, though it is problematic in the present context. In the original case it is *presupposed* that there is a kind of experience that Mary lacks in the room and gains upon her release. Jackson's argument is meant to show that experiential facts in general cannot be deduced *a priori* from physical facts, and so are not physically explainable. It is not meant to establish the existence of any particular kind of experiential fact. It is supposed to show that *if* a property is experiential, then it cannot be physically explained. But it cannot be presupposed that conceptual properties are experiential in this context without begging the question. (McClelland (2016) also makes this point with respect to zombies.) Moreover, if it cannot be presupposed that conceptual properties are experiential, then what it would have to mean to say that Mary never "experienced" thought is that she has never thought at all—which is hardly consistent with her knowing all the physical facts about cognition.

It would be unfair to conclude from this, however, that conceptual properties do not induce an explanatory gap. This particular thought experiment cannot be used to show that they do; but we should no more conclude that they do not than we should conclude that sulfuric acid is not an acid because it dissolves litmus paper before it can change color. Being unable to take a test is not failing it. Jackson's thought experiment is not applicable to conceptual qualities, not because it fails to show that it is possible to know the physical facts about thinking without knowing the phenomenal facts about thinking, but because it cannot be non-question-beggingly set up for them. Conceptual qualities cannot take the test Jackson presents.

And the same is true for zombie thought experiments, which are also designed to show that phenomenal properties are not physically reducible. While it is perfectly conceivable that there be a physical duplicate of a conscious creature who lacks conscious thought, this would show an explanatory gap for conceptual properties only if we assume they are experiential. Again, conceptual phenomenology does not fail the test; it cannot take it without begging the question.

What is required to show the conceivability of conceptually induced explanatory gaps is non-question-begging versions of these thought experiments.

It is widely accepted that thought, unlike sensory experience, can occur unconsciously. So we might imagine that Mary has unconscious knowledge of the physical facts about cognition, but has never thought anything consciously. We could suppose that her room is equipped with a conscious-thought blocker (perhaps some kind of *dampening field* that interferes with Mary's conscious cognitive pathways). We could then argue that she would learn something new about thought—what it is like to think—if the device were turned off, or if she were to leave the room. This certainly seems unproblematically conceivable.

Still, it could be objected that this thought experiment does not hit its mark, since it does not show that thought *content* is gap-inducing. Nothing in the argument shows that the experiential difference is not due to the absence and presence of some kind of non-conceptual phenomenology that accompanies conscious thought. But there is another thought experiment that gets around this objection.

Suppose that the dampening field in Mary's room completely disables her cognitive pathways, so that she has no thought at all (as evidenced, e.g., by her complete lack of response when she is presented with a simple logic problem and asked to solve it). And suppose, further, that the field does not interfere with non-cognitive processes, and does not prevent Mary from having sensory experiences of all the normal kinds (as evidenced by her normal discriminative reactions to various sensory stimuli, including speech and writing). Now we can ask what would happen if *this* field is turned off, and Mary has conscious thoughts for the first time. Will her experience change? Will she learn something new? The proponent of conceptual phenomenology would argue that she does: she learns what it is like to think. Moreover, given that she has had experiences of all the usual kinds while not being able to think, the objection to the previous version of the thought experiment is blocked. (Cf. McClelland 2016: 546.) Her new experience would have to be proprietarily conceptual. There is a non-sensory experience of thinking. The opponent will object that her experience will *not* change, and that it is question-begging to assert that it will. But the point is that the *set-up* is neither question-begging nor incoherent: it does not assume that there is a *sui generis* conceptual phenomenology; and it seems perfectly conceivable. Hence, Carruthers and Veillet's claim that explanatory gaps are inconceivable for conceptual states is false.

We can also construct non-question-begging conceptual zombie thought experiments. Your standard-issue zombie is physically identical to some conscious creature, but lacks consciousness. If we suppose that there can be no unconscious experiences of the familiar types—visual, auditory, olfactory, algedonic, etc.—then these zombies have no experiences at all, and the case delivers explanatory gaps for these various sensory phenomenologies as well as for consciousness itself. (That consciousness is not *identical* to any of these phenomenologies is shown by the fact that any of them can occur consciously in the absence of the other. There are *two* "hard problems.") We can also imagine cases in which physically identical creatures lack some, but not all, of the kinds of conscious experience we have: visual zombies, auditory zombies, olfactory zombies, etc. A conceptual zombie would then be a physical duplicate lacking only conscious thought; and such a creature certainly does seem conceivable. (Cf. Horgan's 2011 Andy thought experiment.)

The possibility of unconscious thought presents a temporary obstacle here, as it did in the Mary case. Zombie scenarios are irrelevant to the question of whether conceptual properties induce an explanatory gap if the absence of *conscious* thought does not entail absence of *thought*. A conceptual "zombie" would have to be a completely *thoughtless* physical duplicate. And it might be objected that such a creature is not in fact conceivable. One might, for example, claim that thinking is *functionally* constituted, and, like biological processes, must of necessity occur in a physical duplicate of a thinker: a thoughtless physical duplicate is no more conceivable than a dead one. However, since it is conceivable that thought is *not* functionally constituted, it is also conceivable that there be thoughtless physical duplicates of thinkers. So there is, at least apparently, an explanatory gap between the cognitive and the physical.

Carruthers and Veillet (2017: 82) argue (against Horgan's Andy example) that a functional duplicate of a thinker would undergo the same "semantic processing," as the thinker, "believe...that he knows exactly what [is] said to him," and be "able to report it...." But this is question-begging. A functional duplicate may *seem* to be doing these things, but is not really doing them unless there is genuine understanding. And it is clearly conceivable that there could be creatures that act, talk and process like they understand, but do not.

Conceptual inversion scenarios also seem to me to be unproblematic. Just as it is conceivable for physically identical perceivers to have different experiential responses to the same kinds of objective stimuli (strict inversion is not required), it is conceivable that physically identical individuals could have different conceptual responses to the same kinds of objective stimuli. For example, just as one perceiver might experience blue while looking at the sky while another experiences yellow, one thinker might think FROG when confronted with instantiations of froghood while another thinks HAMSTER.

One must be careful here, however, since whether or not perceptual inversion scenarios are conceivable depends upon how one individuates perceptual contents. If we suppose, for example, that the content of a visual perceptual representation is the externally instantiated non-experiential property that causes it, then inversion scenarios are coherently conceivable. If blue is an objective property, then two perceivers looking skyward and having qualitatively different experiences could both be in states of perceptually representing blue even if their experiences were different. If, on the other hand, perceptual contents are individuated *phenomenally*, then such scenarios are not coherently conceivable. Individuals having qualitatively different visual experiences could not be representing the same color: they could not be representing the same property differently.

And the same holds for conceptual representations. Physically identical individuals entertaining intrinsically different conceptual representations could be entertaining the same content if conceptual contents are individuated by extrinsic relations, but not if they are individuated by properties intrinsic to the representation. If the contents of the concepts FROG and HAMSTER are determined extrinsically, then they could have the same content in spite of their intrinsic differences. But if their contents are intrinsically determined, they cannot. Hence, the conceptual and perceptual cases are exactly on par with respect to invertibility. (Carruthers and Veillet deny this (2011: 49), but I think they are mistaken.) If, as I have argued, conceptual content is internally individuated conceptual experience, then inversion scenarios are impossible. But this would no more show that there is no conceptual phenomenology than the analogous scenario for perceptual experiences shows that there is no perceptual phenomenology.

2.6.3 Tye and Wright

Michael Tye and Briggs Wright (Tye and Wright 2011) offer several criticisms of the phenomenal intentionality of thought thesis, and of my argument for it in PC. Their "*prima facie*" case against cognitive phenomenology is its *introspective unfamiliarity*—by which I take them to mean that it is not readily encountered in introspection. Whereas the existence of proprietary sensory phenomenologies of the various familiar kinds can scarcely be denied, conceptual phenomenology seems elusive—even among those who are convinced of its existence, or at least not inclined to deny it. I think this is an important challenge. I tried to address it with the contrast cases I presented in section 3 of PC (which were designed to induce examples of the relevant experience, not establish its existence), and in Section 2.7, above. As I said, it may be that it is "diaphanous," and hence difficult to locate—especially amid the hubbub of its more obstreperous companions in consciousness. If one is looking for something as "pugilistic" as, say, a sharp pain, or a thunderclap, one will be bound to miss it. And the problem might be compounded by the fact that we use what we are looking for (thought) to look for it. (Indeed, it is the relative diffidence of conceptual experience that led me to seek an argument for it.)

Tye and Wright also object that in *PC* I adopted a *perceptual* model of introspection, and that such a model mis-locates the phenomenology I argue must exist. Objects of perception are distinct from perceptual experiences of them, and the phenomenal properties apparent in the latter are not (or need not be) properties of the former. So it would not follow from there being a phenomenology of the experience of thinking that thoughts themselves have that, or any other, phenomenology. But I explicitly denied that I was relying a perceptual model (*PC*: 10: "I do not mean to suggest here that simple introspection is simple *perception* of mental particulars, nor that the experience of an occurrent conscious mental particular M is a state distinct from M."). My position in *PC* was, rather, that "to say that one simply introspects a conscious mental particular is to say that one has a conscious experience of which the mental particular is itself a differentiated constituent" (*PC*: 10). Nor am I, my denial notwithstanding, nonetheless committed to one.

My use of Dretske's views on perceptual knowledge perhaps encouraged this misunderstanding. But my use was analogical; and analogies always come with disanalogies. The disanalogy with perception (which I was explicit about) is that in the case of mental states there is no difference between their conscious occurrence and conscious awareness of them. So, just as there is simple (non-epistemic) smelling, i.e., the occurrence of a conscious olfactory experience, there is simple thinking, the occurrence of a conscious conceptual experience. And just as there is no difference between the conscious occurrence of a smell and an experience of it, there is no difference between the conscious occurrence of a thought and an experience of it. In both cases, since one's awareness of the experience is not distinct from the experience, the phenomenal properties one is aware of are properties of the experience.

A further objection is that, as per Peter Geach (1957), thoughts cannot be parts of the stream of consciousness, because they do not *unfold* over time. But if thoughts cannot be part of the stream of consciousness, Tye and Wright argue, they "simply aren't suited to be the bearers of the relevant [i.e., conceptual] phenomenology" (2011: 343). If what they mean by thoughts not *unfolding* over time is that thinking a thought does not *take* time, I think they are obviously mistaken. (Though I am not sure I know what *any* parties to this discussion mean by 'unfolding'.) The duration of an occurrent thought may be very brief, but if thoughts were *instantaneous*—if they took up *no time at all*—they could not be conscious. And if they could not be conscious, something that obviously is possible—viz., knowing that and what one is occurrently thinking through conscious reflection—would be impossible. Thoughts may be more like short, sharp shocks than melodies; but this cannot prevent them from being present within the stream of consciousness. Hence, given that presence within the stream of consciousness is *phenomenal* presence, it follows that thoughts have phenomenal properties. (Moreover, as I have argued in *PC* and elsewhere, it cannot be just the "vehicles" of thought (cf. Soteriou 2009)—e.g., inwardly uttered sentences—that are present in consciousness, since *content* is available to conscious reflection. Indeed, I do not think thoughts have syntactic "vehicles" at all. They are instantiations of meanings, which are pure experiential types.) Furthermore, a conscious thought may be part of a stream of thought by virtue of being one of several that follow upon each other. (Tye and Wright seem to acknowledge this possibility (2011); but, they argue, Geach would have denied it, and, in any case, they have other arguments against conceptual phenomenology.)

Another problem with Tye and Wright's argument is their misunderstanding and misapplication of the metaphysics of persistence. They seem to think that the fact that all of the constituents of a thought must exist at any moment the thought exists means that thoughts can have no temporal extension: thoughts *endure*, they say, but do not *perdure* (2011: 342); "they are wholly present at each moment that they exist" (2011: 342). But being wholly present in *this* sense has nothing whatever to do with the distinction between endurance and perdurance. If a physical object has physical parts, then they must exist whenever it does. But it is a completely separate question whether or not it *also* has temporal parts. The endurantist thesis that physical objects exist wholly and completely at any moment at which they exist is just the denial that they have temporal parts.

A more general problem, which plagues Geach's and Matthew Soteriou's (2007; 2009) discussions as well, is the conflation of *thinking*—entertaining propositional content—with *judging* and *believing*. Judgments may be instantaneous changes in propositional attitude, and attitudes may be standing states (though I deny this; see Pitt 2016), and it may be that because of this they cannot show up in the stream of consciousness. But conscious thoughts, *per se*, are neither judgments nor propositional attitudes. (This is one of many places where the distinction between the phenomenology of *thought* and the phenomenology of *attitude* is crucial.) A judgment may be instantaneous while the thought that is its content is not, just as the diversion of a stream may be instantaneous while what it is a change in, the flow of water, continues through the change.

2.7 Internal Worries

2.7.1 The Matching Content Challenge

Tim Bayne and Tom McClelland (Bayne and McClelland 2016) discuss an important challenge to the phenomenal intentionality of thought thesis. They argue that if intentional content is determined by, or supervenes on, or (as I maintain) is identical to, phenomenal character, then states with the same intentional content should have the same phenomenal character (and, in my case, vice versa). However, there appear to be cases in which this is not so—for example, a visual experience of a particular shade of blue and a concept of that shade. What it is like to have a visual experience of that color is different from what it is like to entertain a concept of it; yet, intuitively, they both have that color as their intentional content (they are both *of* that color). Hence, Bayne and McClelland argue, an advocate of conceptual phenomenology "owes us an account of why the phenomenal character associated with thinking that *p* differs from that which is associated with perceiving that *p*" (2016: 29). And they are skeptical that such an account can be provided.

I addressed this issue in my paper "Intentional Psychologism" (Pitt 2009: 131–3). I argued there that the best way to meet it is to deny that conceptual and perceptual states in general have the same intentional content. In support of this I appealed to the relative richness and density, as well as the potential indeterminacy, of typical perceptual experiential content, as compared with conceptual content. But I think Bayne and McClelland's example of perceptual and conceptual representations of a single property shows that this is not a sufficient response. It does not seem that a pure experience of a particular color is complex in a way that should prevent it from sharing content with a concept of that color. Bayne and McClelland argue that "[a]lthough the specificity of perception *typically* outstrips that of thought, it seems highly unlikely that this fact reflects a deep and essential contrast between perception and thought" (2016: 33). I agree.

I sketched another strategy in my 2009 paper (132–3), on which conceptual and perceptual representations have different kinds of contents because they have different kinds of representational formats. Thoughts, being language-like, have propositional contents, while perceptions, being pictorial or map-like, have non-propositional contents, such as states of affairs, or perceptual scenarios, with structures and constituents matching those of the perceptual state. Bayne and McClelland reject solutions that pin differences in phenomenology to differences in format. They argue that "differences in representational format have a bearing on the matching content challenge only if the phenomenal character of a mental state does not supervene on its content" (2016: 38). But I think this is only true of a view on which format *alone* determines phenomenology. If representations are distinct from their contents, to adopt such a position would be to abandon the connection between content and phenomenology. However, my suggestion was that differences in format entail differences in contents, which is consistent with the thesis that phenomenal character supervenes on (or is identical to) intentional content. (Bayne and McClelland cite Crane (2009) and Heck (2000) as defenders of this approach.)

That said, however, I think this strategy is blocked by the same kind of example that blocked the first one. If simple conceptual and perceptual representations can have the same content—a single property, for example (as opposed to complex propositions or perceptual states of affairs), then an appeal to differences in their format is unavailing, since they do not entail a difference in content.

I still think the best way to respond to the challenge is to deny that perceptual and conceptual experiences can have the same content, however. But the better way to support it is to maintain a sharp distinction between content and reference, and allow that representations with different contents can co-refer. On the view defended in this book, intentional content is essentially phenomenal, and any phenomenal differences constitute a difference in content. And this holds both within and between phenomenal modalities. Hence, a visual experience of blue and a conceptual experience of blue must have different intentional contents, though they both refer to the color blue—just as the concepts BLUE and THE PRIMARY COLOR BETWEEN GREEN AND VIOLET do. They are both *of* blue in the sense that they both refer to blue, but not in the sense that they present blue in the same way.

Some advocates of phenomenal intentionality argue that phenomenal character determines (or supervenes on, or is) only "narrow" content, with "wide" content being determined by extrinsic relations. And it might be thought that this is a better way to go, since it accommodates widely accepted externalist intuitions. One could hold that perceptual and conceptual representations of properties can have the same wide content while having different narrow contents. I resist this move, however, since (as I argue at length in subsequent chapters) I find the narrow–wide distinction to be unmotivated.

Bayne and McClelland consider this kind of response, but reject it (2016: 36–7). They argue that it can only work if it is not possible for conceptual and perceptual representations to represent in the same way, which they deny. In particular, they claim that "it is plausible that our thought represents [e.g.] blueness under just the same mode of presentation as our perceptual experience" (2016: 37).

I am not sure I completely understand Bayne and McClelland's reasoning here. They say that this kind of view (a version of what they call "Unrestricted Fregeanism") "requires either that thought and perception can never represent objects and properties via the same modes of presentation, or that if they did then the content-involving contrast between them would disappear" (2016: 36). They deny that the embedded conditional is true. But I do not see how they can. If modes of presentation are phenomenal (e.g., perceptual or conceptual experiences), then to share them is to share phenomenology—in which case there is no longer a problem with them having matching contents.

In any case, I deny that it is possible for concepts to present their referents in the same way as percepts. As I argue in detail in Chapter 4, conceptual contents cannot be or contain or otherwise be individuated by sensory (or any other non-conceptual) phenomenal properties. Conceptual and non-conceptual *contents* cannot mix—because conceptual and non-conceptual *phenomenology* cannot mix. This strikes me as a fundamental fact about phenomenology. (I call it the Principle of Phenomenal Immiscibility. See Chapter 4 for development.) There can be no cross-modal constitution: a visual experience cannot have an olfactory experience as a constituent, for example. (Note that this is *not* to say that one cannot have an experience part of which is visual and part of which is olfactory. It is to say that no such experience could be either a visual experience or an olfactory experience *simpliciter*.)

There are thus no *concepts* that someone (e.g., Mary) cannot have because they have never had a visual experience. Mary gains new knowledge (phenomenal knowledge) when she leaves the achromatic room; but she does not gain any new concepts. The concept she had of blue in the room is the very same concept she has after seeing something blue. If you asked her to *tell* you (without demonstrating an instance of blue), what blue is after her release, what she can tell you is no different from what she could have told you while still in the room. Indeed, it is no different from what any normally sighted, non-incarcerated individual could tell you (*modulo* the science). (See Chapter 4 for much more discussion.)

Concepts and percepts cannot share phenomenal intentional contents (or modes of presentation), though they may be *of* the same thing in the referring sense of 'of'. The matching content problem does not arise for the advocate of conceptual phenomenology.

2.7.2 Phenomenal Compositionality

One feature that thought is usually taken to have in common with language is *compositionality*. Indeed, the Language of Thought Hypothesis has it that thought, being language-like in certain essential respects, *is* a language. (I prefer to think of language as being thought-like. Thought comes first.) In order to explain the creativity, systematicity and productivity of thought, it seems that we must take the contents of thoughts or complex concepts to be determined by the contents of their constituents and their structural relations—just as we do in explaining the creativity, systematicity and productivity, as well as comprehensibility of novel utterances and learnability, of language. This is especially so if the semantics of language is *grounded in* the semantics of thought. If the meanings of words and sentences are identical to the contents of concepts and thoughts, then if linguistic meaning is compositional, thought content must be compositional as well.

One might worry, however, that complex conceptual phenomenology (the phenomenology of a complex concept or thought) cannot in general be compositional, since phenomenology seems to be subject to contextual variation, or contrast effects.[5] For example, a particular color may look different when seen with other colors. A wine may taste different when tasted with food, and with

---

[5] This concern was pressed upon me, separately, by Adam Arico and Galen Barry.

different kinds of food. A particular chord may sound different depending upon which chords precede it or follow it. And so on. But if phenomenal character can change with context, and a change in phenomenal character entails a change of experience (I consider this non-negotiable), then it will not be true in general that experiences can be combined to form more complex experiences whose constituents are *those very same* experiences. If, when phenomenally individuated experiences combine, their phenomenology changes, they become different experiences. (More precisely, they cease to exist and are replaced by different experiences.) And if this is true of conceptual phenomenology, then the content of a thought or complex concept will not in general be factorable into the contents its constituents have in isolation.

The experienced color of the small square on the left and that of the small square on the right are different.

The one on the right is the same color (and the same size) as the one on the left, but it looks different when embedded in the larger square. Hence, though the look of the combined squares can be factored into the look of the dark gray square and the light gray square embedded in it, it cannot be factored into the look of the dark gray square and the light gray square in isolation (the one on the left).

If there are similar effects for conceptual phenomenology, then we might find ourselves having to say that the content of a complex thought or concept does not include the contents of its constituents. For example, if the thought contents p and q are phenomenally constituted, there would be no guarantee that there is a complex conscious thought whose content is composed of the contents p and q. If conceptual phenomenology is subject to contexts effects, it is possible that when the thoughts that p and q are experienced together their phenomenal characters, and, hence, their contents, change. But if thoughts are individuated by their content, then the original thoughts cease to be thought when one attempts to think them together. In which case, when one is thinking the thought *p and q*, one is not thinking its constituent thoughts p and q. This hardly seems coherent. So if it does happen, it would be a very good reason to reject a phenomenalist account of conceptual content.

Before addressing this worry, it will be helpful to distinguish two kinds of phenomenal compositionality. A complex experience or phenomenal state (I use the terms interchangeably) is *post hoc compositional* if its phenomenology is factorable into constituent phenomenologies, but these constituents are not the phenomenologies of the experiences that came together to form it (*they* had different phenomenal characters). That is, the phenomenology of the complex is determined by the phenomenology its constituents have in context; but it is not determined by the phenomenologies its constituents have out of context (as in, say, Ganzfeld experiences), and it is not constant across all contexts. Let us call this latter kind of compositionality *ante hoc compositionality*. Phenomenology in general, it seems, cannot be assumed to be compositional in this second sense. The experience of the squares on the right is not composed of the experience of the square on the left and the experience of the embedding square on the right. But *ante hoc* compositionality is what is required to explain phenomena like the creativity, systematicity and productivity of thought. If conceptual phenomenology is not *ante hoc* compositional, there would be serious pressure to abandon the idea that it is content-constitutive.

One way to respond to this worry would be to deny that compositionality is typically *ante hoc*. Here one might cite the linguistic phenomena of *topicalization* and *focus*, which involve surface relocation or phonetic stress of a sentential component (without changing its underlying structural relations), as in the following examples:

(1) You can't trust him.
(2) *Him* you can't trust.
(3) *You* can't trust him.
(4) You *can't* trust him.

Some linguists claim that these operations have an effect on the meaning of the sentence. If this is correct, then linguistic meaning cannot be taken to be in general *ante hoc* compositional. And one could argue that the same sort of thing happens with the thoughts these sentences express. And if these phenomena do not spoil compositional explanations for creativity, productivity and systematicity in language, they should not spoil them for thought.

There is, however, an important disanalogy between topicalization and focus and phenomenal context effects. As far as I am aware, topicalization and focus do not affect the meanings of constituent expressions, whereas contrast effects concern the phenomenal character of the components of complex experiences.

Another way to deny that compositionality is *ante hoc* would be to adopt an analogue for thought of Frege's context principle—viz., "it is only in the context of a proposition that words have any meaning" (Frege 1884: section 62). If concepts have content only in the context of thoughts, phenomenal contrast effects would not present a problem for the phenomenal intentionality of thought thesis. If it were true that concepts only have phenomenal properties in context, there would be no contrast effects. I will not pursue this response. I think Frege's motivation for adopting his principle is *ad hoc* (it is introduced only to further his logicist program, and does not have independent support). Moreover, it is patently false that experiential components of complex experiences (such as the gray square on the right) have no phenomenal properties in isolation. The gray square does not disappear if you move away from the larger one.

A more promising route would be to argue that we do not after all need *ante hoc* compositionality to have a theory of thought content that can explain creativity, productivity and systematicity. For, if context effects are not arbitrary—if, that is, there are principles determining when and why phenomenal contents change the way they do in different contexts (as I assume there is for, e.g., colors), then such principles could simply be incorporated into a theory of composition for complex thought contents. And we would have a useful kind of compositionality after all: the content of a complex concept or a thought is determined by the contents of its constituent concepts, their structural arrangement, and the relevant features of the experiential context in which it occurs. On such a view conceptual content would be in part contextually determined, but a complex content would still be determined (albeit in a more complex way) by the contents of its constituents.

Adding a context clause to a definition of compositionality would be like adding a structural relations clause to the simple (and false) mereological rule that the content of a complex expression is the sum of the contents of its constituents. Just as certain semantic evidence (e.g., that 'Tristan loves Isolde' does not mean the same as 'Isolde loves Tristan') would lead one to modify a principle of *mereological* compositionality to get *structural* compositionality (the content of a complex expression is determined by the contents of its constituents and their structural relations), some such evidence could lead one to modify the structural principle of compositionality to get *contextual* compositionality.

However, this approach would not remove the specter of the possibility of thinking that *p and q* without thinking that *p* or that *q*. For, whether or not context effects have principled explanations, if contents can change in context, then it is possible that the contents of thoughts change when they are combined with other thoughts.

I think the best way to handle the compositionality worry is simply to *deny* that there is contextual variation of meaning experience. This is perhaps an empirical question; but I do not think there is any introspective evidence of such variation. Just as it is manifest to linguistic intuition that the meaning of 'chiliagon' (thousand-sided plane figure) is the same in the sentences 'chiliagons have one thousand sides', 'chiliagons are plane figures' and 'Descartes liked chiliagons', it is manifest to introspection that the phenomenal cognitive content of the concept CHILIAGON is the same in corresponding thoughts. We are directly aware of conceptual contents, and directly aware of their sameness and difference. We can know, directly, whether or not our CHILIAGON experience changes with change of conceptual context. Indeed, it is most likely this that allows us to know that 'chiliagon' means the same thing regardless of its linguistic context. Neither linguistic intuitions (speaker judgments about grammatical properties and relations) nor introspective judgments are infallible. However, introspection itself—which is in my view (see *PC*) simply conscious experience—is. We can make faulty *judgments* about our experiences, but we cannot mis-experience them (there is no appearance–reality distinction for appearances). With proper attention and care, our introspective judgments can obtain a high degree of reliability, just like linguistic intuitions.

2.7.3 Complexity and Phenomenal Presence

Mendelovici (2018: ch. 7) objects to the view defended here, on which to consciously think a thought is to consciously token a propositional-phenomenal type. She maintains that the contents of occurrent thoughts are not always completely present in consciousness, and that this is a reason to reject the thesis according to which all thought contents are phenomenal: if not all occurrent contents are present in consciousness, then (unless there is unconscious phenomenology) not all occurrent contents are phenomenal. She thinks this because she thinks thoughts have what she calls "alleged" contents, which are "the contents [thoughts] are often thought to have, either on the basis of intuition or on the basis of philosophical or psychological theory," which "do not seem to be phenomenal contents" (2018: 124). Alleged contents include such things as external objects, kinds and properties. Since these are not phenomenal, they cannot be instantiated in consciousness.

She also maintains that not all occurrent phenomenal thought contents are *conceptual*-phenomenal. "Immediate" contents are those "we are immediately aware of when we are in an intentional mental state...they are the contents that are 'before our mind's eye', or that 'run through our heads'" (2018: 127). However, these are not exclusively, or perhaps even typically, of the proprietarily conceptual kind. She includes among immediate contents experiences such as sensory percepts and images.

I reject both of these claims about possible thought contents. On my view (as argued throughout this book), conceptual contents are internally individuated experiences of the conceptual-phenomenal kind. Mind-external objects, natural kinds and properties are therefore precluded from being conceptual contents, since they are not phenomenal. Moreover, since conceptual contents are constituents of thought contents, they must be *thinkable*. But, though external objects, kinds and properties, and sensory experiences can be thought *about* (i.e., conceptually referred to), they cannot be *thought*. One cannot, for example, think water or the smell of bananas. These are just not the right kinds of things to be conceptual contents, since they are not conceptual-phenomenal.

However, Mendelovici has another, and more challenging, reason to wonder whether conceptual contents are, often enough, not completely present in consciousness, even if they are restricted to purely conceptual experiences. This concerns the entertainment of thoughts of a certain degree of complexity.

Now, surely there are thoughts too long or complex for us to think all at once, or even at all. Molly's monologue, for example (if we take its presentation as a single sentence to indicate that it is meant to express a single thought) expresses a thought that is simply too long to grasp in its entirety in a single conscious act. And the thought expressed by a sentence with seven center-embeddings[6] might not be graspable at all. This is consistent with the phenomenal intentionality of thought thesis, which does not claim that all thoughts, all propositional-experiential contents, are humanly tokenable. On the other hand, just as surely, there are thoughts, like RED IS A COLOR and SNOW IS COLD, that are easily grasped in a single conscious act.

The objection concerns thoughts of intermediate length and complexity whose contents it may seem doubtful we are able to consciously entertain all at once, even while we may be said to be thinking them. Consider, for example, the thought THE SENATE FILIBUSTER EASILY LENDS ITSELF TO PARTISAN ABUSE. This is a sophisticated thought, containing complex concepts (SENATE, FILIBUSTER and PARTISAN). Yet it is one we take ourselves to be able to think all at once, and to express by uttering the corresponding sentence. And it may seem introspectively implausible that the fully articulated contents of all of these concepts are present in consciousness simultaneously at the moment we think that the senate filibuster easily lends itself to partisan abuse: THE PRACTICE OF UNLIMITED DEBATE ALLOWED BY THE RULES OF THE CHAMBER OF THE BICAMERAL UNITED STATES LEGISLATURE CONSISTING OF ELECTED OFFICIALS REPRESENTING ENTIRE STATES... (you get the idea).[7] Is it really true that *all that* is present in consciousness whenever we think that thought? This seems at least questionable. But if we typically do not do what the phenomenal intentionality of thought thesis says we do whenever we consciously think, the thesis is suspect.

I am not convinced that we do not typically consciously entertain such (not too) complex thoughts in their fullness. And it strikes me as implausible that we

---

[6] For example, 'The bird the cat the dog the cow the horse the sheep the lion the elephant chased was flushed by the fox hunters'.

[7] If you do not believe that concepts typically have internal conceptual structure, consider the thought expressed by a very long (but not too long) sentence.

cannot, ever do so. Again, there are human limits; but I do not think the boundaries should be drawn here. Moreover, if there were such a thing as unconscious phenomenology (I consider the question in Chapter 6), the phenomenal intentionalist could claim that much of the content of sufficiently complex occurrent thoughts occurs unconsciously.

However, I have no arguments for the first claim. And unconscious phenomenology is a heavy burden to bear. (Indeed, some might see commitment to it as yet another reason to reject the phenomenal intentionality of thought thesis.) So I will respond in a different way here.

It is worth pausing to wonder why, on the assumption that the content of a thought like the FILIBUSTER thought is too unwieldy to fit in the limited space our conscious attention occupies as we think on the fly, we think that nonetheless anyone should be credited with consciously thinking it. One explanation that seems to me likely is that, all things equal, we generally take one another to be thinking what we say when we utter a sentence, where what we say is what the sentence means in the language we speak. For reasons that I detail in depth in the next chapter, I think that though it is true that we regularly apply this (Burgean) principle to each other in our ordinary interactions, it does not follow that what we say is always what we think. Indeed (as also discussed in the next chapter), it may be that we do so *much* less often than we think we do. We tend to let language do the talking for us, so to speak, even when we do not mean or even know, what our words mean. (Though, in the moment, we would succeed in communicating what the sentence means to our addressees only if *they* could think it all at once.)

So, in the case of a complex thought the full contents of which one may not have the time, patience or competence to entertain, one may only think part of it—the part that is manifest in consciousness, and rely on language to express the rest. This idea is similar to Mendelovici's idea that occurrent conscious thoughts often have "schematic immediate content"—i.e., "an immediate content that is a compressed, gisty, abstract or otherwise schematic version of its corresponding thick or alleged content.... Such contents might include a gisty or abstract characterization of thick contents without including all their details" (Mendelovici 2018: 136). But I would maintain that what one consciously thinks in these cases is neither "gisty" nor "schematic" nor "thin." It is, rather, something else—some other "thick," non-gisty, non-schematic thought that is related in various ways to the thought whose content is the proposition expressed by the uttered sentence. Of course it is possible that one is not *thinking* anything much at all. But one might also mean (think) by 'senate' something like THE GROUP OF SENATORS THAT MEETS IN THE CAPITOL, by 'filibuster' something like DEBATE TACTIC, by 'partisan' something like SELFISH, etc., etc.

Mendelovici suggests that a gisty, schematic thought can carry with it something like a promissory note on a fully articulated one, a feeling that, if asked, one could "cash out" what one was only sketchily thinking in the moment, or had a present disposition to do so. And this, she suggests, can support attributing to an individual a thought only incompletely or sketchily entertained at a particular moment. I wonder, however, how such notes could be issued if the speaker is not aware of what the content of the promise is, or cashed out if the speaker is not, after all, capable of consciously entertaining the full contents of such thoughts as the FILIBUSTER thought in a single mental act. Moreover, being disposed to think that p is not thinking that p. Hence, though I agree with Mendelovici that we often are not thinking what we are saying, I do not see this as a reason to modify or reject the thesis I defend, on which to consciously entertain a thought is to consciously token its propositional-phenomenal content.

Finally, I would remind the reader that the thesis I defend does not entail that any and all thought contents are immediately accessible in introspection to their thinkers in any and all circumstances. The argument for the thesis is based on the claim that it is *possible* to know introspectively and non-inferentially what one is occurrently consciously thinking, and that this depends upon thought contents being distinctively present in consciousness. The thesis is thus consistent with the occurrence of the kinds of situations Mendelovici describes.

3
Externalism

The doctrine that goes by the name "externalism" or "anti-individualism" is most often characterized as the view that factors external to the mind or body of an individual can determine the contents of the individual's concepts (or words). As pointed out by Farkas (2003; 2008a: ch. 4), however, the names as well as the characterization are not entirely apt. What really is at issue between internalists and externalists is whether the content of a conceptual representation (concept or thought) is entirely determined by its intrinsic features, or whether the nature of the things in its extension (or its extrinsic relations generally, which can include relations to other concepts) plays an essential role. Externalist-style thought experiments can be constructed using expressions or concepts of uncontroversially internal things, like brain states or sensations: imagine a twin whose concept PAIN is applied to itches, or whose term 'red' is applied to green afterimages. (See also Farkas's meningitis example, 2008a: 75–6.) The thought experiments introduced by Putnam and Burge can be seen as dramatizing the claim that content-determiners can be representation-external: they need not even be within the *body* of the thinker. The doctrine would, it seems to me, be better termed "relationalism," "extrinsicalism" or "extensionalism."

The thesis of this book, that conceptual content is cognitive-phenomenal (together with the thesis that phenomenology is an intrinsic feature of phenomenal states), is, as noted, fundamentally incompatible with this view. The classic arguments that are supposed to establish the truth of externalism/anti-individualism, due to Putnam and Burge, have been deeply influential in the philosophy of mind. The thought experiments they rest on are widely seen as having considerable, even overwhelming, intuitive force. They are accepted by many, if not most, (analytic) philosophers as having completely changed the way we view the mind and its relation to the world—replacing outmoded Cartesianism with a new understanding of mind as constitutively dependent on and integrated with its natural and social environments, in naturalistically explicable ways.

In this chapter I argue that the classic thought experiments of Putnam and Burge do not motivate their externalist (anti-individualist) conclusions. It follows that any externalist view based upon them (or others relevantly like them) is also unmotivated.

3.1 Putnam

The real moral of Putnam's original (1973; 1975) Twin-Earth thought experiment is, I think, not that "meanings ain't in the head," or that knowing the meaning of a term is not a matter of being in a certain psychological state. Obviously, if meanings are abstract objects, then they cannot be *located* anywhere, including in people's heads. And it is hard to see how a speaker's *knowing* the meaning of a term could not involve being in some mental state that would count as grasping it. (One cannot know a proposition one has never even entertained.) Putnam claims that "Oscar$_1$ and Oscar$_2$ *understood* the term 'water' differently in 1750 *although they were in the same psychological state*" (Putnam 1973: 702; my emphasis). But, again, it is hard to see what understanding could be if not a psychological state. I think it would be more precise to say that the Oscars do not know what their words mean, though in spite of this they succeed in referring to what is in the extensions of their words when they utter them. Indeed, this is what the examples used to motivate the principle of the division of linguistic labor seem to show. In these cases, speakers who do not know the (complete) meaning of a term can nonetheless use it to refer to things in its extension, if they defer to members of their linguistic community who *do* know what it means (either explicitly, or simply by using a word in the language they speak). But Putnam's general conclusion about knowledge of meaning not being a psychological state cannot be inferred from these facts, since, as Putnam recognizes, they are consistent with the meaning of the term (and its extension) being determined by the psychological states of those who know its meaning.

The true target of Putnam's argument is, rather, the traditional idea that linguistic meaning in general is derived from psychological (conceptual) content; and the proper conclusion to be drawn is that meanings ain't *determined by* what's in the head (or, more precisely, that meanings ain't identical to what's *expressed by* what's in the head). (This is how Putnam has been understood by, e.g., McGinn (1977), Burge (1982b) and Crane (1991).)

On the traditional conception, for a term to express a meaning is for it to be used by speakers to express a concept. Thus, 'water' means *water* if speakers use it to express the concept WATER. Concepts, in their turn, express properties (or senses), which are their contents. The concept WATER is the concept it is because it expresses the property (or sense) *water*. There are thus two basic expression relations, one between words and concepts (to be explained within speech-act theory) and one between concepts and contents (to be explained by psychosemantics). The product of these relations is the relation between words and meanings: the meaning of a term is the content of the concept it expresses.

The Twin-Earth cases are more to the point as counterexamples to *this* thesis. There are no experts on either Earth or Twin Earth (in 1750) whose knowledge could supplement that of the Oscars, and thereby save the principle that word meaning is psychologically grounded. It seems in these cases that the environment itself is doing the individuative work. The examples concern psychologically identical twins in environments in which their respective words 'water' have different extensions. Given the second assumption of the traditional theory of meaning—that the meaning of a term determines its extension—the twins' terms must have different senses. Hence, the meanings of words are determined not by psychological content but by (as in the twins' case) such content plus the speaker's environment; and environment-ext can make a crucial difference. (The psychological identity of Putnam's twins includes their both associating the contents *watery stuff*, or *this liquid* with their word-forms 'water'; and this is partly, but not entirely, what their words mean.)

An obvious way for an internalist to resist Putnam's conclusion is to maintain that it is not the principle that meaning is psychologically grounded that should be given up, but, rather, the principle that intension determines extension—at least as it is stated. The conclusion that "meanings ain't in the head" (or entirely determined by what is in there) is certainly startling; but a more conservative moral to Putnam's story is that intension does not determine extension *simpliciter*, but, rather, *relative to context of utterance (tokening)*. The Oscars' word-forms 'water' mean exactly the same thing, since they are psychologically identical; but one and the same meaning can determine different extensions in different contexts.

Indeed, it seems this is precisely the conclusion Putnam ought to have drawn, given his claim that natural kind terms like 'water' are indexical (liquid like *this*; the watery stuff around *here*), and his claim that "[f]or these words [indexicals] no one has ever suggested the traditional theory that 'intension determines extension'" (1975: 234)). But of course this would have short-circuited his thought experiment, since it would have robbed him of his surprising externalist conclusion. If natural kind terms really are indexical, and the intension of an indexical does not determine its reference *simpliciter*, then the fact that the twins' word-forms 'water' have different extensions shows nothing about their intensions.

Oddly, Putnam maintains that the idea that natural-kind terms are indexical "leaves it open" whether or not their meanings change with a change in extension, while also insisting that "difference in extension is *ipso facto* a difference in meaning for natural-kind words," and that we should "[give] up the doctrine that meanings are concepts, or, indeed, mental entities of any kind" (1975).

I suspect that what might have driven Putnam to this paradoxical position is the following kind of Kaplanian intuition. What $Oscar_1$ *says* when he utters "water is wet"—the *content* of his utterance—is that H_2O is wet, while what $Oscar_2$ says when he utters the same words is that XYZ is wet, though their terms have the same *character* (*liquid like this; the watery stuff around here*). If Putnam had appealed to something like a character-content distinction, he could have relativized the sense-determines-extension principle consistent with his semantic externalism (and his claim that meanings are not *entirely* determined by extensions).

It would also have fit nicely with his distinction between 'narrow' and 'broad' mental states. (Maybe this is what he had in mind when he said "Oscar$_1$ and Oscar$_2$ understood the term 'water' differently in 1750 although they were in the same psychological state.")

Without this distinction, however, Putnam's choice between the traditional principles seems arbitrary, and he has not offered a convincing argument for semantic externalism. Moreover, I do not think his arguments can be repaired by slotting in a Kaplanian semantics for natural kind terms, since (as I argue at length in Chapter 4) I think that such a semantics is unmotivated even for ordinary indexicals.

A better way out of these troubles would be simply to give up the idea that natural kind terms are indexical. Burge (1982b) has argued, against Putnam, that the phenomenon of difference of meaning across contexts can be observed to occur with plainly non-indexical and non-natural kind terms, such as 'arthritis' and 'sofa'. In these cases, differences in extension have nothing to do with indexicality: they are entirely due to differences in the speakers' environments. Applying the principle that intension determines extension to Putnam's cases so understood straightforwardly yields the externalist conclusion he wants.

But this still leaves open the internalist option of adopting a relativized intension-determines-extension principle. I hereby adopt it. There is, I maintain, no principled reason for holding that only indexical terms change their extensions across contexts, or for holding that in general a change in extension entails a change in intension. (John MacFarlane (2007) calls a view like this "non-indexical contextualism," and argues that context sensitivity should not be confused with indexicality, which, he says, does involve a change of content. In Chapter 4 I argue that change in extension *never* entails change in content—even for indexicals.) Given a sufficiently liberalized notion of context, it is easy to see that all manner of non-indexical terms retain their meanings in spite of a change in extension. It is clear, for example, that such terms do not change their meanings across possible worlds. (Cf. Lewis 1998: 25: "Contingency is a kind of indexicality." By 'indexicality' he means relativity of truth value, not content.) We do not say that the term 'the president of the United States in 2010' has a different meaning in worlds in which John McCain won the 2008 election. It might be replied that this is true because 'the president of the United States in 2010' is not an indexical, and so its meaning will not change with its extension. But this is question-begging. It is also clear that the meaning of this expression has not changed since 2016 (even as its connotations have). So there can be change of extension across time without a change of intension. The expression 'the president' is also subject to change in extension across worlds and times without change in intension, as well as to changes in extension across locations within a world at a time. (For example, at the time of writing it refers to János Áder in Hungary and to Ellen Johnson Sirleaf in

Liberia.) And the point is as straightforwardly extendable to the contents and extensions of concepts as the thought experiment itself.

It might be objected that these expressions, as used by speakers, have a hidden indexical component ('the *actual* president of the United States in 2010'; 'the *local* president') or are otherwise incomplete because underdetermined by their type-meanings ('the president of *Hungary*'; 'the president of *Liberia*'). But this too is question-begging, since it assumes that the intension of a non-indexical expression must be sufficient to determine its extension independent of context. It is also very implausible as a defense of Putnam-style examples as applied to thought content. For surely it is possible to think that the president is F while having no idea what world one is in (because one does not possess the concept POSSIBLE WORLD), what time it is, or where one is. Moreover, it is obvious that PRESIDENT, ACTUAL PRESIDENT and LOCAL PRESIDENT are different concepts, and, hence, that the thoughts THE PRESIDENT IS F, THE ACTUAL PRESIDENT IS F and THE LOCAL PRESIDENT IS F are different thoughts.

I address these issues at greater length in Chapter 4. But I think it is clear that an internalist can (and should) resist Putnam-style arguments for semantic and psychological externalism by relativizing the intension-determines-extension principle to context of tokening (whether of terms or concepts).

3.2 Burge

The thought experiments of Burge 1979a, 1982b and 1986 are widely held to have established that conceptual content can also be socially determined. (In cases where relations to natural environment have a role in determining content, such relations can also be mediated by social environment (Burge 1982b: 102).) Relations to one's natural environment alone, as well as to one's abstract mathematical environment, can also be content-determinative (Burge 2007: 154). These experiments are meant to reveal that an individual's relations to a linguistic community can fix thought contents as much as they do linguistic meanings. In particular (especially in Burge 1979a), the socially determined meanings of the words linguistically competent individuals use to express thoughts about themselves, others and their physical environment can determine the contents of those thoughts, which contents themselves are thus socially determined.

The cases Burge presents are meant to elicit intuitions which, in combination with a plausible general principle about belief ascription, provide a strong motivation for abandoning the individualist conception of mind. The intuitions concern *what it is natural to say* about what the individuals described in the thought experiments believe, and the general principle is that, *all things being equal*, belief ascriptions it is natural to make are literally true. The intuitions are supposed to override any sense that the *ceteris paribus* clause of the principle is sprung because of the conceptual idiosyncrasies of his subjects: they believe what they say *in spite of* their deviance from the communal norms governing the meaning and usage of their words.

The intuitions about what it is natural to say are undeniably powerful. Burge is surely right that in the situations he describes it is natural to attribute beliefs to his subjects using the very words they utter, even though their understanding of those words is at odds with their socially determined meanings. Nor would the subjects themselves hesitate to describe their thoughts in the same way. This is our practice. Nonetheless, I maintain, these intuitions are not sufficient to establish Burge's thesis. What it is natural to say in a given case need not be literally true; and there may be compelling reasons for thinking that it is not—even if it remains very natural to say it. I will argue that in any case of the kind required by a Burgean thought experiment there is a reason for not taking homophonic ascriptions at face value, which is not neutralized by the intuitive naturalness of making them. Given that it is the strength of these intuitions that accounts for the persuasiveness of the thought experiments, if it can be shown that they do not ensure the literal truth of the ascriptions, Burge's case for anti-individualism ought to seem much less compelling.

3.2.1 The Structure of the Argument and the Role of the Naturalness Intuition

Anna has arthritis. She speaks of her ailment using the term 'arthritis', which, "as used in [her] linguistic community, does not apply to ailments outside joints. Indeed, it fails to do so by a standard, non-technical dictionary definition" (Burge 1979a: 78). Anna says things like "I have arthritis in my ankles," "My grandmother had arthritis, too," and so on, and thereby expresses her (true) beliefs about her condition. One day she develops a condition in her thigh that she worries is the same one she has in her wrists and ankles. She expresses her worry to her doctor, who informs her that this could not be true, since arthritis cannot occur outside of joints.

Counterfactual Anna, who has the same physical makeup and history as Anna up until the moment she expresses her worry to her doctor, is a member of a different linguistic community in which 'arthritis' applies by definition to rheumatoid diseases occurring in joints and bones. In this counterfactual context, none of Anna's 'arthritis' utterances mean what they do in her actual context, and none of her beliefs have their actual content. Since by hypothesis the only difference between the actual and counterfactual situations resides in the practices of the linguistic communities Anna is a member of, we seem compelled to conclude that it is these factors, and not something internal to Anna, that determine the contents of her 'arthritis' beliefs (the beliefs she would express using the term 'arthritis').

More specifically, in both cases the socially determined meanings of the words Anna uses in reporting her beliefs determine her beliefs' contents. Hence, those contents themselves are socially determined. And since similar cases can be described for a very large variety of concepts, the conclusion generalizes: mental content is in general determined socially.

It is essential to Burge's argument that it be literally true in the actual context that, in spite of her confusion, Anna believes that she has arthritis in her thigh. If she does not believe this in the actual case, then the counterfactual case is irrelevant, and no conclusions about social content determination are established by the thought experiment. (In the counterfactual case there is no discrepancy between what 'arthritis' means and what Anna thinks it means.) It is only on the assumption that Anna believes she has arthritis in her thigh that the content-determining role of sociolinguistic context is made salient by a comparison with the counterfactual case.

However, as Burge notes, one might think that the very fact that Anna says that she thinks she has arthritis in her *thigh* is evidence that she does not have the concept ARTHRITIS—since it is a conceptual/definitional truth (in some non-committal sense) that arthritis is a disease of the joints only—and, hence, that she cannot have the belief that she has arthritis in her thigh. After all, in the counterfactual case Anna does not have the concept ARTHRITIS *because* 'arthritis' in the counterfactual community applies by definition to a disease that can occur in bones as well as joints. So why should her belief that 'arthritis' applies to (we may suppose) those very bone ailments not preclude her from having the concept in the actual case?

The reason is, Burge argues, that Anna is not, to our knowledge, an abnormal speaker of English, or obviously deceitful, dissembling or deranged; and there is nothing odd about any of her previous 'arthritis' utterances. So we should take her utterances at face value—what she says is what she believes; and we should take our own ascriptions at face value as well—what she believes is what we say she believes. There is, as Burge says, "a methodological bias in favor of taking natural discourse literally, other things being equal.... Literal interpretation is *ceteris paribus* preferred" (1979a: 88). And we should continue to do this even after we become aware of Anna's misconception, because there is a very strong intuition that the correct way to describe her mistake is to say that she (falsely) believes that she has arthritis in her thigh. It is entirely natural for us to describe Anna—and for her to describe herself, even after she is apprised of her mistake—as believing (or having believed) that she has arthritis in her thigh. And since she could not have this belief without having the concept ARTHRITIS, she must have that concept, in spite of her misunderstanding.

These considerations show that the contrasting counterfactual case is an inessential component of Burge's argument for anti-individualism. The reasons for thinking that the ascription to Anna of the belief that she has arthritis in her thigh is literally true, despite her confusion, are themselves reasons for thinking that psychological content can be (and typically is) socially determined. Given that literal interpretation is preferred even in cases of partial understanding, or misunderstanding like Anna's, and that meaning is determined socially, it follows that the contents of Anna's thoughts are determined socially. The comparison with the counterfactual case is simply a way of dramatizing this conclusion by providing a case in which a *different* content is determined by a *different* linguistic context. The heart of the argument is the explanation of *how* content is determined by sociolinguistic context. Indeed, Burge recognizes the general point in Burge 1978: 134–5:

> Our discussion has brought out the domineering role of the presupposition that speakers are to be taken at their word; that is, literally or homophonically.... When the presupposition is in force, communal conventions about the meaning of a speaker's words tend to override what a speaker mistakenly associates with his words in determining what he says and even, sometimes, what he believes.

Thus, Burge's case for social anti-individualism in "Individualism and the Mental" is just the case for the literal truth of the ascription to Anna. It rests upon the intuitive naturalness of the way we describe her, and the principle that, all things being equal, literal interpretation of natural discourse is preferred—and not, as it might appear, on the comparison of the actual and counterfactual cases.

I take issue with Burge's claims that "the thought experiment does appear to *depend on* the possibility of someone's having a propositional attitude despite an incomplete mastery of some notion in its content" (1979a: 83 (my emphasis)), and that "[i]ncomplete understanding is...the pivot on which the particular thought experiments in 'Individualism and the Mental' turn" (Burge 2007: 175). On the contrary, it seems to me, both the anti-individualist conclusion and the claim about incomplete mastery *follow from* the literal truth of the belief ascription (in conjunction with the assumption of linguistic anti-individualism). If 'Anna believes that she has arthritis in her thigh' is literally true, then the content of its that-clause is the content of Anna's belief. But if Anna believes that she has arthritis in her thigh, then she has the concept ARTHRITIS, despite her misconception. The cogency of the thought experiment depends on the possibility of possession without mastery not as a presupposition, but as an entailment: if possession without mastery is impossible, then Anna cannot believe she has arthritis in her thigh, and there must be something wrong with the intuition that homophonic attribution is appropriate. (Compare Burge 2007: 163 (my emphasis): "My thought experiments *suggest...that* conceptual and linguistic understanding commonly do not rest on the stable mastery of self-evident principles governing use of concepts or terms.")

The principle of literal interpretation (henceforth the "Principle"), as well as the naturalness intuition (the "Intuition"), also apply in cases where speakers understand the terms they use perfectly well, and say nothing that would tempt us to think that they do not possess the concepts the terms express. ("[C]ommunal practice is a factor... in fixing the contents of my attitudes, even in cases where I fully understand the content" (Burge 1979a: 85).) Suppose Anna has complete and accurate knowledge of the communal meaning of the word 'bunion', and we have good reason to think that she does. She has said a lot of true things about bunions, and nothing false or odd. Now consider one of these utterances—say, "My bunions are killing me." On the basis of this utterance, we (naturally and compellingly) attribute to her the belief that her bunions are killing her. We take the content of our ascription to be the content of her thought. Our attribution is literally true, and what it means is what Anna thought. However, since the content of what she says, and thus the content of our homophonic attribution, is determined socially, the content of Anna's thought is determined socially as well. In a counterfactual linguistic community in which 'bunion' means *bialy*, and Anna knows this and makes no mistakes, she would not say, or believe, what she says and believes in her actual linguistic community. In both the 'arthritis' and 'bunion' cases, the social determination of meaning and content is effected through the application of the Principle and the Intuition. These establish anti-individualism in *any* case in which natural discourse is taken at face value. The 'arthritis' case is meant to illustrate just how "domineering" they are supposed to be.

A different kind of example is developed in "Intellectual Norms and Foundations of Mind" (Burge 1986). Here we have a subject (call him "Andy") who is the victim of neither partial understanding nor misunderstanding with respect to the specimen term ('sofa'). Andy knows the meaning of the word 'sofa' in his language. He knows that sofas are by definition pieces of furniture, and he is fully competent in the use of the word. Nonetheless (according to Burge), he doubts that sofas are furniture. Andy has become convinced that they are in fact some sort of artworks or religious artifacts, not meant for the use some people put them to at all, and he expresses his suspicion by saying "Sofas are not pieces of furniture!" He is wrong, however. His belief that sofas are not furniture, which was formed on the basis of systematically misleading evidence, is false. In a counterfactual case, in contrast, we are to suppose that a physically identical Andy says something *true* when he utters the sentence 'sofas are not pieces of furniture'. In the counterfactual language community, the word 'sofa' is applied by definition not to pieces of furniture, but to works of art or religious artifacts, just as Andy suspects. When counterfactual Andy says "Sofas are not pieces of furniture!," his utterance, and the belief it expresses, are both true. (He is wrong in thinking that there is some kind of conspiracy to deceive people into thinking that sofas are furniture.) They do not, however, have the same content as actual Andy's utterances. He counterfactually neither says nor believes that sofas are not pieces of furniture, because 'sofa' in the counterfactual community does not mean *sofa*.

The pattern of reasoning in the Andy case is the same as in Anna's: the difference between the contents of Andy's actual and counterfactual beliefs is due to the actual and counterfactual meanings of the words he utters, which meanings are determined by factors extrinsic to him. Hence, Andy's thought contents are determined by factors extrinsic to him. Moreover, the points made above with respect to the role of the intuition about what Anna believes in the actual case, and the comparison to the counterfactual case, apply to Andy's case as well. The considerations that are supposed to lead us to think that Andy believes that sofas are not pieces of furniture, in spite of the fact that he knows that the word 'sofa' in his community applies by definition to pieces of furniture, are themselves sufficient to show that the content of Andy's sofa thoughts is socially determined. The comparison of actual Andy and counterfactual Andy is not what establishes the anti-individualist conclusion; it merely dramatizes it. That Andy may be correctly characterized as challenging the very practices that determine the communal meanings of the words he uses (Burge 1986: 707) does not prevent those practices from determining the content of his challenge. If it did, then the thought experiment would not show that his thought contents are extrinsically determined: they would be determined by what he thought sofas are.

Further, the point of the Andy case seems to be to provide contrast with ordinary cases as well, since, again, the principles Burge appeals to ought to establish anti-individualism in *any* case in which natural discourse is taken at face value. However, in Andy's case it is not misunderstanding that is overridden by communal meaning, and which provides the essential contrast to the ordinary case—since, by hypothesis, Andy understands perfectly well what his community takes 'sofa' to mean. It is, rather, as Burge says, "nonstandard theory" (1986: 709). Nonetheless, there is an important parallel to Anna's case. Both Anna's and Andy's utterances are *prima facie* conceptually problematic: neither involves a merely empirical divergence from communal standards and belief. Anna's utterance indicates conceptual *confusion*, and Andy's indicates an attempt at conceptual *subversion*. I characterize what the cases have in common as *conceptual dissonance*. In all of Burge's examples it is the fact that the individuals in question think what they say, in spite of the egregious conceptual dissonance of their utterances, that provides the reason for thinking that the Principle has general application because linguistic meaning determines mental content (via membership in a linguistic community). The fact that linguistic meaning trumps individualistic factors in cases of dissonance between what speakers believe about the words they use and what those words mean in their language shows why there is normally a match between linguistic content and mental content: it is not because mental content determines linguistic meaning, or because speakers normally choose their words correctly.

3.2.2 Objections

The inclusion of the *ceteris paribus* clause in the Principle indicates that Burge thinks there *are* conditions under which literal interpretation is not preferred—cases in which the Principle does not override the conceptual dissonance of the thinker's utterance. In such cases, individuals are not to be taken at their word. This might mean that the individuals' words are themselves to be reinterpreted: perhaps one should suppose they are not after all members of one's linguistic community; perhaps they are speaking a foreign language, or a different dialect of English. If, however, one is confident that a speaker is a linguistic compatriot, it is more likely that the speaker's words will be taken to mean what they mean in the language spoken, but that they will not be taken to be an accurate expression of what the speaker thinks. In such cases, the link between the meanings of words and the contents of the thought one wishes to express is broken or otherwise disabled.

Indeed, if we were to hold that there *cannot* be a mismatch between linguistic meaning and thought content, we would be contradicting some very obvious facts. For what then would we say of malaprops, slips of the tongue, phonemic mispronunciations, etc.? To deny that such phenomena justify reinterpretation would seem to imply a kind of infallibility (enforced by language) with respect to one's choice of words in expressing one's thoughts. One simply could not misexpress them. If one's utterance is sincere, then one must be thinking what one's words mean. But this is clearly false; and any view that is committed to it ought to lack any intuitive appeal.

If there can be cases of mismatch between thought content and linguistic content, then, it remains to be seen what sorts of criteria there are for identifying them. What kinds of considerations override our default commitment to taking our fellow speakers at their word? Burge (1978: 134; 1979a: 90–1) mentions utterances involving slips of the tongue, spoonerisms, malaprops and radical misunderstandings as appropriate candidates for reinterpretation. Presumably, at least some of these involve a malfunction of speech-processing mechanisms, and may be to that extent involuntary. Moreover, speakers typically correct themselves ("That's not what I meant!") when they realize or are told of their mistakes. So in such cases there seems to be sufficient reason to excuse them from their *prima facie* commitment to having thought (or meant) what they said. It would be uncharitable to hold speakers to their word in such cases.

In a parenthetical remark (1979a: 91), however, Burge indicates that in fact he thinks utterances involving malaprops or radical misunderstandings are *not* exempt from the Principle. He says that he is "not convinced" that someone who believes that 'orangutan' is a word for a fruit drink and says "An orangutan is a fruit drink" should not therefore be taken to *mean that* an orangutan is a fruit drink and *believe that* an orangutan is a fruit drink. If Burge's argument for anti-individualism really is committed to this, then I think it can simply be dismissed.

If a case of misunderstanding this radical does not trip the *ceteris paribus* clause, then it is hard to imagine what would. Burge claims that his thought experiment depends upon completely ordinary, completely compelling intuitions. But if it depends upon a principle that commits us to the claim that the communal meaning of *any* sincere well-formed utterance is the content of the thought it expresses, then it is completely *counter*intuitive.

But it seems that Burge could reject such cases and still have an important thesis about the determination of mental content. (He has in fact, in conversation, disavowed the intuition about the orangutan case.) He says (1979a: 92): "The thought experiment depends only on there being some cases in which a person's incomplete understanding does not force reinterpretation of his expressions in describing his mental contents. Such cases appear to be legion." I take it that Burge means that his argument does not require commitment to the Principle for every utterance. Standard practice can call for reinterpretation in cases of linguistic incompetence or momentary lapses without spoiling the anti-individualist argument. In such cases all things are not equal, and our commitment to taking speakers at their word is suspended. What the argument requires is cases in which the Principle overrides conceptual dissonance of one (not-too-serious) kind or another. Conceptual dissonance is a *prima facie* reason for thinking that all things are not equal. This is why Burge stresses that the deviance from community norms is not merely empirical. Mere empirical deviance would not raise the issue of non-literal interpretation, and would therefore not provide the resistance needed to reveal the determinative role of the Principle. Since homophonic interpretation is still preferable in these cases, they do show something interesting and important about psychological content.

But why should we think that the Principle applies in spite of the *prima facie* evidence that things are not all equal for Burge's subjects? Why is its *ceteris paribus* clause not tripped by the dissonance of their utterances? How is the resistance to homophonic interpretation overcome? The answer constitutes, I think, the very heart of Burge's arguments for anti-individualism. We do not reinterpret in these cases—we do not choose different words to match the subjects' deviant conceptions—because of the very powerful Intuition about the correct way to characterize them. Anna says "I'm afraid I might have arthritis in my thigh." We know that what she fears cannot be true; we know she has made a mistake. Yet we describe her mistaken belief using the very words she does not understand: we say that she fears she has arthritis in her thigh. Burge (1979a: n. 4) says "I used to believe that a fortnight is a period of ten days." He knows that what he used to believe cannot be true; he knows he made a conceptual error. But he describes what he used to think using the very word he did not understand at the time: he says that he used to think that a fortnight is a period of ten days. Andy thinks everyone is wrong about what sofas are. He knows what 'sofa' means in his language. He knows that it is (something like) definitional that sofas are pieces of furniture. Yet he says "Sofas are not pieces of furniture," and he and we interpret his utterance literally. We might think he is wrong, but we describe him as thinking that sofas are not furniture. These are, as Burge stresses, the utterly natural and intuitively correct things to say. No one without a theoretical ax to grind would question their appropriateness. But this shows that communal meaning trumps individual misconception in determining the contents of a generally competent speaker's thoughts. It is a philosophically surprising but inevitable consequence of our ordinary practice of ascribing thoughts on the basis of sincere utterances that mental content is determined by factors extrinsic to thinkers.

The role of the intuitions Burge evokes should now be clear. The Principle applies in these cases in spite of *prima facie* evidence that all things are not equal because of the clear and firm Intuition about the naturalness of our homophonic ascriptions. The intuitive naturalness of our ascriptions to Anna and Andy prevents the *ceteris paribus* clause of the principle from being tripped. In spite of the fact that their utterances are conceptually dissonant, it still seems perfectly appropriate to use their words in characterizing what they think. The power of Burge's thought experiments lies in the strength of this unspoiled Intuition.

The Intuition is undeniable. I share it. It *is* overwhelmingly natural to characterize mistakes like those made by Anna and Andy using their very words. Nevertheless, I think the Intuition is misleading. It cannot be uncritically accepted as evidence that all things are equal in the situations Burge describes. Countervailing considerations show that what it is overwhelmingly natural to *say* in Burge's cases should not, on reflection, be taken to be literally *true*. The Intuition does not, after all, prevent the *ceteris paribus* clause of the Principle from being tripped. Some of these considerations have been discussed in the literature on Burge's thought experiments (though not always, in my view, as effectively or persistently as they ought to have been), and some are presented here for (to my knowledge) the first time.

Though Burge's precept of upholding the Intuition in the face of theoretical assault should not be rigidly adhered to (after all, it did once seem intuitively obvious that the Sun moves around the Earth), I think the best way to challenge Burge is with intuitions as natural and powerful as the ones he offers. Since Burge's case for anti-individualism rests so fundamentally on the commonsense intuitions he evokes, meeting it on its own terms requires equally natural commonsense intuitions and principles whose application in the situations he describes shows that his conclusions are unjustified.

In what follows I discuss three features of our ordinary belief-ascribing practices that militate against Burge's anti-individualist conclusion. These practices are governed by a principle of charity enjoining ascription of contradictory or incoherent beliefs except in extraordinary circumstances, and also by the principle that utterances betraying linguistic incompetence should not be interpreted literally. In addition, there are many cases in which homophonic ascription is quite natural, but in which there is also a very clear commonsense intuition that on (brief) reflection literal interpretation is not intended. Taken together, these features make a strong case against Burge's argument that all things are equal in his cases with respect to the Principle of literal interpretation.

3.2.2.1 The Principle of Charity

It has been objected to Burge (beginning with Fodor 1982[1]) that all things are not equal in Anna's case because the sentence 'she has arthritis in her thigh' is, *by hypothesis*, self-contradictory or conceptually incoherent, and there is a competing principle governing ordinary discourse that says that one's attributions ought to be charitable. One should not, *ceteris paribus*, attribute contradictory or incoherent beliefs to people, and, *prima facie*, respect their rationality. But to attribute a belief to Anna using the sentence she uttered is to attribute to her belief in a contradiction. Perhaps she could have such a belief;[2] but the intuitively natural assumption is that if a speaker assertively utters a sentence which in the language she speaks is contradictory or incoherent, then she has misexpressed what she thinks. Only in very unusual circumstances would we be willing to suspend the presumption of rationality and attribute a contradictory or incoherent belief.

The question whether or not Anna has such a belief should be distinguished from the question whether or not we attribute one to her in using a homophonic ascription. If Anna utters the sentence 'my arthritis has spread to my thigh', it might be open to question what she actually meant (what she actually thought). But if *we* utter the sentence 'Anna believes that she has arthritis in her thigh', then there is no question that the embedded sentence 'she has arthritis in her thigh' is *for us* conceptually incoherent. For, as Burge makes clear, Anna's error is not an ordinary empirical one; it is a *conceptual* matter that arthritis cannot occur outside of joints. Given that it is reasonable to suppose, as Burge does (1979a: 102), that the kinds of errors he describes are common, to suppose that individuals' words should be taken at face value in such cases is to turn a practice of intending to make sense of their behavior (attitude attribution) into a practice that frequently makes nonsense of their mental lives. But if this is not our practice, then the kinds of cases Burge describes in "Individualism and the Mental" are ones in which

---

[1] See also Bilgrami 1992 and Wikforss 2001. Fodor's paper has languished in obscurity for over forty years. (It is cited by neither Bilgrami nor Wikforss; and Fodor confessed, in conversation, that even he had forgotten about it.) Of course, Fodor went on to accept Burge's argument (if only out of curiosity; see Fodor 1987: 29) and to develop Putnam's distinction between "narrow" and "broad" (or "wide") content. It seems to me, however (as it does to Bilgrami), that this objection is decisive with respect to the thought experiments in "Individualism and the Mental" and "Intellectual Norms and Foundations of Mind."

[2] Whether one can *believe* a contradiction or not is controversial. See, e.g., Marcus 1983 and 1990 for arguments that one cannot. In any case, it must be possible to *think* a contradictory proposition. (Otherwise, how could it be *dis*believed, or used as a premise for *reductio*.)

literal interpretation is not preferable, and the conclusion he wants about the contents of thought does not follow from the naturalness of our attributions. The fact that we find it natural to make them in spite of their incoherence no doubt requires an explanation. But if the principle of charity is upheld, it cannot be maintained that we ought to take them to be literally true.

In discussing another example, Burge (1982a: 290) responds to Fodor by claiming that Fodor mistakenly attributes to him the view that "the fact that contracts need not be written is constitutive of our concept" of contract, whereas he "assumed only that it is not 'constitutive of our concept' of contract that contracts must be written." The concept of a contract leaves it unspecified whether or not contracts can be unwritten. Hence, the sentence 'unwritten contracts do not bind' is not contradictory (unless of course 'contract' just means *binding agreement*): it does not mean *unwritten agreements that need not be written in order to bind do not bind*, but, rather (something like) *unwritten agreements do not bind*. It is, thus, simply false. Presumably, Burge would claim that an analogous point applies in the 'arthritis' case: the fact that arthritis cannot occur outside of joints is not constitutive of the concept ARTHRITIS; rather, it is simply not constitutive of ARTHRITIS that arthritis is a disease of the joints only. Applicability of 'arthritis' to ailments occurring outside of joints is undetermined by the term's content. So Anna's utterance of 'I have arthritis in my thigh' is not contradictory or incoherent; it is just mistaken.

I think Burge is wrong about this (at least in the case of 'arthritis'). Though the definition of 'arthritis' as an inflammation of the joints does not explicitly state that it can only occur in joints, this is implicit—just as it is implicit in the definition of 'retinitis' (*an inflammation of the retina*) that it only can occur in retinas.

Moreover, if Burge were right, it is hard to see how "any dictionary could have told" Anna that she could not have arthritis in her thigh—how, that is, mastery of the term 'arthritis' would have enabled her to avoid her mistake. If Anna's error is not an ordinary empirical (theoretical) one—because such an error would not drive intuitions in the direction of anti-individualism—then it must be a conceptual one. An ordinary empirical error (such as, for example, the belief that only old people get arthritis) would not provide the *prima facie* reason for thinking that Anna does not have the concept ARTHRITIS (the conceptual dissonance) the overcoming of which by the naturalness of homophonic ascription shows the "domineering" role of the Principle. And, given what Burge says about dictionaries, it is hard to see how Anna's utterance could fail to be conceptually incoherent.

Moreover, the distinction between its being constitutive of a concept that things in its extension are not *F* and its not being constitutive of a concept that things in its extension are *F* cannot serve Burge's purposes. It is not enough that it not be constitutive of the concept ARTHRITIS that arthritis can only occur in joints for

Anna's utterance to be conceptually anomalous. Compare: the concept LONELY is not a constituent of the concept BACHELOR; yet the sentence 'bachelors are lonely' is conceptually consonant. Generally, if a concept G (or *not-G*) is not constitutive of a concept F, it does not follow that the sentence 'F is G' is in any way conceptually problematic. So to counter Fodor with the claim that POSSIBLY UNWRITTEN is not constitutive of CONTRACT takes the teeth out of the example. If an utterance does not suggest lack of mastery of a concept, then it should come as no surprise that an individual could have a belief of which the concept is a constituent. If there is no conceptual dissonance, there is no reason to think that the match between socially determined linguistic content and mental content is due to anything other than the individual having chosen the correct words.

Now, Burge explicitly disavows (for Quinean reasons) any commitment to a view on which one concept may be a constituent, or be constitutive, of another. But what then does it mean to say that it is *definitional* that Fs are not G—that "any dictionary could have told you" that Fs are not G? If there is nothing like a constitutive connection between a concept F and a concept *not-G*, then how is an utterance of the sentence 'Fs are Gs' to indicate anything other than a factual error? Perhaps something like a meaning postulate, of the form $(x)(Fx \rightarrow \neg Gx)$, could provide such a (non-constitutive?) connection. But then any expression of the form *a is F and G* (e.g., 'my ailment is arthritis and is in my thigh'), while not explicitly contradictory, would in combination with the meaning postulate entail the explicitly contradictory expression '*a* is F and G and not G'. And anyone who had completely mastered the term '*F*' would know this. So the problem Fodor raises remains: though Anna might not know that her belief involves this conceptual problem, we who ascribe it to her do.

There would seem to be a dilemma here for Burge (cf. Wikforss 2001: 221–6). If there is no conceptual as opposed to factual problem evinced by Anna's utterance, then the thought experiment does not show anything about the constitution of mental content. On the other hand, if Anna's utterance does involve a conceptual error of the kind Burge relies on, then homophonic ascription violates the principle of charity, since *by the ascriber's lights* the content clause of the ascription is incoherent.

Burge does accept that charity precludes ascription of explicit contradictions (1982b: 291–2), but he denies that the utterances in his examples are explicitly contradictory. If by 'explicit' Burge means *formal*, then he is surely right. Even assuming that CANNOT OCCUR IN BONE is a constituent of ARTHRITIS, 'arthritis can occur in bone', unlike 'a disease that cannot occur in bone can occur in bone', is not a *formal* contradiction. But neither is 'a disease that can only occur in joints can occur in bone'. And if it is obvious to the fully apprised user of this last sentence that it is contradictory, then it ought to be obvious to the fully apprised user of 'arthritis can occur in bone'—in particular, to the ascriber of the belief that she has arthritis in her thigh to Anna—that it is also contradictory. And that ought to be sufficient for the principle of charity Fodor reminds us of to spring the *ceteris paribus* clause of the Principle of literal interpretation. All things are not equal in Anna's case because literal interpretation of homophonic ascription violates the presumption of rationality.

Still, Burge could concede to Fodor that the cases presented in "Individualism and the Mental" do not survive his criticism and continue to maintain that social/linguistic anti-individualism is true. For he could dismiss such cases as involving linguistic incompetence (anyone who was really competent with 'arthritis' would not believe it could occur in thighs), and argue on the basis of completely ordinary, unproblematic utterances (as he does in describing Anna before introducing the problematic belief) that what someone thinks is determined by what they (we) say, given the Principle and the intuitive naturalness of our ordinary ascriptions. He could further claim that part of what it is to be a member of a linguistic community is to be fully competent in the language of that community.

But we have already seen that non-dissonant examples do not make Burge's case, since there is an obvious alternative explanation of the match between thought content and utterance content. (Thinkers tend to choose the correct words to express what they are thinking.) Moreover, it would not help in the case of Andy, since it is assumed that he is fully apprised of the meaning of, and hence fully competent in the communal use of, the word 'sofa'. So it can be argued that the principle of charity prevents attribution of the belief that sofas are not furniture to Andy since, *by the ascriber's lights*, that belief is conceptually incoherent. Indeed, one could argue that the case as conceived is incoherent even independent of principles governing third-person attributions of thoughts to Andy. For, given that Andy knows that sofas are by definition pieces of furniture, how could he consistently believe that they are not pieces of furniture? And how could we, who do not share Andy's subversive tendencies, attribute such a belief to him without impugning his rationality?

Nonetheless, I think the charity objection does not really get to the bottom of the kind of case Burge wants to make for anti-individualism. Given the role the examples are supposed to play in the thought experiments, it really is not necessary that they involve the sort of *prima facie* conceptual incoherence Burge's actual examples exhibit. The examples are supposed to illustrate the domineering role of the Principle by presenting it with a serious obstacle to overcome. They are supposed to show that even when an individual's errors raise the specter of reinterpretation, homophonic attribution is completely natural and compelling, and therefore the Principle still applies. I have argued that the 1979a and 1986 cases run afoul of the principle of charity. But that might only show that Burge's examples were not well chosen. If Burge can accept (because he can explain away) cases of conceptual dissonance in which reinterpretation is forced because there remain so many cases in which it is not, then giving up

Burge's examples would not spoil the argument for anti-individualism, if there are others that can play the same role.

The problem with Burge's examples is their conceptual incoherence. But since it is conceptual dissonance that is doing the work, and since incoherence and dissonance are not the same thing, there may be examples that make Burge's point without violating the principle of charity. In Section 3.2.2.2 I consider such dissonant-but-coherent utterances, and argue that, in every sort of case I could think of, though homophonic ascription seems natural and inevitable, there is a clear intuition that literal interpretation is not preferred. I think this shows that the naturalness of homophonic ascription and the appropriateness of literal interpretation are subject to different standards, and, hence, that an inference from naturalness to literal truth is invalid.

3.2.2.2 Malaprops, Misnomers and Other Miscellaneous Mistakes

Consider Mona (an actual person, who actually said this). After surgery, Mona goes on vacation to recuperate. At the airport, she repeatedly sets off the metal detector. Later, Mona says "I began to worry that maybe the doctor left a scaffold in me." (It is not a slip. When pressed ("The doctor left a *scaffold* in you?!"), Mona does not retract her statement.) If we say that Mona *said that* she feared the doctor might have left a scaffold in her, it seems clear that what we are saying is literally true. That *is* what she said—in the sense that this is what the words she uttered mean in the language she speaks. Moreover, it seems, intuitively, entirely natural to *say that* Mona feared the doctor might have left a scaffold in her. Mona is confused. She thinks 'scaffold' is a term for a piece of surgical equipment; but she is mistaken. We describe her confusion using her own words, just as we do in the case of Anna. And after she has been corrected Mona might describe her misstatement using the words she uttered, just as Burge himself did in the 'fortnight' case.

Mona's utterance is sufficiently dissonant to raise suspicions about her competence with the term 'scaffold', and, hence, to present a *prima facie* obstacle to literal interpretation. But it does not run afoul of the principle forbidding casual attribution of contradictory or conceptually incoherent thoughts. It is not at all plausible that Mona's surgeon would have left a scaffold inside her; but it is not conceptually or logically impossible. (The scaffold would just have to be very small.) So perhaps this is just the kind of example that Burge needs. It does not involve a contradiction, but neither is it an ordinary empirical error. It is a rather extraordinary one: scaffolds are not kinds of things surgeons use. It is bizarre to think that a surgeon could leave one in a patient. Anyone who seriously says so thereby provides *prima facie* evidence of not knowing what a scaffold is—of not being competent with the concept SCAFFOLD. However, since the Intuition applies in Mona's case, the Principle ought to apply as well, and Mona ought to have the concept SCAFFOLD, and fear that the doctor might have left a scaffold in her, in spite of her confusion. The domineering role of the Principle would thus be highlighted, and the social anti-individualist thesis confirmed.

Another sort of example escapes the charity problem but, arguably, does not involve conceptual dissonance at all. Suppose Mona says "Pat Boone was an early American frontiersman." We would not reinterpret her as having said that *Daniel* Boone was an early American frontiersman. She may have meant to say something about Daniel Boone, but she did not, because she did not use his name. Moreover, though the oddness of Mona's utterance might lead us to suspect that she is confused about who Pat Boone is, it is nonetheless intuitively very natural to *say that* she believes that Pat Boone was an early American frontiersman. She made a jarring error; but it is natural to describe it using the very sentence she uttered. And again, if the Principle applies, we can conclude that Mona believes that Pat Boone was an early American frontiersman.

Constructing a Burgean thought experiment using examples like these not only avoids the charity objection (at least as it concerns incoherence and contradiction); it also comports more comfortably with Burge's Quinean repudiation of a sharp distinction between conceptual truth and empirical truth. It might seem that only constitutive conceptual errors—i.e., only errors of (roughly) the form *Gs are F*, where NOT-F is a constituent of the concept expressed by *G*—can support Burgean conclusions about mental content. But the examples of this section show that this is not the case. Clearly, ordinary empirical errors do not serve Burgean purposes very well (if at all). If someone says "Aluminum does not conduct electricity" or "Water freezes at 33°F," there is no special reason to doubt that the speaker has the relevant concepts, and no hesitation to overcome in attributing a belief with the content of the uttered sentence. It would be *prima facie* pretty implausible to maintain that these errors were due to a misunderstanding of one or more of the terms contained in these sentences. Yet one need not insist that the examples involve incoherence or contradiction, or that the concepts involved have analyses, or (perhaps) even that the examples have to involve confusion about a concept at all. A Burgean error just has to be odd enough to raise suspicion about an individual's competence with a particular term, so that the Intuition can sweep it away and the Principle can show that the individual *thinks* what is *said* in spite of the confusion. The Mona examples seem to do this, without running into trouble with the principle of charity.

But there are strong counterintuitions in both sorts of cases. In the malaprop case, if we reflect and ask ourselves if Mona really was thinking that the doctor left a *scaffold* in her, I think the answer has to be "No." This really is not what she thought. (She was not thinking what *we* think when we think that Mona's doctor left a scaffold in her.) She simply misexpressed herself. She had a false belief about which word to use to say what she was thinking, and that belief led to her anomalous utterance. (Cf. Bach 1988; Crane 1991; Segal 2000.) In spite of the fact that the Intuition holds, the *ceteris paribus* clause of the Principle is activated:

all things are not equal in Mona's case, because she is not fully competent with the words she uses. She does not know what some of them mean.

Since Burge accepts that malaprops are evidence of a lack of the minimal competence required for an individual to be subject to the Principle (1979a: 90), he ought to agree that it is not literally true that Mona believes her doctor left a scaffold in her. The crucial point here, however, is that *it is nonetheless intuitively completely natural to say that this is what she believes.* It is as natural as describing Anna's confusion, and Andy's subversion, using their own words. In Mona's case it is clear that we do not accept our homophonic ascription as literally true. We know that she meant to say 'scalpel', and that this is what she was actually thinking. We know that she did not *really* think the doctor left a scaffold in her. We realize, on (brief) reflection, that we should not take what it is intuitively natural for us to say about her to be literally true. So the presence of the Intuition provides no assurance that we should apply the Principle in spite of a speaker's errors. But Burge's argument for anti-individualism depends on this: naturalness of homophonic ascription is supposed to overpower any inclination to reinterpret. Cases of this type show that the Intuition concerns only what it is natural to *say*, since, on reflection, we do not take our ascriptions to be literally true. The Intuition does not prevent the *ceteris paribus* clause of the Principle from being sprung.

There is a strong counterintuition in the misnomer case as well. On reflection, what it is natural to say Mona thought is not an accurate description of her. If Mona is *that* confused about Pat Boone, then she really does not know whom she is talking about, and should not be said to believe that Pat Boone was an early American frontiersman. Though she may refer to Pat Boone by using his name, and though one might hold that her utterance expresses a singular proposition one of whose constituents is Pat Boone, I think it is intuitively natural to say that she was not really thinking of him when she said what she said. She was really thinking of Daniel Boone, but used the wrong name to express her thought. If we tell her that 'Pat Boone' is the name of a smarmy mid-twentieth-century American crypto-fascist pop vocalist, and that the name she wants is 'Daniel Boone', she will no doubt say that the latter is whom she meant. She did not mean to say (though she did say it)—because she was not thinking—that Pat Boone was an early American frontiersman. Hence, once again, literal interpretation of a spontaneous homophonic attribution is, on reflection, precluded. In both sorts of cases, the Intuition holds, but the Principle does not.

Indeed, I would argue that the Intuition applies in virtually all of the cases Burge explicitly exempts from the Principle. (It might not apply to slips of the tongue that are immediately corrected by their utterers.) Suppose little Oskar is taken to the zoo, having been told that, among other fun things, he will get to ride a big escalator (out of the subway, at the Bronx Zoo). After passing a number of cages containing large animals, Oskar asks, excitedly: "Which one is the escalator?

When do I get to ride it?" It seems entirely natural to describe Oskar as having mistakenly believed that escalators are animals. This is a perfectly intuitive way to describe the mistake he made, even though his is a case in which "mastery of the language and responsibility to its precepts have not been developed; and mental content attribution based on the meaning of words uttered tends to be precluded" (Burge 1979a: 90). But surely Oskar was not thinking what *we* would be thinking if we thought that escalators are animals.

Burge's own initial acceptance of literal interpretation in cases of radical misunderstanding shows just how powerful he thinks the Intuition is. It *is* natural to say that the person who says "An orangutan is a fruit drink" believes that an orangutan is a fruit drink. Our spontaneous impulse is to describe this individual using the very words that were uttered. Burge's hesitancy with respect to the example, and his subsequent rejection of it, however, suggest that he (at least tacitly) appreciates the gap between the Intuition and the Principle. We naturally describe the errors of malapropists, misnamers, children, foreigners, spoonerists and the radically confused homophonically, even while we explicitly exempt them from the Principle. We think that Oskar has not the slightest idea what 'escalator' means; so we do not really think he thought that escalators are animals. We *say* he did, and the intuition that our description is appropriate is very strong. But we do not mean it literally. The fact that homophonic ascription is natural in so many cases in which literal interpretation is precluded shows that the Intuition cannot do the work the Burgean thought experiments require it to do. It does not show that the Principle applies in spite of incompetence. Hence, it cannot be relied upon to make the case that socially constituted linguistic meaning determines psychological content.

3.2.3 Anti-Individualism without the Principle and the Intuition?

In his "Postscript to 'Individualism and the Mental'" (Burge 2007: 151–81), Burge regrets his emphasis on ascriptions—and, by implication, the Principle and the Intuition—in presenting his case for anti-individualism. He says that "[a]lthough discussion of ascriptions looms large in the article – too large – it is not essential to the force or purpose of the main line of the argument" (2007: 162). The fundamental reasoning is, he says, not about language, but "concerns the conditions under which one can be in certain sorts of mental states, or have certain concepts" (2007: 162). The relevant conditions, however, are sociolinguistic. In all of Burge's thought experiments concerning conceptual content, the difference between actual and counterfactual languages is what explains the difference in actual and counterfactual conceptual content. But what is it that establishes the determinative connection between what a term means in one's language and the concept one expresses in uttering it? It cannot be (as Burge realizes) *just* membership in the linguistic community. As noted above, that would make it impossible for speakers to make mistakes in expressing their beliefs: what one says would be, necessarily, what one thinks.

Burge claims that the connection is established by dependence upon others in one's linguistic community, which dependence is itself established through "certain types of causal relations to them" (2007: 176). The question remains, however, how it is that one's involvement with others in one's community can—in the relevant way—determine the contents of one's mental states. It has something to do with shared language. But what is the mechanism by which public meaning comes to be the content of private mental states? In "Individualism and the Mental" (and "Intellectual Norms and Foundations of Mind") it is the naturalness of homophonic attribution, by individuals in the imagined scenarios (or by the reader). This supports literal interpretation, which in turn supports the anti-individualist conclusion. If the Intuition and the Principle are abandoned, there is nothing to override the equally plausible principle that conceptually dissonant utterances are evidence of conceptual confusion, and the natural intuition that such confusion prevents possession of the relevant concept. As a result, the motivation for drawing the anti-individualist conclusion is lost.

The following passage from Burge 2007 (175, my emphasis) is illuminating:

> Reading "Individualism and the Mental" again, I was struck by my insistent emphasis on the idea that one can have thoughts that one incompletely understands. This emphasis had an autobiographical root. A primary impetus for my discovering the thought experiments was recognizing how many words *or concepts* I went around using which I found, on pressing myself, that I did not fully understand.

I once recognized the same thing about myself. I use a lot of words I do not completely understand—in the sense that I do not know exactly what they mean in the language I speak. But I drew the opposite conclusion—that I was not, in fact, using concepts whose contents matched the meanings of many of the words I used, when I used them. What I said was very often not what I thought—the former in many cases being far more nuanced than the latter. (For example, though I use (and love) the words 'rebarbative' and 'execrable', what I usually mean by them both is just *bad*.)

I suspect that what is at the root of a response like Burge's is a tendency to identify, or to overemphasize the connection between, thought and inner speech. If thought were just inner speech, then, given that the meanings of the words one uses are socially determined, it would follow directly that the contents of one's thoughts are socially determined.

But thought is not inner speech, and the connections we find between language and the more sophisticated thoughts we are capable of are not content-constitutive. It may be that we need language to help us grasp relatively complex thought contents and keep them before our minds, as something like scaffolding upon which to hang their constituents.[3] (And this may be because we are, in fact, not all that good at thinking.) But it no more follows that the sentences we lean on are thoughts, or that saying them to ourselves is thinking, than it does that crutches we lean on are legs, or that they walk.

I conclude, then, that Burge has not made a convincing case for psychological anti-individualism with respect to conceptual content.

3.2.4 Perceptual Anti-Individualism

Though (again) my main concern in this book is with conceptual, not perceptual, intentionality, I would like to make a few remarks about Burge's anti-individualist views on perception. Burge claims (1986, 1989 and 2010) that the contents of an organism's perceptual states are (at least in part) individuated with respect to relations to objects in its environment (relations to other states and capacities may also be individuative). The basic idea is that of the teleological versions of the causal-informational theory: a perceptual state represents a kind of object or property with which the organism (or its ancestors) has had sustained contact, such that it has acquired the function of indicating that kind of object or property. The content of such a state is determined to be the kind of object or property it has the evolved function of indicating in normal conditions in its environment. As such, it inherits the problems of these approaches detailed above.

What I would like to address here, however, is Burge's explicit denial of any content-constitutive role for perceptual phenomenology. He writes (2010: 76, second emphasis mine): "Qualitative or phenomenal features of perceptual states do not *in themselves* bear *any* explanatory relation to the environmental properties that perceptual states represent." (This is imprecisely stated. It is clear from the context that what Burge means is that qualitative features of perceptual states bear no explanatory relation to the *representation of* environmental properties, not to the properties themselves; 'the' should be replaced by 'which'.)

Burge recognizes that a stable relation between tokenings of a mental representation type and an object (kind) or property is not by itself sufficient to determine the content of the representation. For he adds that the representation must be such as to *specify* the kind of object or property it represents and attributes to things in the organism's environment (it must be a representation *as of* (2010: 82)). Furthermore, he insists that *veridical* representation is foundational in determining content (2010: 68). Thus, it would seem that

---

[3] I agree with Burge when he says, "Language and mind inevitably become intertwined at relatively sophisticated levels" (2007: 180). See also Jackendoff 1996.

in order for a stable causal relation between an organism's perceptual representations and its environment to feature in the individuation of their contents, the representations must accurately attribute properties to objects in its environment.

But how do they do this? And, in particular, how do conscious perceptual representations do it? Unless we maintain that conscious perceptual experiences reliably caused by external environmental stimuli are not conscious perceptual representations of them, we may ask how those experiences attribute properties to those stimuli. Suppose we have an organism for whom interactions with oval leaves of a particular plant common in its environment reliably result in conscious visual experiences that accurately attribute their shape, color, texture, size, etc. to them. How should we understand what it is for the experience to do this? I think we must say that *how* the organism is experiencing the leaves—the phenomenology of its experience of them—plays an essential role. For, imagine another organism in the same environment whose interactions with those leaves reliably result in conscious visual experiences indiscriminable from accurate experiences of clown emojis. This is not a one-off misperception (which Burge allows for). It is the way this organism always responds to the leaves. (Never mind how this came to be, or how the organism managed to survive long enough for a stable relation to be established between the leaves and the clown emojis. Maybe it does not matter to its well-being how the leaves are represented. Or maybe it was deliberately engineered to respond this way.) It is very difficult to resist the conclusion that this individual is *mis*representing the leaves—*mis*attributing properties to them—*because of* the phenomenal character of its experience. But if this is correct, then we have good reason to assign phenomenal experiential character a central role in explaining what it is for a conscious perceptual state to represent and attribute *accurately*. (See also the discussion of Montague in Chapter 1.)

One can accept that the properties of the objects of perception dictate the terms for accurate representation of them: what counts as a veridical perception is determined by the way the objects of perception are, not vice versa. But it does not follow that such properties exclusively individuate the contents of the perceptual states they cause, or that the phenomenal character of a conscious perceptual state is explanatorily irrelevant.

3.2.5 Externalism without Thought Experiments?

Juhani Yli-Vakkuri (2018) has recently argued that externalism can be established without the use of thought experiments, "by a straightforward deductive argument from premises widely accepted" (2018: 82) by internalists and externalists alike. He argues that the following three principles are inconsistent:

Narrow$_C$: Necessarily, corresponding beliefs of duplicate subjects have the same contents.

Broad$_T$: Possibly, corresponding beliefs of duplicate subjects do not have the same truth value.

Trans: Necessarily, the truth value of a belief is the same as the truth value of its content.

and that neither Broad$_T$ nor Trans(parency) can reasonably be given up. Specifically, he argues that the conjunction of Narrow$_C$ and Trans entails the negation of Broad$_T$—i.e., that if content is narrow and a belief has the same truth value as its content, then it is *not* possible for corresponding beliefs of duplicate subjects to have different truth values. But since Broad$_T$ and Trans have considerable intuitive support, Narrow$_C$ must go.

I agree that giving up Broad$_T$ and Trans would be too high a price to pay for Narrow$_C$; but I do not think Yli-Vakkuri's argument shows that they are inconsistent. As stated, the argument is invalid. It does not follow from that fact that duplicates have beliefs with the same contents, and that the truth values of contents are the same as the truth values of their beliefs, that their beliefs cannot have different truth values. The argument requires the further premise that the content of a belief determines its truth value *absolutely* (*simpliciter*). If that is so, then if duplicates have beliefs with the same contents, their beliefs must have the same truth value. But if content determines truth value *relative to context*, then it is possible for the duplicates to have content-identical beliefs with different truth values. Though he does not include the principle that content determines truth value absolutely explicitly among his premises, Yli-Vakkuri recognizes that it is possible to reject it. However, he maintains, to adopt a principle of relative truth is to deny Trans. But it is not. Trans is a principle concerning a relation between beliefs and their contents. And it remains true even if the truth values of the contents of duplicates' beliefs can be different in different contexts. What the argument needs is the following principle:

Broad$_C$: Necessarily, the contents of corresponding beliefs of duplicate subjects have the same truth values.

But Broad$_C$ cannot be derived from Narrow$_C$, Broad$_T$ or Trans: it may be true that beliefs have the same truth values as their contents, but it does not follow that if two beliefs have the same contents their contents have the same truth value. To adopt Broad$_C$ as an independent premise is, quite obviously, to beg the question against the internalist. I suspect that what is really doing the work in Yli-Vakkuri's reasoning is a monadic conception of truth. Such a conception would justify Broad$_C$, and rule out the relativist response to his argument; but he offers no support for it in this paper. (In correspondence he has claimed that Broad$_C$ needs no support, since it is a theorem of first-order logic. It seems to me obvious that it is not.)

3.3 Phenomenal Externalism, the Paraphenomenal Hypothesis

SAM: Say, Abe; can you explain to me how the telephone works? I don't get it.

ABE: Sure. Imagine you've got this gigantic dog. It's so big, it can stand in Manhattan with its head in Brooklyn and its tail in the Bronx.

SAM: Uh huh?

ABE: So, when you talk to the head in Brooklyn, the tail wags in the Bronx.

SAM: Ah, okay; I see now. Very nice. But what about wireless? Can you explain to me how that works?

ABE: Simple. It's the same thing, only you don't have the dog.

In *The Concept of Mind*, Gilbert Ryle accused Descartes of advancing what Ryle called the 'paramechanical hypothesis', according to which the structure and operations of the mind can be understood on the model of the structure and operations of a physical system. The body is a complex machine—"a bit of clockwork"—that operates according to laws governing the mechanical interactions of material things. The mind, on the other hand, according to Ryle's Descartes, is an immaterial machine that operates according to formally analogous laws governing the paramechanical interactions of immaterial things—"a bit of not-clockwork." In other words, mental processes are the same as physical processes, only you don't have the matter.

I do not know whether Descartes actually thought this. But, surely, if he did, he was making some kind of logical or conceptual error. Mental processes *cannot* be *the same as* physical processes, minus the matter, since the matter matters. The properties of physical systems have physical explanations, which are explanations in terms of physical properties and physical laws. But it is absurd—a category mistake—to suppose that mechanical explanations could apply to immaterial things with no physical properties, subject to no physical laws.

Now, whether or not Descartes made this mistake, I think contemporary reductive representationalists make a precisely analogous one in their account of non-veridical perceptual experience. These theorists hold that the phenomenology of perception (and of introspection and proprioception) can be reduced to a kind of non-phenomenal intentionality, which in turn can be explained in naturalistic causal-informational-teleological terms. The qualitative features associated with an experience are properties, not of the experience, but of the worldly (or bodily) things it represents. The blue that characterizes what it is like to see a clear sky at noon, for example, is a property, not of one's *experience of* the sky, but of *the sky*. Its relevance to the characterization of the experience of a clear sky at noon is due to the fact that one's experience *represents* it, not that one's experience *instantiates* it. These views are externalist about qualia (see Dretske 1996, Byrne and Tye 2006, Tye 2015).

According to these views, to suppose that experience instantiates perceivable properties is to commit what U. T. Place (1956) termed the "phenomenological fallacy"—that is, to conclude that properties of experienced objects are properties of experiences of them (because experience is required for awareness of them)—and to court all of the mysteries and explanatory dead ends of ontological dualism. Sound scientific philosophy requires that we give materialistic explanations of all phenomena, including mental ones. The mind is (or arises from, or supervenes on, or is realized in—or something) the brain; mental processes are brain processes; mental states are brain states; etc. Your brain does not turn blue when you look at a clear sky at noon; it does not taste like chocolate when you eat chocolate; and it does not sound like the Beatles when you listen to *Revolver*. All of those properties are out in the world, though they are *represented by* what is in the head. One's perceptual representation of the sky is no more blue than one's conceptual representation of snow is white, or cold.

However, a *prima facie* problem for views like this is the existence of illusions, dreams and hallucinations—cases where there *is not* anything out there that is the bearer of the properties we are aware of in experience. If you have ingested a hallucinogenic substance, you might have an experience just like one you would have if you were floating downstream, or surrendering to the void, in the absence of any such things within sensory range. But how could this be, if the qualitative properties characterizing experience are properties of things perceived?

According to Place, what is common to veridical and non-veridical experience is the brain processes underlying each, regardless of the presence or absence of the objects or properties you seem to be seeing. When you have veridical experiences, your brain processes represent external objects and their properties, which latter you mention when characterizing how it is with you, experientially. And when you have non-veridical experiences, the same brain processes occur, but in the absence of the external objects and their properties. Hallucinating a clear blue sky at noon is (internally) the same thing as perceiving it, only you don't have the sky.

But where is the *blue* in such a case? On this view, it is not in the brain (it *never* was); and it is not in the world. But it is still in your *experience,* in the sense that you are still consciously aware of blueness. You would (*pace* Fish 2008) describe your experience in exactly the same way as you would if you were not hallucinating: what it is like to see the sky at noon and what it is like to hallucinate the sky at noon are subjectively indistinguishable. And, one may suppose, they are subjectively indistinguishable because they are phenomenally identical. But now there is no place to put the property you would mention in describing what your experience is like. It cannot be the same thing, only without the sky, since the sky was where the qualitative feature you experienced was supposed to be located. This para*phenomenal* hypothesis is no more plausible than the paramechanical one.

Some reductive representationalists, in particular Dretske (1995, 1996, 1999), Bill Lycan (1987, 1996, 2001, 2008) and Tye (2000, 2015), propose that in cases of non-veridical experience there *is* something that exists contemporaneously with your experience, and which is represented by it—though it is not the same as what is represented in subjectively indistinguishable veridical perceptions. For Dretske and Tye, non-veridical experiences represent *uninstantiated universals*; whereas for Lycan they represent *properties instantiated by non-actual objects in non-actual possible worlds*. The non-veridical experiential states are intrinsically just like the veridical ones, and represent the same objects and properties; but the objects do not actually exist and the properties are not instantiated (at least not locally).

Intuitively, it may seem unproblematic to speak of non-veridical experience in this way. If you hallucinate a baboon wearing a pink party hat in the living room, it seems perfectly natural to say that your experience represents an object that might have been, but is not, in the living room, and a color that might have been, but is not, locally instantiated. But interpreting this to mean that your experience represents an object that is located in the (or a) living room in some other possible world, or an uninstantiated color, is not consistent with the reductive representationalist's claim that the qualitative features of experience are features of the objects of experience, and not experience itself. For uninstantiated blue and pink are not colored blue and pink, and neither other-worldly objects nor uninstantiated properties appear to us the way actual objects and instantiated properties do. Indeed, they do not *appear* at all. Neither merely possible baboons nor uninstantiated colors look like anything. We cannot *see* them. The reductive representationalist says that in veridical experience objects appear to us in certain ways, but that these ways are properties of experienced objects, not our experience of them. But if the things that have the properties that appear to us are removed—either by simply eliminating them or by replacing them with things that do not have appearance properties—then the basis for a reductive account of the phenomenality of experience goes with them. Saying it's the same thing, only the baboon is in another possible world, or baboonhood is not instantiated, is just as bad as saying it's the same thing, only you don't have the dog. If there is no actual *baboon*, there is no sense to saying it is the same thing.

The same problem besets McGinn's (1999) and Gottlieb and Rezaei's (2020) 'clusters of properties', and Johnston's (2004) 'sensible profiles'. The point is that when the object goes, the properties that are supposed to be the phenomenal character of the experience go with it. What is essential is the absence of properties, not things that instantiate them.[4] Gottlieb and Rezaei miss this point. They claim that my argument against reductive representationalism does not go through because I do not recognize that on (their version of) the cluster theory the relevant properties "may or may not be instantiated in the subject[']s environment" (2020: 2). They argue that according to this view "objects never mattered to the phenomenal character of experience to begin with" (2020: 6). (Moreover, this is true "*irrespective of whether the experience is veridical or hallucinatory*" (2020: 6, my emphasis). One wonders, then, what distinguishes veridical from hallucinatory experiences, if neither the presence of an object nor the instantiation of phenomenal properties does.) But, again, it is not the objects that matter. What matters is the instantiation of properties, since locally uninstantiated properties do not *appear* any way to local perceivers.

Given that veridical and non-veridical experiences can be phenomenally identical,[5] the claim that the latter represent what might have been is plausible only on a *non*-reductive version of representationalism (e.g., Loar 2003), according to which experiences instantiate phenomenal properties which are themselves intrinsically representational. (This point is made in Thompson 2008, which makes many of the points I make here. Thompson does not, however, bring out the *absurdity* of the reductive representationalist's position.) If what might have been veridically perceived, but is not, is experientially identical to what is veridically perceived, then it cannot be that the properties in virtue of which the experiences are identical are themselves experientially distinct. But instantiated pink and uninstantiated pink *are* experientially distinguishable—both subjectively and objectively—as are actual and merely possible baboons. We cannot see counterfactual apes, and we cannot see uninstantiated colors. We *can*, however, according to the *non*-reductive representationalist (and anyone else who holds that phenomenal properties are intrinsic properties of experience) have qualitative experiences *as of* baboons and pink party hats where and when there are none, since the properties that characterize what the experience is like *are* instantiated—just not in the external world.

Dretske's, Tye's and Lycan's proposals cannot account for the subjective indiscriminability of veridical and non-veridical experience. If subjective sameness of experience is understood in terms of the ways things appear, and uninstantiated properties and non-actually-existing objects do not appear, and do not instantiate perceivable properties, then dreaming or hallucinating and perceiving cannot be

---

[4] If properties could be instantiated absent anything that counts as a non-qualitative basis, as some trope theoretic bundle theories suggest, one would speak of local non-co-instantiation or non-compresence of the properties.

[5] In fact, total phenomenal identity of veridical and hallucinatory experience is not required for counterexamples to reductive representationalism (and direct realism). All that is needed is experience as of properties that are not instantiated in the spatiotemporally local environment. Illusions and dreams are enough.

the same, minus the external object, any more than a mental process can be the same as a physical process, minus the matter, or wireless can be the same as telephone, minus the dog. They are guilty of advancing an absurd paraphenomenal hypothesis.

It might be thought that this problem can be avoided by going disjunctivist. According to disjunctivism, veridical experience is 'a basic, unanalyzable metaphysical condition' (Brewer 2008: 170; see also Martin 2002) of experientially apprehending facts about the external world. Subjectively indiscriminable non-veridical experience is metaphysically distinct, since the relevant worldly facts are no longer involved. Perception and hallucination do not have a substantive common nature: hallucination is not the same thing as perception, minus the world. If they are subjectively indiscriminable, it is only because they share the disjunctive property of being either veridical or non-veridical. Nothing more can be said by way of *explaining* their subjective indiscriminability. In particular, it is not due to their instantiating or representing the same phenomenal properties. Thus, attempts like Dretske's, Tye's and Lycan's to explain indiscriminability in terms of objects and properties represented are quixotic, since there is in fact nothing substantive to explain.

I do not think this can be right. In general, the idea that indiscriminability of veridical and non-veridical experiences—or of anything else—could be due to nothing more than the sharing of disjunctive properties is very hard to believe. Moreover, to say that perception is indiscriminable from hallucination when the subject cannot tell whether an experience is a perception or a hallucination—when all that can be known is that the experience is either a perception or a hallucination—is not to give an *explanation* at all, even a superficial one.

Furthermore, the metaphysical version of the argument from hallucination is based on the premise that it is possible for veridical and non-veridical experiences to *be* phenomenally identical (from which it follows that they are subjectively indiscriminable; the converse need not hold). A disjunctivist would, then, have to argue that this is in fact not possible—that veridical and hallucinatory experiences must differ in their intrinsic phenomenal character. Then it could be denied that it is possible for one to be having the very same experience one has of the external world while hallucinating.

But how is this claim to be made out? Either, I think, by maintaining that hallucinations have phenomenal character which is (perhaps detectably, perhaps not) relevantly different from that of veridical perceptions, or by maintaining that hallucinations have no phenomenal character at all—i.e., that there is *nothing* it is like to hallucinate. (Bill Fish once held this view (Fish 2008). I believe he no longer does.) The main problem with the former strategy is that it will not help the reductive representationalist, for whom, if an experience has a correct phenomenal characterization at all, it is in terms of the qualitative properties of the objects experienced. However, the phenomenal characterization of the experience will either mention properties that are instantiated by objects one perceives or not. In the former case, we no longer have a hallucination. In the latter case, the problems detailed above remain. As long as there is something it is like to hallucinate, the problem of the *location* of the properties experienced will arise.

So it seems the only option for a disjunctivish solution to the reductive representationalist's problem is to deny that there is any phenomenology of hallucinations (or dreams, or, to the relevant degree, illusions) at all. Once hallucinations are phenomenally characterized, the problem of the placement of the mentioned qualitative properties arises. So the only way out of it is to deny that hallucinations have phenomenal characterizations. But surely it is a *reductio* of disjunctivism, as well as reductive representationalism, and any other qualia-externalist view (including at least some versions of direct and naive realism) to deny that there is something it is like to hallucinate, or to dream.

4
Indexical Thought

Intentionality is, originally and essentially, a mental phenomenon. We do not have a mind-independent conception of it that conceptual representations must somehow measure up to, any more than we have a conception of a world of perceivable objects that precedes our experience of them, that perceptual representations have to capture. The very idea of intentionality, of meaningfulness, like the very idea of a world of perceivable objects, arises from our experience of it.[1] Intentional states are not theoretical entities. Moreover, since linguistic intentionality is derived from mental intentionality, and not vice versa, theorizing about the semantics of natural languages should be constrained by facts about the concepts and thoughts natural language expressions are used to express. It is, thus, in my view, a mistake to base a theory of linguistic meaning on an account of how language is used in communication (as, for example, Grice does). Meaning is not a third-person phenomenon. What expressions mean is grounded in what thinkers mean by them, which is in turn grounded in what thinkers think. And it is independent of expressions' being put to use by anyone, for any purpose, and independent of considerations concerning how a speaker is to be interpreted by someone else in various circumstances. What semantics is really about is the structure and content of thought (in the sense of *what is thought*, as opposed to *what is thought about*), and a successful semantic theory must answer to the facts about them. Thought is not language-like. Language is thought-like. Intuitions about the use of natural language expressions and the interpretation of speech acts cannot be the foundation for theorizing about mental or linguistic content.

I have argued that the contents of thoughts, given that they are introspectively and non-inferentially accessible, must be phenomenally constituted. This includes indexical thoughts (thoughts expressed using indexicals, including demonstratives). This is *prima facie* incompatible with the standard semantics for indexical expressions, on which their contents are *referent-dependent*—i.e., determined with respect to the referents of their constituent indexicals (perhaps by *including* them). These theories are thus extensionalist, and, *de facto*, externalist. For example, if you and I simultaneously utter the sentence "I'm fed up," we have, intuitively, said

---

[1] Cf. Kriegel 2011b: ch. 1; Mendelovici 2018: ch. 1. It might be objected that the "very idea" of intentionality arises from reflection on language (or signs and symbols in general), and that the idea of mental intentionality is thus derivative from the idea of linguistic intentionality. I do not think this is the case. To reflect on the fact that a sign or symbol means something is already to experience meaning independently of its association with anything symbolic. Language is not intentional on its own.

different things.² And since the only difference between our utterances is the referents of our 'I' tokens, it seems reasonable to conclude that you and I are constituents (or otherwise determinants) of the contents of those utterances.

The phenomenal intentionality of thought thesis, on the other hand, is committed to internalism (and intensionalism)—given that phenomenal properties are intrinsic to the states that have them, and hence not individuated extensionally (including externally). Yet, the intuitions that motivate extensionalist/externalist semantics for indexicals might appear to be equally sound when applied to thought. My *thought* I'M FED UP and your thought I'M FED UP are, intuitively, different thoughts, because mine is about me and yours is about you (because our I-concepts refer to different individuals).³ Likewise, my thought THIS IS WHY WE CAN'T HAVE NICE THINGS thought of your chronic drunkenness and my thought THIS IS WHY WE CAN'T HAVE NICE THINGS thought of your inveterate clumsiness are different thoughts, because the constituent 'this' concepts are about (refer to) different states of affairs. Again, it seems reasonable to conclude that indexical thought contents are individuated in terms of what their constituent indexical concepts refer to. If, however, thought contents are individuated by their intrinsic phenomenology, our thoughts I'M FED UP and my thoughts THIS IS WHY WE CAN'T HAVE NICE THINGS ought to have the *same* contents, in spite of being about different individuals or states of affairs.

Similarly, it looks like intuitions about the counterfactual evaluation of indexical thoughts mirror those about the counterfactual evaluation of indexical sentences. Suppose I think I AM SOMETHING THAT YOU'LL NEVER COMPREHEND. We can ask whether or not what I have thought in the actual world, the content of my actual thought, is true or not at some other world. But the counterfactual truth value of what I actually thought is, intuitively, determined by whether or not *I* am something that you'll never comprehend in a counterfactual circumstance; and it seems the only way to secure that I am the referent of the I-concept in that circumstance is to make me its content. Whatever descriptive content (*character*) the I-concept may have cannot be relied on to pick out *me* when applied to another world. Indeed, it will not pick out *anyone* without specification of a context; and the right context to specify is one in which I am the agent. Moreover, allowing modal operators to operate on the descriptive contents of

---

² Cf. David Kaplan:

"What is said in using a given indexical in different contexts may be different. Thus if I say, today

    I was insulted yesterday

and you utter the same words tomorrow, what is said is different" (Kaplan 1989: 500).

³ In the paper this chapter is adapted from (Pitt 2013) I used what I called sentences in "thought quotes"—^ ^ ("little thinking caps")—to refer thoughts (and concepts), as they occur in thinkers' minds. Here I use small capitals for the same purpose.

indexical concepts results in absurdities such as that the thought POSSIBLY I DO NOT EXIST is necessarily false (since it is necessarily false that the agent of a context does not exist in that context). (The example is, of course, adapted from Kaplan 1989.) So, the descriptive/phenomenal "character" of the I-concept cannot be part of *what I have thought* when I think I AM SOMETHING THAT YOU'LL NEVER COMPREHEND—it is not a constituent of the *content* of my thought.

Furthermore, it might be argued (as Evans (1982) and McDowell (1984) have with respect to indexical sentences) that unless one knows what the referents of the indexical concepts in an indexical thought are (by, e.g., being *acquainted* with them), one does not *understand* what one has thought—just as one would not understand what has been said by an utterance of an indexical sentence if one did not know what the referents of its constituent indexicals were. If I do not know what you are thinking about (what your indexical concept refers to) when you think YOUR VIEW GIVES ME HIVES, then I will not know what you have thought, just as I would not understand your utterance of 'Your view gives me hives' without knowing who the referent of your token of 'you[r]' is. And this would apply in one's own case as well. One will not understand what one has thought if one does not have a referent in mind for YOU[R]. But if we assume that understanding a thought is knowing what its content is, then it would appear that the contents of indexical thoughts are referent-dependent and, thus, cannot be purely phenomenal.

Finally, the way we attribute propositional attitudes appears to entail that the content of an indexical thought is individuated in terms of the referents of its constituent indexical concepts, and not its intrinsic phenomenal features. The way for a third party to report my thought MY VANITY SAVED MY LIFE is *not* (at least in English) to say "He's thinking [that] my vanity saved my life," but, rather, "He's thinking [that] his vanity saved his life." To get the content of my thought right, any third-person ascription must replace 'my' with a term that, in the mouth of the ascriber, refers to what 'my' referred to in my mouth (viz., me). The descriptive content of the part of the third-person ascriber's utterance that specifies the content of my thought must be different from that of mine in order for the ascription to be correct. To capture the content of my thought your term must agree in reference, not conceptual content, with mine. (Cf. Frege 1918.) And this suggests that the content of my thought contains (or is otherwise individuated by) the referent of my I-concept.

My concern in this chapter is to blunt these intuitions, and to defend a conception of indexical thought content that is entirely phenomenal and internalist. On this view, when you and I think I'M FED UP, we are thinking the same thought.[4] The

---

[4] David Lewis (Lewis 1998: 41) calls this "the proper naïve response" to Kaplan's claims about "what is said." He characterizes this view of the semantic values of indexical utterances as "constant but complicated," as opposed to Kaplan's (and Stalnaker's) "variable but simple" view, and claims that there is no basis for a choice between them. Obviously, I think there is.

fact that my thought is about (refers to) me and yours is about (refers to) you, and that mine might thus be true while yours is false, does not give them different contents and does not make them different thoughts. I am thinking I'M FED UP of me, and you are thinking it of you, and that accounts for the possible difference in truth value of our utterances. Nor does modal evaluation of indexical thoughts require that their contents be individuated by the contextually determined referents of their constituent indexical concepts. One cannot determine the truth value of an indexical thought in the actual world without a specification of its context (a thinker, a time, a place, an addressee, etc.); and the same is true for evaluation of that thought in any other possible world. The fact that the relevant context is otherwordly does not entail that indexical contents are referent-dependent any more than contextual sensitivity in the actual world does. And there is no *semantic* necessity that the object I pick out in another world be the very object referred to in the actual world. Moreover, ignorance of the referent of an indexical concept does not prevent its containing indexical thought from being understood. Such knowledge may enrich one's overall conceptual take on things, but only through the introduction of further thoughts. Finally, the constraints our propositional-attitude ascribing practices are subject to are pragmatic rather than semantic. Our interest in what others are thinking is influenced by factors that do not affect the individuation of their contents. Needless to say, my arguments have direct application to the semantics of indexical expressions.

4.1 What Is Thought

A standard move for anyone who accepts externalist/extensionalist intuitions about mental content, but nonetheless thinks there is something content-*like* that thoughts can have in common, is to make a distinction between "narrow" and "wide" (or "broad") content. Narrow content is intrinsically individuated, and can be common to thoughts with different wide contents, whereas wide content is extrinsically individuated, and cannot be common to thoughts about different things. Accordingly, it might seem that the best way for the phenomenal intentionality of thought thesis to accommodate intuitions about indexical thought is to make a Kaplanesque character-content distinction for indexical thoughts, and identify conceptual phenomenology with (the conceptual equivalent of) character. One could then say that what our thoughts I'M FED UP have in common is their propositional character, though not their contents, and that they are, in one sense, the same thoughts, but in another sense not the same thoughts.

Now, thoughts can be individuated in any number of ways, depending upon one's interests and purposes, and this way might serve some perfectly well. But I do not think it is the *right* way to individuate thoughts, since it does not capture what they *are*. Thoughts are not theoretical posits whose natures are determined by theories about them, or whose existence we accept because of their usefulness in explaining and predicting behavior. They are objects of intimate acquaintance in experience. They are states of *minds*, and, as such, are (I have argued) intrinsically constituted, and knowable from the first-person point of view. That (mind- and language-independent) propositions could be referent-dependent or referent-involving is, perhaps, unproblematic. And such singular propositions can be put to good use (as *referents* of sentences and thoughts; I return to this idea in the next chapter). But if thought contents are propositional-phenomenal types (and thoughts are tokens of those types), then they cannot be individuated non-phenomenally. They cannot have non-phenomenal constituents or depend for their identity on non-phenomenal entities, and neither can their tokens. (This *Principle of Phenomenal Purity* is another basic law of experience. I develop the point further in the discussions of demonstrative concepts, below, and nominal concepts, in the next chapter.) It could not be literally true that one has a concrete (or abstract) object, such as an individual or a time (or a number or a universal), in mind, or that some extrinsic, non-phenomenal entity could affect the intrinsic nature of a mental state. If thought contents are phenomenal types, they cannot be referent-involving; and if phenomenal properties are intrinsically determined, they cannot be referent-dependent.

So I have a reason for questioning the motivation for making a narrow/wide or character/content distinction in the first place—i.e., for introducing a two-factor theory of content—that is, of *meaning* (as opposed to *reference*). It seems to me that a theory that postulates only one kind of mental content, distinguishes it from mental reference, and identifies it with propositional phenomenology—a theory that allows that distinct tokens of the same thought could have different referents, truth conditions and truth values—is all the theory we need. I argued for this kind of approach in the previous chapter with respect to externalism about non-indexical concepts. Here I apply it to indexical concepts.

In part, resistance to this approach is rooted in the intuition that, since content determines reference, if two concepts have different referents, they must have different contents. So, your and my tokens of the I-concept, having different referents, must have different contents. It cannot be that our thoughts have exactly the same contents but different referents, truth conditions and possible truth values. But I do not think this is correct. The argument is that, e.g., our I-thoughts have different contents *because* their constituent I-concepts have different referents. But, as I argued in the previous chapter, it is not true *in general* that thoughts with constituent concepts having different referents or extensions must have different contents, and be different thoughts.

Suppose I think CENTENARIANS ARE RARE in 2000 and then again in 2024. The extension of CENTENARIAN in 2000 is not the same as its extension in 2024. But have I thought different thoughts? Has my *concept* CENTENARIAN changed its content? I have a strong intuition that I do not, and it has not. Do my thoughts have different truth conditions? Well, you might think they do not, since they are, in both cases, just that the set of centenarians is a subset of the set of rare things, and in both cases the conditions are fulfilled (so that difference of *extension* is not sufficient for difference of truth conditions). On the other hand, if you think that the truth conditions of the 2000 thought CENTENARIANS ARE RARE involve the set of the centenarians that there are in 2000, and those of the 2024 thought the set of the centenarians that there are in 2024, then the thoughts do have different truth conditions—though they are still, I maintain, tokens of the same thought type. In either case, however, the truth *values* of the thoughts could be different: people get older. And this ought to be enough, on the view I am challenging, to conclude that they have different contents. But they do not. General concepts (as argued in the previous chapter for natural kind concepts) do not change their contents with changes in their extensions.⁵

Here is another example. In 1972 I think THE PRESIDENT OF THE UNITED STATES IS A CRIMINAL. In 2020 I think THE PRESIDENT OF THE UNITED STATES IS A CRIMINAL. Have I thought the same thing or not? It seems to me that I have thought *precisely* the same thing on both occasions, in spite of the fact that in 1972 I am referring to a different criminal than the one I am referring to in 2020, and, hence, that it is possible for what I thought in 1972 to differ in truth value from what I thought in 2020. (This intuition would not be defeated by a Russellian construal of definite descriptions, since it would still be the case that these thoughts would be about, in the sense of being made true by, different individuals—the values of the existentially quantified variables.) Difference in reference of definite-descriptive concepts, and the consequent difference of truth conditions and possible truth values of the thought tokens, do not result in thought tokens with different contents either. (Compare MacFarlane 2007; 2014. MacFarlane does not accept the extension of his view to indexicals (personal communication).)

Now, it might be maintained that the contents of the above thoughts are insufficiently specified, because they contain a hidden indexical concept—e.g., CURRENT—and, hence, are in fact indexical thoughts. (In which case it would be question-begging to deny that their contents are different.) But the concept PRESIDENT is not the same as the concept CURRENT PRESIDENT, and, hence, it is possible to think that the president of the United States is a criminal without thinking that the current president of the United States is a criminal.

It might also be argued that the contents of these thoughts are insufficiently specified because the *complete* content of any thought includes an indication of the time at which it is thought, so that, e.g., my 2000 and 2024 centenarian thoughts

---

⁵ I think the notion of truth conditions is far too vague to be of any use in determining meaning or content. That a particular object has some property (or is a member of some set) does not determine which of the many different ways of thinking of that object or property a thinker might deploy.

have different (non-indexical) contents, and that is what allows them to have different truth values. From a first-person perspective, however, the view that thought contents always include time indications, and hence are true or false once and for all (a doctrine sometimes called "eternalism," and contrasted with "temporalism") is quite implausible. I might think CENTENARIANS ARE RARE and have no idea what the current date is. And even if I know the date, I need not think of it whenever I think CENTENARIANS ARE RARE. Moreover, parity of reasoning would seem to require "ubiquitism"—the view that thought contents include *place* indications, and hence are true or false at every location—as well as "necessitarianism"—the view that thought contents include *world* indications, and hence are true or false at every possible world. But my thought THE KING IS IN HIS COUNTING HOUSE (NB: not THE LOCAL KING IS IN HIS COUNTING HOUSE) could be true if I thought it in Saudi Arabia, though false if I had thought it (at the same time) in the United States. And I could think it without having any idea where I am. And even if I do know where I am, I need not think that I am there when I think THE KING IS IN HIS COUNTING HOUSE. Similarly, necessitarianism has the consequence that all of my thoughts are either necessarily true or necessarily false, since it is true (false) at every possible world that my thought is true (false) in the world in which I am thinking it. And a parallel point holds for the possibility of thinking a thought without thinking of the possible world I am in—or even having the concept of a possible world.

Analogous considerations hold for difference in reference or extension *across worlds*. We do not suppose that general concepts change their meanings across worlds in which they have different extensions. My otherworldly twin may be thinking of other centenarians, but he thinks exactly what I think when he thinks CENTENARIANS ARE RARE. Nor do we suppose that the content of definite-descriptive concepts changes with changes in their referents—e.g., THE KING OF AMERICA does not *mean* something different at worlds in which the United States is a monarchy; and THE KING OF AMERICA IS MAD does not mean something different at worlds at which it is false. Similar responses are available to the claim that such thoughts contain the implicit indexical concept ACTUAL.

Though I have given reasons for thinking that the (controversial) thesis that reference, extension and truth are always relative to something is correct, in fact my argument does not depend on it. The essential point is that such relativity does not *entail* relativity of content: one may consistently endorse the claim that the extensions of general and definite-descriptive concepts typically vary with respect to places, times and worlds while denying that their contents do. Hence, some rationale is required for thinking that indexical concepts are exceptional in this regard. In the absence of such a rationale, they may be treated as differing only with respect to the *scope* of their relativization. Whereas general and (indexical-free) definite-descriptive concepts have extensions relative to worlds, and times and places within worlds, indexical concepts have extensions relative to times, places, speakers, addressees, etc. within worlds. True demonstrative concepts such as THIS and THAT have extensions relative to an even more deeply world-embedded index, viz., a perceptual-attentive state of an individual. (A rough gloss on the content of simple demonstrative concepts is THE THING I AM ATTENDING TO.)[6] The fact that our indexical thoughts have constituent indexical concepts with different referents, and hence different truth conditions or truth values, does not entail that they have different contents.

4.2 Modality

The standard modal motivation for a referent-dependent semantics of indexical expressions is that the actual referent of any indexical must be a constituent of what is evaluated at other worlds in order to get the truth conditions of modal indexical sentences to come out right. (From here on I will be focusing on the referent-*involving* version of referent-dependence, since, for one thing, it seems the more commonly accepted view. Adjustment of the points I make to address Evans–McDowell-style referent-dependence is straightforward.) Analogous considerations would seem to apply to indexical thoughts. This intuition is widely accepted; but I think some reflection shows that it is not inevitable. There are intuitively satisfying ways to understand the counterfactual evaluation of indexical thoughts (and sentences) without individuating them referentially.

Suppose you and I both think I'M ITCHY. On the view I am defending, your token of the I-concept has exactly the same content as mine, or anyone else's. 'I' is (like definite descriptions) referentially singular, but conceptually general: its tokens refer to individuals, but its content is such that different tokens can refer to numerically distinct but relevantly qualitatively identical individuals. (Concepts like CENTENARIAN are both referentially and conceptually general.) *What* we have thought, the shared content of our token thoughts, is, on my view, the propositional-phenomenal type I'M ITCHY. And our thoughts—our individual, unshareable, unrepeatable, dated cognitive episodes—are tokens of that type. (They *have* their contents by *being tokens of* their contents.)

The truth values of our thought tokens are determined by the states of the referents of their token I-concept constituents; and the referents of our token I-concepts are determined by their contents—relative, of course, to some parameter (a world, time, person, place, etc.). Insofar, there is no difference from truth value determination for non-indexical thoughts: contents determine referents and

---

[6] Arguments that indexicals are essential (e.g., Perry 1979)—i.e., that they are never replaceable by non-indexical descriptions—do not show that indexical contents are not descriptive. While it may be true that complex descriptive indexical contents always include indexicals (e.g., THE THING I AM ATTENDING TO), indexical contents need not be complex. Descriptive contents in general can be (indeed, some *must* be) primitive.

extensions relative to some parameter, and the relations of referents and extensions determine truth values. As noted above, where indexical contents differ is only in the scope of their relativization—as it were, the *size* of the context to which their reference is relativized. Concepts have referents or extensions relative to contexts, and contexts come in various sizes, from individual acts of attention to possible worlds to the space of all possible worlds (and perhaps beyond). General concepts have extensions at worlds and, typically, times within those worlds. Definite-descriptive and indexical concepts can have referents at proper parts of worlds—places (HERE, THE KING), times (NOW, THE PRESIDENT), individuals (I, YOU) and acts of attention (THIS, THAT). And just as you and I can think the same *non*-indexical thought—i.e., token the same thought type—with different truth values, we can think the same indexical thoughts with different truth values: my token of I'M ITCHY can be true while yours is false—since the referents of their constituent I-concepts are different, and the states of those referents may be relevantly different.

The same parity holds for the evaluation of thoughts at other possible worlds. In order to evaluate a thought at a world, one must determine extensions for its constituent referential concepts. For some concepts, specification of a world may be enough. In the case of indexical concepts, specification of a world is normally not sufficient to determine referents, and so not sufficient to determine truth value. One must also specify a relevant context within that world—a person, place, time, etc. But it does not follow that indexical referents must be constituents of the contents of indexical thoughts evaluated at a world—whether it be this world or some other. And it does not follow from its being the case that an individual must be specified in order to evaluate an indexical thought at a counterfactual circumstance that the referent of its *actual* token must be specified.

I can sensibly ask whether what I thought in a particular context in the actual world is true in some context, in the actual world or in some other world. If I think I'M ITCHY, I can ask if what I thought is true of you: *not* (NB), is my *token* true of you (we may assume it could not be); but, supposing you are also thinking I'M ITCHY, if *your* token of the I-concept is true of you. This is exactly parallel to the situation in which I, in the United States, and you, in Saudi Arabia, in 2016 think THE KING IS IN HIS COUNTING HOUSE. The thought type we have tokened contains the place- (and time-)sensitive concept THE KING. Hence, since my token occurred in the U.S., the default assumption is that it does not refer to anyone (yet), while your token of the very same concept (at the same time) refers to Salman bin Abdulaziz Al Saud. And I can ask whether what I thought—the content I tokened—is true when tokened by you. And what is true across contexts within a world is also true across worlds. I can sensibly ask with respect to some other world whether what I actually thought is true of me or you or someone else, or at some time or place, in that world. By which I would mean: if the thought type I tokened in some particular actual context were tokened in some context in some other world, would it be true in that context (*of* the chosen individual, time, place, etc.) in that world?

If I ask whether what I thought when I thought I'M ITCHY is true at possible world *w*, the answer depends upon which individual in *w* is assigned as the referent of my I-concept. Though I am semantically constrained to refer to myself when I token this concept, I am not semantically constrained evaluate the *content* of my I-thought at another possible world with respect to *me*. And even if I were so constrained, it would not follow that the content of my I-thought is referent-involving. The I-concept could be construed as having, for each individual, a *de facto* rigid descriptive content—though at the high cost of each of us having our own unshareable self-concept. Indeed, the same would seem to be the case if we individuate our I-concepts referentially, given that an individual's I tokens are, necessarily, self-referential.

But it is a mistake to hold that no two individuals can have the same self-concept. It may be true that each of us is presented to him- or herself in consciousness in a way in which we are not, and could not be, presented to anyone else, and in which no one else is, or could be, presented to us. But this is not due to the nature of our self-*concepts*: you or anyone else can think about yourself in exactly the same way as I can think about myself. It simply does not follow from the fact that I cannot think about you by tokening the I-concept that *you* cannot think about you by tokening the very same concept. Indeed, the way in which one is presented to oneself in consciousness—*viz.*, *self-consciousness*—is a type as well: though it is a relation one can stand in only to oneself, others can stand to themselves in precisely the same relation. (It is like identity. There is not a distinct identity relation for every object.) The token I-concept in my token of I'M ITCHY must *refer to* me. But since its content is general (in the sense specified above), it can have tokens that do not refer to me. Which context I select at a given world will be determined by whom I am interested in. If I want to know whether or not what I thought of me in the actual world is true of me at another possible world, then I must specify a context in that world of which I am the agent. I must find me there (or take me there) and examine my qualities there. It might be that when I or anyone else asks whether what I thought is true at world *w*, we are most often concerned with whether or not what I actually thought of myself (necessarily) is true of me at *w*. But this is not semantically required, any more than it is required of my thought THE KING IS IN HIS COUNTING HOUSE. There may be a pragmatic presupposition—even a very strong one—that questions about the (actual and) counterfactual truth value of what I thought will be anchored to the referent of my actual tokening of THE KING, but there's no semantic necessity that it be. It is not determined by the content of the concept. The fact that I-concept *tokens* must refer to their actual tokeners is a red herring. As we learned from Kaplan, it is essential to distinguish the logical status of indexical tokens from the logical status of their contents.

I cannot falsely think 'I' REFERS TO ME; but it is not a necessary truth that the I-concept refers to *me*.

The evaluation of general thoughts at other worlds works the same way. In order to determine the truth value of CENTENARIANS ARE RARE at a world, we must determine the extensions of CENTENARIAN and RARE in that world. (We may need to consult specific contexts as well, since the extensions of these terms vary over time.) It is true at the actual world iff the actual extension of CENTENARIANS is a subset of the extension of rare. To determine the truth value of this thought in some other world, we must assign extensions to CENTENARIANS and RARE in that world. It is perhaps the default assumption that we are interested in whatever extensions those concepts happen to have in counterfactual worlds—because we are typically interested in the modal properties of centenarians *per se*. But we could also inquire about the modal properties of some centenarians *in particular*. We might be interested in knowing whether CENTENARIANS ARE RARE is true in some other world where CENTENARIAN has the *same* extension it has here—that is, whether the centenarians we have picked out in the actual world are rare in some other world. The default assumption for indexical concepts is just the reverse: counterfactual questions concern their actual token referents. But in both cases it is possible—it is coherent (even if strange or typically pointless)—to cancel the default assumption. It is not ruled out semantically.

The pragmatic nature of the presupposition that, when one asks of an indexical thought (or utterance) whether it might have been true or false, one is asking about the actual referents of tokens of its constituent concepts, is perhaps plainer in the case of indexical concepts whose token reference is not so semantically constrained as the I-concept. Suppose there are two tall males before us, and I say to you "He's tall." If I do not indicate to you to whom I am referring (say, by directing my gaze, or pointing), you will not know of whom I have said it. And if I had said it twice (referring the second time to the second individual, without indicating him to you), you would know that I had said the same thing twice—though not whether about the same individual, or one then the other. As we saw above, the fact that these sentence tokens can have different truth values, and that their constituent 'he's can have different referents, does not, *per se*, give them different contents. (Indeed, I could utter the same sentence falsely, of one and the same individual, at different times. Should we conclude that what I have said has changed?) *What* you said is independent of *whom* you said it of. If I then say "Possibly, he's not tall" (or, more colloquially, "He might not have been tall"), there is nothing in the *content* of my utterance to determine which of the two guys I am talking about. I might have been referring to either (or even to neither, some additional individual having come to my attention). And if I do not direct your attention to one or the other, you will not know to whom I was referring, or whether or not what I said is true. I could have said the very same thing about the other. Whom I am referring to, in any case, including a counterfactual one, is determined by whom I am interested in. But this is a pragmatic matter; it is not determined by the content of my utterances. Your not knowing whom I have referred to by my utterance of 'he' does not entail that you do not know what I said. You just do not know whom I have said it of, or whether or not it is true (supposing you have the relevant information). It might be *odd* to go from thinking HE'S TALL of one person to thinking POSSIBLY, HE'S NOT TALL of some other person—especially if the latter were thought of someone not present. But it is not semantically impossible. (Cf. Bach 1994: ch. 9.)

Indeed, it seems to me that it is not conceptually impossible to think HE'S TALL or POSSIBLY HE'S NOT TALL about *no one in particular*—i.e., just to *think* it; just entertain the thought (the way you just did). In fact, such an "empty" thought might even be construed as having a determinate truth value. What one might be thinking in such a case—rather abstractly (and probably idly)—is whether there is a possible world at which a male (at some time) is not tall. This would be to address the purely general content of the thought *as such*. There may not be much point to wondering this; and it is certainly an *unusual* (not to say *mad*) thing to think. But the fact that it is possible shows that the contents of indexical concepts are as general as their non-indexical cousins.

Of course Kaplan objects to this sort of construal for indexical expressions. He calls intensional operators on characters "monsters," and accuses them of wreaking semantic and metaphysical havoc. If, for example, we suppose that 'possibly' operates on the character of an indexical sentence instead of its referent-involving content, we end up with absurdities such as (as previously discussed) that 'Possibly I don't exist' (and, of course, POSSIBLY I DON'T EXIST) is *false*, since, according to Kaplan, any context "appropriate" (to use his term) for the evaluation of an 'I' sentence will contain an agent, which is the referent of the occurrence of 'I' in that context, and, hence, 'I exist' will be true in every such context. Thus, 'I exist' will be true in every possible (appropriate) context, and 'Possibly I don't exist' will be false. But, obviously, it is possible for such contingent beings as us not to exist (Kaplan 1989: 498).

Such problems can be avoided by making indexical contents their contextually determined referents and the content of my utterance of 'I don't exist' the singular proposition consisting of me, the property of existence (supposing *arguendo* that existence is a property) and negation. We can then approach a world (a circumstance of evaluation) with this proposition, and ask whether or not *it* is true at that world. If I am not to be found in that world (at a specified time), then the proposition, hence what I said, is true at that world (at that time).

But monsters are only a problem on the assumption that indexical contents are referent-involving. This is clear from the passage in "Demonstratives" (1989: 510) in which Kaplan responds to the question

Are there such operators as 'In some contexts it is true that', which when prefixed to a sentence yields a truth if and only if in some context the contained *sentence* (not the content expressed by it) expresses a content that is true in the circumstances of that context?

as follows:

Let us try it:

(9) In some contexts it is true that I am not tired now.

for (9) to be true in the present context it suffices that some agent of some context not be tired at the time of that context. (9), so interpreted, has nothing to do with me or the present moment. But this violates Principle 2!

But Principle 2 is just the thesis that indexicals are directly referential. If we do not accept it, then the fact that (9) evaluated with respect to other contexts might be true of someone else is not problematic. I might be most interested in what is the case with *me* in some other context in evaluating (9), in which case I can pick contexts in which I am the agent. But—or so I have argued—the *semantics* of indexicals does not force this.

Likewise, if we do not suppose that the content of a tokening of the I-concept by me is *me*, but, rather, (something like) SELF (a reflexive self-concept; or perhaps it has a primitive content) then POSSIBLY, I DON'T EXIST *can* come out true even if POSSIBLY is monstrous. Of course, this concept cannot be tokened in any context lacking a thinker (*no* concept can). But tokening of concepts is like utterance of sentences, and we can follow Kaplan in maintaining that it is not utterances of sentences containing indexicals that get evaluated at counterfactual contexts, but *occurrences*. If we took evaluation to concern utterances, then 'Possibly I am not speaking to you now' would be in the same sinking boat as 'Possibly I don't exist'. So the question becomes, are there true occurrences of I DON'T EXIST (understood as having (something like) the content THERE IS NO SELF)? Clearly there are—namely, occurrences evaluated at any context in a world without selves. If there is no self for an I-concept to refer to, then I DON'T EXIST IS TRUE. No *token* of I EXIST can be false—just as no token of 'I am speaking to you now' or I AM THINKING NOW can be false. But it does not follow that its *character* cannot be false. It is false at all contexts in worlds with no agents—just as 'I'm speaking' is false at all contexts in worlds with no speakers.

Again, what one is most likely interested in with respect to one's thought POSSIBLY I DON'T EXIST is not worlds in which there is *no one at all*, but worlds in which one is oneself not to be found. But this can be accommodated. One can ask, "Is what I thought *of me* true *of me*?"—that is, is there a possible world in which the individual about whom I thought the thought, viz., me, does not exist?

And the answer is (alas) *yes*. The fact that it might be extremely *odd* for someone to ask whom you are thinking about when you wonder whether POSSIBLY I DON'T EXIST is true does not entail that it is semantically incoherent. If you are interested in what is true at some other world of the individual you actually referred to, you do not have to put that individual in the *content* of the utterance in order to take them there. You can take them along as the *referent* of your actual indexical token.

I conclude that modal considerations do not yield decisive reasons for thinking that the contents of indexicals are referent-dependent. One need suppose neither that indexical concepts are directly referential, in the sense that what they contribute to what is thought by their tokening (the *content* of their tokens) is just their contextually determined referents, nor that they are *rigidly* referential, i.e., that an indexical concept token must refer to the same thing at every possible world. (With the exception of the I-concept, of course—though, as argued above, this token referential rigidity does not prevent the concept from having a constant content.) They are as general in content and as variable in their reference as their non-rigid relatives. *This very* token indexical concept that I entertain, with its actual content, can have different referents in different possible worlds/contexts. So modal considerations do not show that indexical contents are referent-involving, and do not militate against the thesis that (the contents of) indexical thoughts are intrinsically, phenomenally individuated.

The lesson here is that indexical contents are *thin*. But it is their very thinness that makes them so useful—so *portable* (i.e., applicable, on the fly, to things about which one has minimal information). We should resist the temptation to fatten them up with referents in response to extra-semantic considerations having to do with the way we typically *use* them.

4.3 Understanding

The third motivation for supposing that the contents of indexical thoughts are referent-dependent is the claim that unless one knows the reference of an indexical concept one does not understand the thought it is a constituent of. If you or I think (or try to think), for example, THIS IS A FINE RED ONE or HE'S A LOUSE without having any particular individual in mind as referents for THIS and HE, then neither of us will understand what either of us has thought. Moreover, if we tried to express our thoughts by uttering the relevant sentences without identifying referents for their constituent indexical terms, we would fail to understand what we had said, as would anyone else who could not identify such referents.

My response here is a quick one: understanding comes in degrees, and whereas there might not be much information associated with an indexical thought of whose indexical referents one is not apprised, or conveyed by its linguistic expression, it is far from clear that *nothing* has been thought or understood or communicated. Say you hear an utterance of the sentence "He's here!" and you have no idea who said it, where it was said, or whom it was said about. Do you nonetheless not know that someone has said that some male has arrived (or is located) at some location? You will have a much better idea of the nature of the state of affairs that this sentence refers to if you know who *he* is and where *here* is. But it does not follow either that you do not understand the utterance, or that if you repeated it yourself (perhaps replacing 'here' with 'there') you would not understand what you said, or, indeed, that you have not succeeded in saying anything.

Likewise in thought. I can very well think HE'S A LOUSE having no one in particular in mind as the referent of HE and have thought something determinate—if only that some male is contemptible. And I can have absolutely no idea where I am (I was transported in an opaque hood) or what my surroundings are like (it is pitch-dark), and still think something determinate in thinking I REALLY DON'T LIKE IT HERE. I know that HERE refers to the place where I am, even though that is the only information I have. If someone turns the lights on, my understanding of the place HERE refers to would increase, but only in the sense that further thoughts would be directed toward the place where I am, and would be known to be about the same place. My thought I REALLY DON'T LIKE IT HERE, in the dark, with no knowledge of the referent of HERE beyond its being the place where I am, though surely paling in comparison with what I can think about where I am when the lights go on, is nonetheless a real thought. I do succeed in thinking something in such a case, and I do understand what I am thinking, even if what I am thinking is relatively jejune and uninformative. The content of what I thought in the perceptually impoverished environment (I REALLY DON'T LIKE IT HERE) does not change when the lights go on.

Again, conceptual indexical contents are very thin. We do not suppose that acquaintance with the extensions of definite-descriptive or general concepts, or knowledge of truth values of the thoughts containing them, is required for determinate thought or understanding. It is only the relative informational paucity of indexical concepts that tempts us to treat them otherwise.

4.4 Attitude Reports

It appears that getting the contents of indexical thoughts right in third-person ascriptions depends upon identifying the referents of their constitutive indexical concepts, not their descriptive content. In order to report what you think when you think I'M HUNGRY, I must capture the referent of your tokening of the I-concept, not its descriptive content (its character). Thus, the conceptual-phenomenal content of the I-concept—the mental analogue of character—is not part of what is thought, the content of the thought. The contents of (token) indexical concepts are referent-involving, and so cannot be phenomenally constituted.

I think this is a *non sequitur*. We could have a primary, even *overriding*, interest in the referents of others' concepts—which things in the world they are thinking about—without its being the case that content itself is referent-dependent. Interest in a thinker's referents is perhaps to be expected, given the relation of propositional attitudes to behavior, and our interest, perhaps typically, in what someone is going to do, has done, or is doing, and to whom—i.e., which objects in our shared environment (including, especially, ourselves) the individual's actions will affect. If our main reason for wanting to know what someone is thinking is that we wish to know which objects they might be acting upon, then we may be less concerned with *how* they are thinking of them, i.e., with what their thought actually *is*. But our practical interests in the referents of an individual's thoughts should not be the basis for an account of the nature of the thoughts themselves. The pragmatics of propositional-attitude ascriptions should not be allowed to dictate the metaphysics of propositional attitudes. There are ascriber-independent facts about what individuates a thinker's thoughts *per se*—independent as much from the interests of others as from the referents of their constituent concepts. We should not conflate interest in what someone is thinking *about* (in the sense of what the referents of his concepts are) with interest in *what* they are thinking. Indeed, even if our concern is primarily external, if our expectations, predictions or explanations are thwarted by an individual's behavior, we will recur to an interest in *what* they are thinking.

4.5 Agreement and Disagreement

If we do not appeal to the referents of indexical concepts in the individuation of indexical thoughts, then, one might think, there will be cases in which we cannot make sense of thinkers agreeing and disagreeing in what they indexically think (believe).[7] Suppose I believe I WAS BORN IN THE '50s. If you want to agree with me—if you want to believe what I believe—you will, intuitively, have to think what I think: our beliefs will have to have the same content. On the view defended in this chapter, that would mean that you would have to think I WAS BORN IN THE '50s. But if you think *that*, you would not, intuitively, be thinking what I am thinking, since you would be thinking about someone else (not me). In order to think what I think, you would have to think (of me) a different thought—e.g., HE WAS BORN IN THE '50s. But the thoughts I WAS BORN IN THE '50s and HE WAS BORN IN THE '50s cannot have the same content (be the same thought) unless

---

[7] This section and the next were prompted by objections raised independently by David Chalmers and Paul Boghossian, in conversation.

they are individuated referentially—e.g., as having the singular proposition featuring me and the property of being born in the '50s as their common content. Individuated intrinsically (propositional-phenomenally), on the other hand, these thoughts are *different*. But if our thoughts are different, then we do not agree—we do not accept the truth of the same thought.

Likewise, suppose Arthur thinks THE WORLD WILL END TOMORROW on Sunday, and Marvin thinks THE WORLD WILL END TOMORROW on Monday. Intuitively, it seems that Arthur and Marvin disagree (about when the world will end). But according to the approach advocated in this chapter, the thought Arthur affirms is the very thought Marvin affirms; so, it seems, they agree. If we are to honor the intuitive facts, again it looks like we have to take Arthur's and Marvin's thoughts to be individuated referentially: the thought content Arthur affirms has (the relevant) Sunday as a constituent, whereas the one Marvin affirms has (the immediately following) Monday as a constituent. Since, on this way of individuating thoughts, the thought Arthur affirms and the thought Marvin affirms are different thoughts, the truth of each of which implies the falsity of the other, they disagree.

This objection is based on the assumption that agreement among thinkers requires that they affirm the same thought, and that disagreement requires affirmation of different, logically incompatible, thoughts. But this does not in general seem to be the case. Agreement need not involve thinking thoughts with the same content, and disagreement need not preclude it. If we are to agree, I submit, all that is required is that the referents of the referring constituents of our thoughts, and the properties we attribute to them, be the same. And if we are to disagree, all that is required is that we attribute incompatible properties (or attribute and deny the same property) to the same things. Agreement does not entail that we refer or attribute in the same way, and disagreement does not entail that we refer or attribute in different ways.

For example, you and I can agree on the nationality of Marie Curie, I by believing THE ONLY PERSON EVER TO WIN NOBEL PRIZES IN TWO DIFFERENT SCIENCES WAS POLISH, and you by believing THE DISCOVERER OF POLONIUM WAS POLISH (or THE DISCOVERER OF POLONIUM WAS A CITIZEN OF THE COUNTRY WHOSE CAPITAL IS WARSAW), though the contents of our beliefs (our thoughts) are different. (Whether or not we *know* we agree depends on whether or not we know that the referents of our referring concepts and the extensions of our predicates are the same.) And we can disagree about the employment history of the Ukrainian president, I by believing THE UKRAINIAN PRESIDENT IS A FORMER COMEDIC ACTOR AND LAWYER in 2022, and you by believing THE UKRAINIAN PRESIDENT IS A FORMER COMEDIC ACTOR AND LAWYER in 2018. Agreement does not entail that thinkers grasp the same content, and disagreement does not entail that thinkers grasp different contents: agreement requires thinking thoughts that attribute the same property to the same individual, and disagreement requires thinking thoughts that attribute incompatible properties to the same individual. And this applies to indexical thoughts as well.[8]

If you and I both think the indexical thought I WAS BORN IN THE '50s, we are, I maintain, thinking the same thought. But it does not follow that (if we both affirm it) we agree. I am (necessarily) thinking it *of me* and you are (necessarily) thinking it *of you*. It is not possible for me to think I WAS BORN IN THE '50s of you, or for you to think it of me: this is a case in which we *cannot* agree by thinking the same thought. In order to attribute the property of being born in the '50s to me, you would have to use a different concept that refers to me, and, hence, think a different thought. Agreement does not require that we grasp the same indexical content. We can agree by thinking different indexical thoughts that attribute the same property to the same individual. We do not have to make my thought I WAS BORN IN THE '50s and your thought HE WAS BORN IN THE '50s have the same content. And if I think THE WORLD WILL END TOMORROW on Sunday, and you think THE WORLD WILL END TOMORROW on Monday, we have disagreed, though we have thought thoughts with the same content—because we have thought them about different days, and the world cannot come to an end twice.

4.6 Tautology, Contradiction, Analyticity and Antonymy

Referential individuation of indexical thought contents would also appear to be required in order to accommodate the possibility that a token of a demonstrative thought such as THIS IS THIS could be false, and a token of THIS IS NOT THIS could be true. If the contents of all THIS tokens were the *same*, then it would seem that any thought of the form THIS IS THIS would be necessarily true, and any thought of the form THIS IS NOT THIS would be necessarily false. But there is ready evidence to the contrary. For example, if I think of my left thumb that it is my right thumb, by thinking THIS [attending to my left thumb] IS THIS [attending to my right thumb], what I have thought is *false*; and if I think of my left thumb that it is not my right thumb by thinking THIS [attending to my left thumb] IS NOT THIS [attending to my right thumb], what I have thought is *true*. So it cannot be that the contents of the two tokens of the indexical concept THIS are the same. If we suppose that the contents of token indexical concepts are individuated referentially, then the fact that the referents in the first case are different and in the second case the same entails that the thoughts have different contents. So there is no problem with their having different truth values.

However, if we suppose that the contents of indexical concepts are referentially individuated, then tokens that have the same referents have the same contents,

---

[8] Cf. Lewis 1986: 59: "...we agree not when we think alike, but when we ascribe the same properties to the same things."

and tokens that have different referents have different contents. In which case, if I were to think THIS [attending to my left thumb] is NOT THIS [attending, again (inadvertently) to my left thumb], I would be thinking something contradictory, and we would have to explain why I might nonetheless be rational. Likewise if I were to think THIS [attending to my right thumb] IS THIS [attending (inadvertently) to my left thumb]. The problem is not dissolved by adopting a character-content-like distinction for concepts; for then thoughts with contradictory characters could have true content, and thoughts with analytic characters could have false contents (e.g., the thoughts YOU ARE NOT YOU and YOU ARE YOU thought of two different individuals).

This problem can be avoided if we stick to the idea that indexical contents are non-referentially individuated, and rethink the relation between content and reference. If we suppose that THIS has a constant content, and that, therefore, THIS IS THIS is *analytic*, are we constrained to think that it, or any of its tokens, is necessarily *true*? I think not. Analyticity is not necessary truth in virtue of meaning. There are in fact thoughts which are analytic and *not true*—for example, THE PRESENT KING OF FRANCE IS MALE, and ROUND SQUARES ARE RECTANGLES. Analyticity is an entirely internal, structural relation among the component contents of thoughts, which in itself does not determine reference or truth value. The content of THIS is not such as to determine the *same* referent on every occasion of its use. Certainly the contextual features relevant to the determination of the referent of an indexical concept can change mid-thought—as in, for example, the (true) thought NOW IS NOT NOW; indeed, given that thinking takes time, the features relevant to the interpretation of tokens of NOW are constantly changing. Even if one observes Kaplan's distinction between an utterance and an occurrence, one would not be constrained to assign the same referent to, for example, both occurrences of this in an occurrence of THIS IS THIS.

Similar considerations apply to non-indexical singular concepts as well. Consider the thought THE KING IS DEAD; LONG LIVE THE KING. Though the content of THE KING is the same in both of its occurrences, the sentence is not contradictory, since the referents of the occurrences are different. The content of THE KING does not determine that the referents of all of its occurrences must be the same. (In my view, the only expressions whose contents determine the same referents for every occurrence are *de facto* rigid designators.) It is simply left open whether or not a thought like THE KING IS THE KING or THIS IS THIS is true, in spite of the fact that both tokens of its constituent concepts have the same contents. Likewise, it is left open whether a thought like THE KING IS NOT THE KING or THIS IS NOT THIS is false. In both cases sameness of conceptual content does not entail sameness of conceptual referent; hence, analyticity does not entail truth, and antonymy does not entail falsity.

And the same holds true for general thoughts such as CENTENARIANS ARE CENTENARIANS. If this thought is true iff the extension of the first occurrence of

CENTENARIAN is identical to the extension of the second, then, given that this might not be the case (some centenarian dies in the middle of my thought), the thought might not be true. (And the same would be true on a *conditional* interpretation of CENTENARIANS ARE CENTENARIANS—viz., *if something is a centenarian then it is a centenarian*—if this is taken to mean that if something is a member of the set of centenarians, then it is a member of the set of centenarians. The concept THE SET OF CENTENARIANS does not necessarily determine the same extension at every occurrence.)

What of the thought I AM HERE NOW? Kaplan argued that the corresponding sentence is a truth of the logic of indexicals. Though the singular proposition it expresses is not a necessary truth, it is necessarily the case that any occurrence of 'I am here now' is true. It has a necessary character, but not a necessary content. If, however, one identifies character and content, as the account I am defending does, then would it not have to be that the content of my thought I AM HERE NOW *is* necessarily true? But the intuition that it might not have been the case that I was in that place at that time, which is clearly correct, seems to rule this out.

According to Kaplan, the character of 'I' is a function from a context to the agent of the context, the character of 'here' is a function from a context to the place of the context, and the character of 'now' is a function from a context to the time of a context. Contexts are represented by *indices*, which are n-tuples of (perhaps among other things), a world, an agent, a place and a time. He therefore builds it into his system that any occurrence of 'I am here now' will, necessarily, be true—since the agent, place and time of a given context are, necessarily, the agent place and time of that context.

This construction is based on the intuition that 'I am here now' is "deeply, and in some sense,... universally, true.... One need only understand the meaning of [it] to see that it cannot be uttered falsely" (Kaplan 1989: 509). On the contrary, I would argue, intuitively, 'I am here now' *can* be uttered falsely—if, for example, one moves while one is speaking. Intuitively, the characters of 'I', 'here' and 'now' are such as to determine as referents, respectively, the utterer of 'I', the place at which 'here' is uttered, and the time at which 'now' is uttered. But since there is no guarantee that a person who utters 'I am here now' is at the time he utters 'now' in the place he was in when he uttered 'here', the logic of indexicals does not guarantee that any utterance of 'I am here now' is true.

Of course Kaplan makes a distinction between *utterance* and *occurrence*, and one may say that it is not utterances of 'I am here now' which cannot be false, but occurrences. But this just formalizes the intuition that one cannot utter 'I am here now' falsely, and builds it into the system.

While it does seem to be true that the utterance *as a whole* will take place wherever it does, whenever it does, I do not think this can be attributed to the characters of the indexicals. It is a *metaphysical* fact that one is wherever one is when one is there; and this fact may be expressed by saying 'I am here now'—but *only* if one does not move! (If one takes the place denoted by 'here' to be large enough, perhaps it would be (physically, not logically) impossible for one not to be at the place of utterance at the time of utterance.)

4.7 Phenomenal Demonstratives

A popular response to Jackson's Knowledge Argument is to claim that Mary does not acquire new factual knowledge when she leaves the black-and-white room, but, rather, comes to know facts she already knew in new ways, by virtue of acquiring a special kind of concepts, *phenomenal concepts*, that she previously lacked. Phenomenal concepts in the relevant sense are concepts of phenomenal properties whose content is in some way determined by experience of the properties, and which cannot therefore be possessed in the absence of such experience. This way of resisting Jackson's argument is known as the "Phenomenal Concept Strategy," and a prominent version of it takes phenomenal concepts to be kinds of demonstrative concepts.

I think there cannot be phenomenal demonstrative concepts of the kind needed by phenomenal concept strategists. This is not to say that there cannot be concepts, both demonstrative and non-demonstrative, whose *referents* are phenomenal properties and states. Clearly there are such concepts. Rather, I want to argue that there are no concepts the grasp of which requires experience of the phenomenal properties they are of, and no special conceptual knowledge of what it is like—no phenomenal thought. (More precisely, there can be no *non-conceptual*-phenomenal thought. On the view defended in this book concepts and thoughts are themselves phenomenally constituted, so of course there are phenomenal concepts and thoughts in *this* sense. This qualification applies throughout this section.) There is nothing Mary can *think* once she has experienced red that she could not think before she experienced it.

There are intuitively good reasons for thinking that, in general, concepts cannot *be* (non-conceptual) sensory experiences or images. Concepts and sensory experiences, or images, are fundamentally different kinds of things. We can think about, and have concepts for, things that cannot in principle be perceived (and, hence, not imagined), such as transfinite ordinals, ten-dimensional spaces and (non-actual) possible worlds. We can also think about, and have concepts for, things that can be perceived, but which cannot be imagined, such as chiliagons and ten-thousand-six-speckled hens. If we can think about things that cannot be perceived or imagined, then we have concepts of those things. But if we cannot perceive or imagine them, we do not have percepts or images of them. Hence, our concepts of them cannot be percepts or images of them.

Moreover, it seems obvious that perceiving and imagining are possible without thinking—as, for example, when one absent-mindedly enjoys the breeze, or listens to music in one's head. These are, apparently, activities one can engage in without deploying any concepts at all. And it certainly seems that there could be non-human creatures capable of perceiving and imagining but not of conceptualizing (or vice versa), as well as that there could be (perhaps there are) humans who can do one but not the other.

A deeper, but still, I think, intuitive reason for maintaining that concepts cannot be percepts or images is that concepts (i.e., conceptual contents) must be *thinkable*, while percepts and images are not. It is nonsense, a category mistake, to say that what I was thinking (or part of what I was thinking) was the smell of lavender or the sound of a distant trumpet, or that the concept I was entertaining was rose-tinted or bored. It is true that I can think *about* these things, but only in the sense that I can have otherwise-content-individuated concepts that *refer to* them. Concepts (their contents) must be things capable of being thought—in the course of thinking a complete thought of which they are constituents, or merely *entertained*—i.e., simply had in mind or considered.

My tendentious explanation for all of this is that thinking is a proprietary kind of experience, that distinct kinds of experience are distinguished by distinct kinds of phenomenology, and that phenomenal properties of different determinable kinds (visual, auditory, etc.) can only be experienced in their proper modalities. One can no more think colors or smells than one can hear pains or itches. These kinds of experiencing are constituted by the instantiation of radically distinct kinds of phenomenal properties, each with its distinctive experiential modality. There can be no cross-modal experiences. One cannot experience olfactory percepts or images in the way one experiences colors, or experience colors in the way one experiences sounds. Seeing is not smelling or hearing. Confused interpretations of synesthesia aside, it is absolutely impossible to smell colors, hear flavors, etc. Thus, if thinking is a distinctive fundamental kind of experience, one cannot *think* any of these things either. Nor can thoughts and concepts be seen, heard or smelled, tasted, etc. No one, not even a telepath, could *read* someone else's mind (or their own, for that matter). And no one can ever *hear* themselves think (no matter how quiet it is), or hear someone else's thoughts.

I also think it is untendentious and intuitively clear that experiences of different phenomenal modalities cannot *mix*. Not only can one not smell colors or hear thoughts, there cannot be conscious states of any of these phenomenal kinds partially constituted by instantiations of different kinds of phenomenology. There cannot be a sound *part of which* is a smell, or a sight *part of which* is a taste. There may be experiences that have sounds, smells, sights and tastes as constituents (as, for example, one's total experience at a given moment). But their constituents remain metaphysically independent. Experiences of different modalities cannot *combine* in the way experiences of the same modality can—for example, in the way the taste of chocolate and the taste of orange combine, or the way the sound of a tympani roll followed by the sound of a pizzicato double-bass line can be temporal parts of a single auditory experience. The orange–chocolate taste is still a taste; and the tympani–bass sound sequence is still a sound. There can be no orange–bass tastes (or sounds), or tympani–chocolate sounds (or tastes).

I call this general fact the *Principle of Phenomenal Immiscibility* (it is another basic law of experience). Just as there can be no water that is part oil, or oil that is part water—though there can be quantities of liquid that are part oil and part water, there can be no experiences of kind K that have parts that are non-K experiences—though there can be experiences with K and non-K constituents.

One version of the phenomenal demonstrative strategy has it that the concepts Mary acquires upon her release are "quotational" demonstrative concepts (Balog 1999, 2012; Block 2007; Papineau 2002). These concepts in some way "contain" samples of the phenomenal properties they are concepts of. Beyond the obvious problem that this account builds in more or less intimate relations to phenomenal properties that Mary had not experienced before her release, and so still face the problem it is supposed to finesse (i.e., the metaphysical status of those properties), this strategy is ruled out by the facts about experience, concepts and thought detailed above.

The Principle of Phenomenal Immiscibility, together with the phenomenal intentionality of thought thesis, precludes the possibility of quotational demonstrative concepts. Concepts are cognitive-phenomenal experiences; colors (sounds, smells, . . .) are not. So colors, etc. cannot be constituents of conceptual contents.[9] There is no special red-percept-or-image-containing concept that Mary acquires upon experiencing red for the first time. Such things are not possible. What *is* possible is for there to be a phenomenal sample (a percept or an image) that one is thinking *about*—applying a concept to. But the *content* of the concept THIS or THIS COLOR—or RED, for that matter—cannot involve non-conceptual phenomenology, because conceptual content is cognitive-phenomenal and phenomenal properties of different kinds cannot mix. Such concepts are also ruled out because their contents, not being cognitive-phenomenal, cannot be *thought*— i.e., cognitively experienced.

Mary acquires no concepts of this kind when she leaves the black-and-white room. There is nothing she can *think* upon her release that she could not already think in the room. (Though she nonetheless does, as I will argue below, acquire new *knowledge*.) When it comes to *saying* what red is, pre-release Mary is as conceptually competent as any unconfined, normally sighted person. If you were to ask immured Mary to tell you about red, she would tell you exactly what you would tell her if she asked you to tell her about red. The differences between you are not *conceptual*, they are *perceptual*. Indeed, a congenitally blind person can have the same concept RED as a normally sighted person, and think the same

---

[9] Here I part company with Professor Woodworth: "*In addition to sensorial elements*, thought contains elements which are wholly irreducible to sensory terms" (Woodworth 1906, emphasis added).

thoughts with it, including demonstrative thoughts like THIS IS RED. The fact that sighted people know how red things look and Mary and blind people do not does not entail that they have different *concepts*.

The phenomenal intentionality of thought thesis also precludes concepts whose contents are individuated by their referential relations to percepts or images (or to anything else, for that matter), whether these be Evans–McDowell referentially-sense-individuated concepts (Evans 1982; McDowell 1984) or Sainsbury–Tye "originalist" concepts (Tye and Sainsbury 2011). Anything non-cognitive-phenomenal is the wrong kind of thing to be a conceptual content individuator, just as anything non-sensory is unsuited to be the content of a sensory experience. Conceptual contents are cognitive-phenomenal types, individuated entirely phenomenally, and phenomenal properties in general are not individuated relationally. The pain of a sunburn, for example, is not *per se* different from the pain of a windburn or an iceburn because it was caused by the sun and not by wind or ice. The same holds for conceptual experiences. The phenomenal demonstrative concept THIS PAIN does not change its content depending upon its referent, or its origin, any more than (see above) the concept THIS THUMB or THE PRESIDENT. THIS PAIN applied to a burning pain is the same concept as THIS PAIN applied to an ache. And the thoughts I DON'T LIKE THIS PAIN thought of the burning and the aching are the same thought, thought about different things.

I also reject Loar's recognitional concept strategy (Loar 1997). Loar's recognitional concepts bear a special relation to experiences one has had, in virtue of which they are "triggered" by subsequent experiences of the same kind. These would be analogous to, say, the concepts of middle C and the B-flat below it that people with perfect pitch have: they hear the pitch; they automatically token the concept MIDDLE C or B-FLAT BELOW MIDDLE C, and on the basis of this come to know what the pitch is. But I do not think that people with perfect pitch have a different *concept* of middle C from me. The fact that they can instantly identify the pitch when they hear it does not make their concept different from mine. What is different between us is their automatic and infallible *application* of it. Their concept of MIDDLE C is like my concept RED. I recognize red on sight; but I do not have a different concept from someone who is color blind, or totally blind. Moreover, Loar's idea (1997) that the phenomenal properties that are the referents of recognitional phenomenal concepts are also their modes of presentation looks to make his view susceptible to the problems that beset quotational accounts.[10]

If one recognizes that thinking is a fundamental kind of experience, irreducible to and immiscible with any other fundamental kind of experience, it becomes very clear that not everything that is happening in the conscious mind can be treated as

---

[10] Topic-neutral, or inferential-role, characterizations of phenomenal concepts face the objection that since such concepts do not require experience, they cannot be used to account for the fact that Mary learns something that a zombie could not (cf. Chalmers 2007: 178–9).

part of what one is consciously *thinking*. I may have visual experiences Mary does not have, but it does not follow that I have *conceptual* experiences she does not have. To be sure, I know propositions she cannot know. But, as I have been arguing, this is not because I can think things she cannot think—because I have concepts she does not have. I may be able to think things *truly* that she cannot—as, for example, that *this thing* is red. In *this* sense I may be capable of knowing things Mary cannot know. But it is not in virtue of my being able to deploy concepts she cannot deploy. It is simply a mistake to assimilate the perceptual differences between us to differences in what we can think. It is a mistake to assimilate all knowledge to knowledge *that*. The various kinds of experiencing must be kept strictly apart when theorizing about mental content.

The knowledge that I can have that Mary cannot have is knowledge of *what it is like* to see chromatic colors. Such knowledge is, as I argued in Chapter 2, acquaintance-knowledge, and is non-conceptual.

5
Thinking with Names

The majority view about the semantics of proper names is that their meanings—that is, what they contribute to the contents of (propositions expressed by) sentences containing them—are just their referents, and, hence, that those contents are singular propositions. This is typically taken to be because proper names are Millian: they have no descriptive meaning to contribute; though it would also be the case if proper names had descriptive *character* that functioned in the way Kaplanian indexical characters do. In either case, names are directly referential.

On the assumption that linguistic meaning is derived from mental content, the majority view suggests that the concepts expressed by names (I call them "nominal concepts") are also directly referential. Their semantic contribution to the contents of the thoughts expressed by utterances of the name are their referents (I call these "nominal thoughts," and the sentences that express them "nominal sentences"), and the thought contents themselves are also singular, object-containing propositions.

This is *prima facie* inconsistent with the view of thought and thinking I am defending in this book. If thought contents are propositional experiences, then the contents of nominal concepts cannot in general be their referents, since these are typically not experiences at all, and so nominal thought contents cannot be the singular propositions direct reference theorists say are the contents of nominal sentences. Acceptance of the phenomenal intentionality of thought thesis thus entails a commitment to some kind of conceptualism about the contents of nominal concepts and (probably) the meanings of proper names. Nominal concepts must have conceptual contents, and conceptual contents must be cognitive-phenomenal. Conceptual contents are, moreover, descriptive (even if they are primitive). Hence, what the phenomenal intentionality of thought thesis requires is a descriptive theory of nominal concepts and, by extension, a description theory of the meanings of names.

Many philosophers of language think the description theory of names was refuted by Kripke. However, the Fregean problems for direct referentialism have lingered. It is not the majority view that direct reference theorists have provided satisfying accounts of the difference in epistemic status of identity statements whose terms are the same name and those whose terms are distinct but co-referring names, the failure of substitutivity of co-referring names in certain linguistic contexts, or the meaningfulness of sentences containing non-referring names. These remain serious outstanding challenges to the view. Furthermore, there is a burgeoning consensus among philosophers and linguists that names can occur as predicates, and thus have predicative (descriptive) meanings or semantic values. So it is far from clear that descriptivism has been completely swept aside by the New Theory of Reference. Which is good news for the phenomenal intentionality of thought thesis.

In this chapter I develop and defend a version of the description theory that, I argue, is resistant to Kripke's criticisms, and can be adapted to fit with the phenomenalist view of thought content I am defending in this book.

5.1 Metalinguistic Descriptivism

According to the description theory criticized by Kripke, a description that gives the meaning of a name must be sufficient for determining the name's referent: it must be uniquely satisfied by the name's bearer. In order to do this, it must be substantive: it must encode enough information about the referent of the name to pick *it* out, and nothing else. On metalinguistic views, in contrast, the descriptive content of a name is minimal, predicating of its bearers only the property of being its bearers, and does not have the function of determining the name's reference.

The most developed versions of this view are due to Kent Bach (1981, 1994, 2002; Bach calls his theory "nominal descriptivisim") and Jerry Katz (1990, 1994, 2001; Katz calls his theory "pure metalinguistic descriptivism"). (Earlier endorsers of the idea include Burge (1973), Russell (1911: 1918–19), Kneale (1962) and Loar (1976).)

Since the meanings of names on these views are not their referents, but metalinguistic descriptive senses, the Fregean problems are avoided. Different names have, *eo ipso*, different senses, so true identity statements whose terms are distinct but co-referring names are not knowable *a priori*, and the substitutivity *salva veritate* in propositional attitude and modal contexts of co-referring names is not guaranteed. And since empty descriptions can be meaningful, so can sentences containing non-referring names.

On the version of the metalinguistic description theory I develop here, the meaning of a name N (and the content of the nominal concept it expresses) is given by the indefinite description 'a bearer of "N".' In this I differ from (almost all[1]) other theorists, who hold that the content of a name N is given by the definite description '*the* bearer of "N"' (at least when N appears in argument position). I think there are good reasons to prefer the indefinite description.

The justification for the use of the definite article is usually put in terms of "uniqueness of reference." I assume this is meant to reflect the fact that a name is

---

[1] Burge (1973) maintains that the predicative content of a name N is **that bearer of 'N'**.

properly used to refer to one and only one thing.² But it is misleading to characterize this feature of names in these terms, since names can (and typically do) have multiple bearers. The feature of names that is supposed to be captured by 'the' cannot be uniqueness of bearer. However, the use of the definite article in giving the meaning of a name suggests that it is, since it represents uniqueness of bearer as a feature of the name as a type.

It may be replied that uniqueness of reference is really uniqueness of reference on an occasion of use—i.e., that use of a name in a context is correct if and only if there is one and only one bearer of N in that context. But this can be accomplished as well by an indefinite description, without the misleading suggestion of general uniqueness of reference.

The property of names that needs to be captured is, rather, *singularity* of reference on an occasion of use. Names are properly used to refer to one and only one of their bearers at a time. And this does seem to be a semantic property of names, as types. It is not just that we do not use a name to refer to more than one of its bearers at a time; we cannot. Names are, semantically (and syntactically), singular terms. But singularity does not imply uniqueness. And singularity—the one-bearer-at-a-time constraint—is captured by the indefinite article. We use an indefinite description when we mean to be referring to one of (possibly) many things that satisfy it ('a friend of mine', 'a rift in the space–time continuum'). If our intention is to refer to more than one thing, we are using the wrong kind of description. The presence of the indefinite rather than the definite article builds in to the meaning of a name that it has (can have) more than one bearer, but that a proper (literal) use of it can refer to only one of them.³

Indefiniteness is also implicated by what it is to think a nominal thought and understand a nominal sentence. Suppose you hear, from a room you cannot see into, someone say "Never fear, Smith is here!" You do not see who is speaking, and you do not see or otherwise know who is being spoken about. Surely, however, you understand the utterance. You understand it as meaning that a person named 'Smith' has arrived at some location (probably the location of the speaker). And this is what you think. You may want to know more about who and where Smith is, but, as in the I DON'T LIKE IT HERE example from Chapter 4, it is not the case that you have understood or thought *nothing*. Moreover, what you understand (what you think) is not that the unique bearer of 'Smith' (there is no such) or the unique bearer of 'Smith' in the context of utterance (there might not be such) has arrived. You understand that someone named 'Smith'—*a* bearer of 'Smith'—has arrived. This is what the words mean, and what you think when you understand

---

² Plural names, such as 'the Beatles' and 'the Smiths', are still singular in the sense that they are collective, not distributive, and cannot be used to refer to more than one collection at a time. 'The Smiths' cannot be used to refer to a rock band *and* your neighbors on the same occasion of use.

³ Like their definite cousins, indefinite descriptions also have generic uses, as in 'a dog is a good companion' (compare 'the dog is a quadruped'). I will not be concerned with such uses here.

them outside the immediate context of their utterance. And, I submit, this is *all* you would understand by the utterance *even if* you were perceptually embedded in its context—you see who is speaking, you know where he is, and you see the Smith in question, or otherwise know who he is from contextual cues. You may have a lot more information about Smith and the state of affairs surrounding his arrival, and many associated thoughts, images or emotions concerning him, but your understanding of the utterance itself, and the thought you would express if you uttered it, is identical to what you understood and thought when you were (partially) isolated from the context of utterance. And the same is true, I would argue, when you use the name in thought. To think something about a Smith using his name, even one you are well acquainted with, is just to think of him as a bearer of the name 'Smith'.

It may be objected that indefinite descriptions are not referring expressions, and, hence, that they cannot give the meanings of names, which are. Such descriptions are, logically, as Russell recommended, best understood as essentially quantificational. So, for example, what one says when one says that a cat has wandered into the yard is that there is a cat which is such that it wandered into the yard $((\exists x)(Cx \& Wx))$. Here 'a cat' is a predicate ('x is a cat'), not a referring expression.

But one may also say of some particular cat one observes wandering into the yard that it has wandered into the yard. In such a case, I maintain, the indefinite description is used as a referring expression. It is intended to pick out the errant cat. And the indefiniteness of the description is meant to convey that it is, as far as one knows, but one cat of many. (One may also say that *the* cat wandered into the yard, though this seems appropriate only if it is a cat of one's previous acquaintance.) Hence, indefinite descriptions have both predicative and referential uses. (See, e.g., Chastain 1975, Donnellan 1978, Strawson 1974 and Wilson 1978 for arguments and examples.) And there is evidence that names do as well.

One can say, for example, that some Smiths have the same last name, that everyone loves a Smith, that one thinks we are all Smiths on this bus, etc. The most obvious interpretation of these predicative uses of 'Smith' is one on which their extensions are individuals who bear the name 'Smith'. For, what is it to be a Smith? Under what conditions is one in the extension of predicative 'Smith'? To be a Smith is just to be a bearer of the name 'Smith'. One is in the extension of predicative 'Smith' if and only if one is a bearer of the name 'Smith'. It makes sense, then, to say that 'Smith' means *a bearer of* 'Smith'. Recently, following Burge (1973), a number of authors, including Geurts (1997), Elbourne (2005), Matushansky (2005, 2008), Sawyer (2010), Leckie (2013), Gray (2014), Rami (2014), Fara (2015a, 2015b) and Schoubye (2017), have claimed that names can appear as predicates and have name-involving descriptive contents.

Though these uses provide evidence for assigning metalinguistic contents to names, there are important differences between predicative and referential uses of names that suggest that the analysis I have offered may not be correct.

If the meaning of a name *N* is *a bearer of 'N'*, then 'N' and 'a bearer of "N"' are synonymous, and they ought to be interchangeable *salva felicitate* in all contexts. But this is not the case. For example, whereas (1b) is a synonymous and acceptable transformation of (1a), the substitution does not preserve grammaticality in (2b) (I follow the linguist's practice of marking ungrammatical or otherwise infelicitous sentences with an asterisk):

(1a) István lives in Úrhida
(1b) A bearer of 'István' lives in Úrhida
(2a) Every Kati I have met is Hungarian
(2b) *Every a bearer of 'Kati' I have met is Hungarian

Thus it seems that when names appear in argument positions, their meaning involves the determiner, whereas when they appear in predicate positions, they do not.

This syntactic difference has been addressed by the philosophers and linguists mentioned above who think that proper names can appear as predicates. There is disagreement among them as to whether or not names are always predicates, or are syntactically ambiguous between their predicative and referential forms, and as to the proper way to account for their syntactic behavior. According to Delia Graff Fara (Fara 2015a), a proper name *N* is always a predicate, and is equivalent to *thing called N*. It is not clear to me whether or not Fara intends the description to give the meaning of the name (the content of the nominal concept), as I do, though the following remark suggests that she does:

> According to the being-called condition, a name '*N*' is *semantically equivalent to* the predicate 'thing called *N*'. (Fara 2015a: 70; my emphasis)

It is also worth mentioning that in Fara's "being-called condition" a name is used, not mentioned, which suggests that her view is not metalinguistic. However, the quotation above continues as follows:

> This latter predicate ['thing called *N*'] is equivalent to 'bearer of "N"'...

which suggests that her view *is* metalinguistic. In any case, her analysis of the syntax of names in predicate and argument positions is relevant to the view I am proposing.

On Fara's view, when a name appears in an argument position it is a predicate embedded in what she calls a "denuded definite description." Predicative names in argument positions cannot be replaced by the phrases they are semantically equivalent to, *salva felicitate*:

(3a)   Alfred was a famous logician

(3b)   *Thing called Alfred was a famous logician

Moreover, predicative names do not have the definiteness required of referring expressions. Fara proposes that in such contexts a name N is semantically equivalent to the definite description *the N*. However, (3c) seems no less infelicitous than (3b) as a way of saying what (3a) says:

(3c)   *The Alfred was a famous logician

Names *can* appear with definite articles when they are part of longer descriptive phrases, such as in the following:

(4a)   The Alfred who emigrated from Poland was a famous logician

which is equivalent to

(4b)   The thing that is called Alfred who emigrated from Poland was a famous logician

but they cannot when they are "bare" (Fara's term), as in (3a).

Fara proposes that in such cases the determiner is syntactically and semantically present but phonologically unrealized ("denuded"). Thus, (3a) has the surface form given in (5), but the underlying form (LF?) given in (6):

(5)   [$_S$ [$_{NP}$ Alfred] [$_{VP}$ [$_V$ was] [$_{NP}$ a famous logician]]]

(6)   [$_S$ [$_{DP}$ [$_D$ $\emptyset_{the}$] [$_{NP}$ Alfred]] [$_{VP}$ [$_V$ was] [$_{NP}$ a famous logician]]]

This strikes me as an *ad hoc* solution to the problem. The definite determiner must be semantically present if 'Alfred' in (3a) is to have the required definiteness. But if the NP 'Alfred' in (5) *means the same as* the DP 'the Alfred' in (6), which seems likely if (5) and (6) have the same meaning, then why should it be that the definite article cannot be phonologically realized? It seems odd to say that a constituent of the meaning of an expression cannot be made phonologically explicit. That, though 'Alfred' in (3a) means *the Alfred,* the 'the' cannot be pronounced, seems to me as implausible as saying that though 'bachelor' means *unmarried man,* 'Anders is a bachelor' is fine, but 'Anders is an unmarried man' is not. It ought to be the case that if two expressions are synonymous they are interchangeable, *salva felicitate,* in any context.

There are, of course, cases of phonologically unrealized syntactic elements. For example,

(7) Alfred promised Kurt to be on time

is standardly analyzed as having an unpronounced syntactic element, PRO, co-indexed with 'Alfred' (indicating that it is Alfred who is to be on time):

(7) [$_S$ [$_{NP}$ Alfred$_i$] [$_{VP}$ [promised Kurt] [$_{TP}$ [PRO$_i$ to be on time]]]

But PRO sentences differ from Fara's in two important respects. First, PRO is not a *morpheme*, while 'the' is. Second, the morpheme that is its anaphor, 'Alfred', can be brought to the phonological surface (with a bit of adjustment):

(8) Alfred promised Kurt Alfred would be on time

or (if this ruled out by binding theory)

(9) Alfred promised Kurt he would be on time

I also find Fara's solution puzzling for a different reason. On her analysis the full meaning of 'Alfred' is *thing called Alfred*. But note that if we take 'thing called Alfred' to be the complement of the definite determiner, the resulting sentence is perfectly acceptable:

(10) The thing called Alfred was a famous logician

So maybe the problem is in not making the meaning fully explicit; or in making only a part of it fully explicit; or in making the wrong part of it fully explicit. (Or something.) Maybe (3c) has the same problem as (3d):

(3d) *Called Alfred was a famous logician

It would not make much sense to say that (3d) is unacceptable because 'called' must be phonologically null. That is not the problem.

In any case, this issue does not arise for the analysis of names as indefinite descriptions. (3a) is (to my ear) unproblematically equivalent to both (11) and (12):

(11) An Alfred was a famous logician
(12) A bearer of 'Alfred' was a famous logician

However, the indefinite description view still faces the problem mentioned above—that (e.g.) (13a) (= 2a) and (14a) are acceptable but (13b) (= 2b) and (14b) are not:

(13a) Every Kati I have met is Hungarian
(13b) *Every a bearer of 'Kati' I have met is Hungarian
(14a) The first István I met does not live in Budapest
(14b) *The first a bearer of 'István' I met does not live in Budapest

That is, my view might work for referring names, but not for predicative names. And it might seem that Fara's denuded description view, or some version of it, on which names are always predicates, may be the way to go after all. But I still have worries about the *ad hocness* of Fara's phonological repression strategy.

Fortunately, there is another option—namely, taking names to be *ambiguous* between their referential and predicative forms. When 'N' appears as a predicate, it means *bearer of 'N'*; but when it appears as an argument, it means *a bearer of 'N'*. The main reason Fara offers for the thesis that names are always predicates is that it simplifies theory. But if simplification obscures a real difference, it is not a virtue.

Anders Schoubye (2017) maintains that names are type-ambiguous between their referential and predicative forms. He argues, further, that their predicative forms are derived from their referential forms. I am inclined to agree. It seems to me, intuitively, that saying that someone is an Anders is slightly strained—not quite literally true. (To my ear it *sounds* derived.) Schoubye's approach also has the advantage of avoiding the problems Fara's encounters. Following Schoubye, I can say that *predicative N* and *referential N* are of different syntactic categories, and that the former means *bearer of 'N'*, while the latter means *a bearer of 'N'*.

I do not need to take sides here, however, since the view I am defending could easily be slotted into any of these approaches. It is distinctive only in its claim that the metalinguistic descriptions associated with names are indefinite. I could say either that names are always indefinite descriptive, and that the determiner is phonologically repressed when they appear in predicative positions, or that names are always predicates, and that they are embedded within (non-denuded!) indefinite descriptions when they appear in referential positions, or (as I prefer) that names are type-ambiguous. On any of these accounts, the *prima facie* syntactic issues would be addressed (if not definitively resolved).

5.1.1 Kripke's Objections

5.1.1.1 Modality

Kripke (1980) famously argued that description theories of proper names are subject to the following, fatal objection. If the meaning of a name N is given by a description d, then sentence 'N is d' is true by virtue of meaning (analytic), and hence ought to be necessarily true (true in all possible worlds). But no such sentence is necessarily true. There are possible worlds in which such sentences are false. So no description *d* gives the meaning of a name *N*.

Prima facie, the objection applies to metalinguistic description theories as well. If we suppose that the meaning of 'Igor' is *a bearer of "Igor"*, it follows that the sentence

(15) Igor is a bearer of 'Igor'

is analytic, and hence necessarily true. But of course it is no more necessary that Igor is a bearer of 'Igor' than that he was born in Russia. (15) is contingent; so it cannot be analytic—necessarily true by definition.

One way to respond to Kripke's argument is to claim that names always take wide scope, and that on wide scope readings sentences like (15) do not come out as necessarily true. This approach, preferred by Michael Dummett (1973) and Bach (1994), is not without its problems (see Soames 1998). Another way to avoid the objection, preferred by Katz (1992), is to adopt a notion of analyticity that does not entail necessary truth. I think Katz's response is more productive.

Kant has been interpreted as offering two distinct characterizations of analyticity. On the first, a judgment is analytic if its predicate concept is (covertly) contained in its subject concept.

> If I say, for instance, 'All bodies are extended', this is an analytic judgment. For I do not require to go beyond the concept which I connect with 'body' in order to find extension as bound up with it. To meet with this predicate, I have merely to analyze the concept,.... (Kant 1781: 49)

On the second, a judgment is analytic if it is necessarily true, because its denial is a contradiction. These characterizations are obviously not equivalent. The former entails the latter, but not vice versa. But it is not clear that Kant meant to be introducing a distinct characterization of analyticity when he says:

> I have only to extract from it [the concept of body], in accordance with the principle of contradiction, the required predicate, and in doing so can at the same time become conscious of the necessity of the judgment. (Kant 1781: 49)

That is, he can be read as claiming only that analytic judgments are necessary, not that necessary judgments are analytic. Indeed, he famously claimed that '5 + 7 = 12' is necessarily true but *not* analytic. Nonetheless, it is this latter conception, on which an analytic statement is one whose denial is a contradiction, or one that can be reduced by definition to a logical truth, that has gained the most traction in philosophy of language (principally due to Frege, who wanted arithmetic truths to be analytic, and Quine, who wanted to put an end to the whole business). On this conception, every necessary truth is analytic. I think it is clear that this is not what Kant meant by analyticity. In any case, if analyticity is supposed to have something to do with semantic relations among terms—for example, names and descriptions—then I think it is best understood in the first way.

On Katz's conception, analyticity is not necessary truth in virtue of meaning. It is a purely structural relation (containment) holding among the senses of terms, which does not in and of itself make a sentence true. Indeed, there are analytic sentences that are not true—because they are either false or truth-valueless (depending upon one's view of *prima facie* empty referring expressions). Consider:

(16) The present king of France is male

Given that 'king' means *male monarch*, (16), (17) and (18) are analytic.

(17) Kings are male
(18) The king is male

On anyone's account, however, (16) is not true at all, much less necessarily true. For Frege, it is not true because it has no truth value, because 'the present king of France' is a vacuous referring expression. For Russell, it is not true because it is false; and it is false because it asserts that there is presently a king of France, which is false. Hence, analyticity is not truth in virtue of meaning. It is, again, a *structural* relation among constituents of sentence meanings, and entails nothing about whether or not the terms expressing them actually refer to something (which is a necessary condition for truth). The possibility that a sentence is false does not entail that it is not analytic; and the impossibility of its being false does not entail that it is.

Analyticity does not entail necessary truth. What it does entail is what I call "truth-security" (Katz (2004) calls it "security from falsehood"). If a sentence is analytic, then, necessarily, if it has a truth value at all, it is true: it is "truth-secured." Nor does necessary truth, or truth-security, entail analyticity. A sentence may be necessarily true, or truth-secured, if its terms are not analytically related.

So, if we suppose that the sense of 'Igor' is *a bearer of 'Igor'*, then (15), though analytic, is not *ipso facto* true. And the possibility of its being false does not entail that 'a bearer of "Igor"' does not give the meaning of 'Igor'. However, since analytic sentences are truth-secured, it does follow that any referentially successful utterance of 'Igor is a bearer of "Igor"' is, necessarily, true. Still, it does not follow that it is necessarily true.

Compare

(19) Igor exists

If 'Igor' refers, then, necessarily, 'Igor exists' is true (it is not logically possible to *refer to* something that does not exist). But it does not follow that 'Igor exists' is analytic, or necessarily true. And the same is true of (15). If a literal token of the name 'Igor' refers, then its referent is, necessarily, a bearer of 'Igor'. Hence, a referentially successful utterance of (15) must be true. But the proposition it expresses (that Igor is a bearer of 'Igor'), like the proposition expressed by (19), is contingent. (And the same is true of 'If Igor exists, then Igor is a bearer of "Igor".)

The situation is analogous to the one Kaplan pointed out for:

(20)   I am here now

This sentence cannot be falsely uttered (or, rather, it cannot have a false Kaplanian *occurrence*; if you move while you are saying it, it will be false). But it does not follow that it is necessarily true. The proposition it expresses is contingent. Nevertheless, the logic of demonstratives determines that, necessarily, that contingent proposition is true when it is the content of an utterance of (20). Kaplan calls 'I am here now' a truth of the logic of demonstratives. I submit that 'Igor is a bearer of "Igor"' is a truth of the logic of names.[4]

So, the metalinguistic description theory of names is not subject to Kripke's modal objection. It does not entail that (15) (or any other analytic nominal sentence) is necessarily true, by definition.

5.1.1.2 Kneale

It is also not subject to the kind of criticism Kripke offered of Kneale's (1962) view. Kripke objects to Kneale's argument that 'Socrates' must be analyzed as 'the individual called "Socrates"' because there is no other way to explain why "it is trifling to be told that Socrates is called 'Socrates'" (Kripke 1980: 69). He notes that by the same reasoning one could conclude that 'horses' means *the things called 'horses'*, on the basis of the fact that 'horses are called "horses"' is trifling. Clearly, however, 'horse' does not mean *thing called 'horse'*. Hence, he concludes, "[t]here is no more reason to suppose that being so-called is part of the meaning of a name than of any other word" (Kripke 1979 (2011: 132, n. 12)).

Kripke is right that this is not a good argument for a metalinguistic view of the meanings of names. And it would be equally misguided to conclude from the fact that 'Socrates is a bearer of "Socrates"' is truth-secured that 'Socrates' means *a bearer of "Socrates"*. 'Socrates is called "Socrates"' would be trifling, and

---

[4] The sense of 'Igor does not exist' is *a bearer of "Igor" does not exist*, or, *there is no bearer of 'Igor'*. Given that 'Igor' has multiple bearers, the truth of 'Igor does not exist' depends upon which bearer (or alleged bearer) of 'Igor' a speaker (thinker) has in mind, which will be determined by the descriptive information the speaker (thinker) associates with the use of the name.

truth-secured, even if 'Socrates' did *not* mean *a bearer of "Socrates"*. Any sentence of the form '*t*s are called "*t*"s' will be truth-secured, since the term mentioned is the same as the term used. If a term *t* (literally) refers, then, necessarily, the things it refers to are referred to as '*t*'s. But this does not make '*t*s are called "*t*"s' necessarily true; and it cannot be concluded from the fact that it is truth-secured that it is *analytic*, and, hence, that *t means* 'called *t*'. As Kripke notes, this cannot be "the only explanation for why it is trifling to be told that Socrates is called 'Socrates'" (ibid.). Truth-security is necessary, but not sufficient, for analyticity. There must be independent reasons for proposing a metalinguistic analysis of names—such as the ones given above.

5.1.1.3 Non-Circularity

Kripke also objects that Kneale's view violates the non-circularity condition which he takes to be a condition of adequacy on a theory of reference. He argues that the sense of a name should tell us whom the user of the name refers to. However, the meaning *the man called 'Socrates'* does not, since it is trifling:

> Taking it in this way it seems to be no theory of reference at all. We ask, 'To whom does he refer by "Socrates"?' And then the answer is given, 'Well, he refers to the man to whom he refers.' If this were all there was to the meaning of a proper name, then no reference would get off the ground at all.
>
> (Kripke 1980: 70)

However, as Bach (1994: 159–61) and Katz (1994) have pointed out, the metalinguistic description theory is meant to be a theory of *meaning*, not of reference. And the meaning of a term need not by itself be sufficient to determine its reference. Given that names typically have multiple bearers, the meaning of a name can provide at best a *necessary* condition on what it can be used literally to refer to. It does not include information about *which* of its bearers is the intended referent on a given occasion of use. This is determined by the user of the name. Nor does it entail that a name in fact refers to anything. Kripke's criticism therefore misses its mark.

Moreover, the metalinguistic theorist is not constrained to endorse the circular answer "He refers to the man to whom he refers." One may answer the question "To whom does he refer by 'Socrates'?" by saying "He refers to a man who is a bearer of 'Socrates'." It may not convey the information the questioner seeks—viz., *which* bearer of 'Socrates' the speaker is referring to; but this is a practical problem (a violation of a Gricean maxim). Moreover, it does not violate Kripke's non-circularity condition. The property of being a bearer of a name does not *per se* involve the notion of reference. It is a non-referential relation between an individual and a name. Of course, a name may be *used* to refer to one of its bearers; but being referred to by a name is not an essential feature of bearing it.

5.1.1.4 Ignorance and Error

Bach (1994: 157-9) has shown that Kripke's objection from ignorance and error does not apply to his nominal description theory. He argues that if it were discovered that an individual to whom we had been referring using a name N were not in fact a bearer of N, we would withdraw the name. Kripke may be right that "[i]f a Gödelian fraud were exposed, Gödel would no longer be called 'the author of the incompleteness theorem', but he would still be called 'Gödel'" (Kripke 1980: 87). But, Bach argues, if the fraud involved not the appropriation of the discovery of the incompleteness of arithmetic by someone who did not discover it, but the appropriation of the name 'Gödel' by someone not named 'Gödel', its discovery would occasion withdrawal of both the description and the name. The impostor would not still be called 'Gödel', precisely because he would not be 'a bearer of "Gödel"' (Bach 1994: 159). I find this convincing.

5.1.2 Back to Frege?

It might seem that the conception of analyticity I have adopted allows a return to Frege-style views of the meanings of proper names. One could say, for example, that 'Aristotle' means *the teacher of Alexander the Great*, and, hence, that (21) is analytic,

(21)   Aristotle was the teacher of Alexander the Great

but that this does not entail that it is necessarily true—or even actually true. However, the metalinguistic description view as developed here does not allow this. What it says is that if a description d gives the meaning of a name N, then the sentence 'N is d' is truth-secured. But it is not the case that, necessarily, if 'Aristotle' refers, then (21) is true. Hence, 'the teacher of Alexander the Great' cannot give the meaning of 'Aristotle'. And the same may be said for any other substantive description that might be suggested as giving the meaning of 'Aristotle'.

5.2 Direct Reference, Rigidity and Necessity

It may be objected that if names have metalinguistic descriptive content, they cannot be rigid designators. Metalinguistic descriptions are not *de facto* rigid, and it is controversial whether or not rigidifying them would suffice to explain the modal intuitions that rigidity due to direct referentiality is supposed to explain (see, e.g., Nelson 2002 and Soames 2002). I do not think any of this matters, however, since I do not think that names are in fact rigid designators.

It is commonly held that if a name is directly referential then it is rigid. Like any other expression, a name means with respect to the description of any possible world just what it means in the actual world. But what a directly referential name means in the actual world is just the thing it refers to in the actual world. So it refers to that thing with respect to every possible world. (Or every possible world in which the thing exists. I ignore the difference between persistent and obstinate rigidity where it is not relevant.) I deny that names are directly referential; but even if they were, it would not follow that they are rigid. Since names may, and typically do, have multiple bearers, there is no one thing a name would directly refer to (mean) in the actual world, and, hence, no one thing it would mean (directly refer to) with respect to every possible world. So direct referentiality is not sufficient for rigidity.

The possibility of multiple bearerhood also blocks Kripke's original arguments. As has been pointed out by a number of his critics, the examples Kripke uses involve names of famous people who are likely to be the only bearer, or one of very few bearers, of the name known to the reader. But this is artificial. Most names have many bearers; and even if a name in fact has only one, it could have more. And this fact makes much of what Kripke says about names implausible. (Imagine his examples with the name 'John' substituted for 'Aristotle', 'Gödel', 'Moses', etc.)

Neither of Kripke's suggested responses to the objection from multiple bearers is satisfactory. One involves maintaining that different bearers of a name in fact have different names. The problems with this counterintuitive view are well known (see, e.g., Bach 1994: 167–9; Katz 1994), and I will not rehearse them here. On the other, Kripke claims that multiple bearerhood is irrelevant to the question of rigidity, since in a given context it will be clear which bearer of a name is the subject of discussion, and thus how the statement in question is to be interpreted. Once the interpretation is fixed, Kripke writes, "[f]or each...particular reading separately, we can ask whether what is expressed would be true of a counterfactual situation if and only if some fixed individual has the appropriate property. This is the question of rigidity" (Kripke 1980: 9). However, as was pointed out by Bach long ago (Bach 1981), this trivializes the rigidity thesis. Before we ask about the counterfactual truth value of a statement containing a name, we must referentially interpret the statement by assigning a bearer to the name. Then we ask about the truth value of the sentence on that interpretation with respect to some possible world. But this amounts to saying that when we are referring to a particular individual, and ask what is true of *that* individual in some possible world, it is *that* individual, and not some other, that we are asking about. This is true, but tautologous. ("If you want to know what is true of *this* individual in some other world, consider what is true of *this* individual in that world.") It is hard to see how anything philosophically significant about language or metaphysics could follow.

It is certainly the case that once we select a referential interpretation for a name in a nominal sentence we may choose to evaluate that sentence with that interpretation at another world. Moreover, doing so may be the default assumption. But nothing in the semantics of names requires that we do. With this suggestion Kripke seems to be conceding that what was supposed to be done semantically, by the *name*—picking out a particular individual to be held constant across worlds—is being done by the *user* of the name, in which case sameness of reference in other worlds becomes a pragmatic phenomenon. It is a matter of speaker reference, not semantic reference. But then we have no more reason to think that names are semantically rigid than we do to think that definite descriptions are, because *they* can be used referentially. Notice that Kripke says that we *can* ask whether what is expressed by a given use of a name in a sentence would be true of a counterfactual situation if and only if some fixed individual has the appropriate property. It does not follow that we *must* ask whether what is expressed is true in some counterfactual situation of the same individual it is meant to be about in the actual world. (Compare the Ronald Reagan example in Bach 1994: 153. See also Burge 1979b: 412.)

Since names as types do not have fixed, unique bearers, nominal sentence types do not have fixed *singular* truth conditions. They do have *general* truth conditions, however. The sentence type 'Aristotle is an oenophile' is true just in case a bearer of 'Aristotle' is an oenophile. Nominal sentence *tokens* can have singular truth conditions, though mere tokening is not sufficient to create them. If one says "Aristotle is an oenophile" with no particular Aristotle in mind, one has said simply that a bearer of 'Aristotle' is an oenophile, and what one has said is true just in case a bearer of 'Aristotle' is an oenophile. Names are like indexicals in this respect. One can meaningfully say "He is tall" without having any particular individual in mind. In such cases what one says is that a male is tall, and it is true just in case a male is tall. If I simply utter 'Aristotle is an oenophile' or 'he is tall', without intending it to be true *of* some individual, it is not the case that my utterance has no content—that I have said *nothing*—or that anyone hearing me will have no idea what I have said. One might wonder why on Earth I would say such a thing, given that the primary use of names and indexicals is to refer to particular things a speaker has in mind. But atypical use, even blatant misuse, of an expression does not rob it of meaning. Though it is hard to see what the point would be of uttering a nominal or indexical sentence with no particular individual in mind, nothing in the *semantics* of either indexicals or names prevents such utterances from being meaningful (and expressing thoughts). They are pragmatically odd, but not semantically misbegotten.

It is easier to accept this in the case of thought. There may be an intuitive barrier to accepting that someone who *says* "Aristotle is an oenophile" can have said no more than that a bearer of 'Aristotle' is an oenophile. Surely, however, one can simply *think* ARISTOTLE IS AN OENOPHILE while having no particular Aristotle in mind. One clearly can simply entertain the proposition that a bearer of 'Aristotle' is an oenophile. (One can, for example, think that the proposition can be true only in worlds in which there is someone who is a bearer of 'Aristotle'.) And though one may think this of a particular individual (Aristotle or not) one has in mind, the having in mind of that individual is, I maintain, a distinct mental act.

In order for (a thought expressed by) an utterance of 'Aristotle is an oenophile' to have singular truth conditions—in order for it to be true just in case some particular Aristotle is an oenophile—it must be said of some particular Aristotle the speaker has in mind. A speaker must have a singular intention in uttering it in order to be saying something about an individual, just as in the case of an indexical sentence. And one's utterance will not be true or false *simpliciter*, but true or false of the particular bearer of 'Aristotle' one has in mind. The very same utterance, as such, might have been true or false of a different bearer: one might have produced that very utterance with a different singular intention.

The actual truth value of an utterance, with singular intention (I refer to these as "singular utterances"), of 'Aristotle is an oenophile' depends upon which bearer of 'Aristotle' the speaker intends the utterance to be about. Likewise, the counterfactual truth value of the utterance depends upon which counterfactual Aristotle (if any) the utterance is intended to be about. But since the meaning of a name is not its bearer, the fact that we describe another possible world using our language with our meanings does not entail that the bearer of a name we assign to utterance of it in the actual world is, without further ado, the bearer assigned to it in any other possible world. If we ask of a particular singular utterance of 'Aristotle is an oenophile' whether it is true in some world w, we have not asked a complete question. Since it is not true or false *simpliciter* in the actual world, it will not be true or false *simpliciter* in any world. It is true or false *of* some individual x in the actual world. However, to ask if the utterance, true of x in the actual world, is true in world w is still to ask an incomplete question. A singular utterance must be evaluated with respect to a particular referent, in any world. Hence, the complete question is "Is that utterance, true of x in the actual world, true of y in world w?" Choosing the same bearer for otherworldly evaluation as we do for this-worldly evaluation may be the default assumption. (As it is when we maintain a referential interpretation of a name in a given discourse context.) And it may seem odd to answer the question "Is that utterance, true of x in the actual world, true in world w?" with the question "True *of whom*?" However, since, again, the meaning of a name—either type or token—is not its bearer, there is no semantic necessity that x be y. Whatever unusualness there may be is pragmatic.

Hence, to hold an interpretation of a name constant for counterfactual evaluation of a singular utterance is in fact to *reassign* the same referent with respect to each possible world, since no particular referential interpretation is built in to the meaning of the name. A *user* of the name 'Aristotle' may, so to speak, bring a particular Aristotle along with a sentence containing his name to some other possible world for evaluation. But the *name* 'Aristotle' does not do this.

This does not preclude asking counterfactual questions about a particular Aristotle, or attributing necessary or contingent properties to him. But we cannot do these things simply by asking whether or not, for example, the sentence 'Aristotle was the teacher of Alexander the Great' is contingent or necessary—any more than we could determine the modal status of a given female's height by asking whether 'she is tall' is contingent or necessary. Neither the semantics of indexicals nor that of names does this for us. It may be that, by default, a referential interpretation is held constant within a discourse, unless explicitly canceled. But, as above, to hold an interpretation constant is to reassign the same referent, even if one need not announce that one is doing so. And it is always semantically possible to shift referents midstream, whether one is talking about the actual world or another possible world.

Names in natural languages are thus not like individual constants in standard formal languages. Let us say that a singular term is *logically singular* if it cannot, as a matter of the interpretive rules of a language, be assigned to more than one individual. In standard formal languages, individual constants are logically singular terms. (They are also logically proper, in Russell's sense, since they must be assigned referents.) Since any individual constant has only one referent in any interpretation, any formula of the form $a = a$ will be true on any of them, and, hence, logically true. Logical singularity does not entail rigidity, however, since a logically singular term need not be assigned to the same thing in every interpretation. Logically singular terms refer to one and only one thing in *any* interpretation, whereas rigid singular terms refer to the same thing in *every* interpretation (possible world). The converse entailment does hold, however: if a term is rigid (it has one and only one referent in every possible world), it is logically singular (it has one and only one referent in any possible world). Since names in natural language are not logically singular, using our language with our meanings to describe non-actual possible worlds does not entail that a given name will refer to one and only one thing in *any* of them. And since they are not logically singular, they are not rigid.

If names are not rigid designators, then identity sentences whose terms are names (I call these "nominal identity sentences") are not necessary. They are not necessarily true if true, or necessarily false if false. According to Kripke, a nominal identity sentence N is M is, if true, true necessarily, because names are rigid designators. If N and M refer to the same thing in the actual world, then they refer to the same thing in every possible world, since they refer to their actual referents in every world, and N is M is true just in case N and M refer to the same thing. Likewise, on Kripke's view, a nominal identity sentence N is N will be true in every world. And here we may say not that N is N is, if true, true necessarily, but, rather, that it is necessarily true if N refers.

None of this is the case on the view I am defending. And this may seem difficult to accept. The intuitions that *N is N* is necessarily true (if *N* refers) and that *N is M* is necessarily true (if *N* and *M* refer to the same thing) are hard to shake. For it seems such sentences merely predicate identity of a thing with itself, and self-identity is necessary. So, they must be necessarily true. And it might seem that this ought to be the case even if names are *not* rigid. For whether or not a name names the same thing in every world, it names what it names in the actual world, and that thing is necessarily identical to itself.

If names have non-rigid descriptive contents, however, we should no more think that, for example, 'Ringo Starr is Richard Starkey' is necessarily true because 'Ringo Starr' and 'Richard Starkey' refer to the same individual than we should think that 'the first woman in space was the pilot of Vostok 6' is necessarily true because 'the first woman in space' and 'the pilot of Vostok 6' both refer to Valentina Tereshkova. It is a contingent fact that 'Ringo Starr' and 'Richard Starkey' refer to the same individual. It is also a contingent fact that in a given utterance of 'Ringo is Ringo' the 'Ringo's refer to the same individual. And even if names were directly referential, the fact that they are not logically singular would still entail that no sentence *N is N* is guaranteed to be true.

So how should the intuition of necessity be accommodated?

I suggest the following. Let us cast *n*-tuples of objects and properties—aka Russellian propositions, or singular propositions—in the role of *referents* of sentences. Many follow Frege in taking the referents of (declarative) sentences to be truth values. But we need not do this. Indeed, there are reasons not to. As has long been recognized, on the Fregean conception every true sentence has the same referent, as does every false sentence. This is counterintuitive, given the differences in the referents of the parts of the sentences. The constituent referential structure of a sentence is obliterated in the compositional process: the referent of a sentence is an unstructured entity that contains none of the referents of its constituents, and from which those referents cannot be recovered. This makes it obscure how the referent of the complex is determined, and violates to some extent at least the spirit of referential compositionality.

If a complex referring expression has referring constituents, then one would expect to find their referents in (or, at least, to be able to recover them from) the referent of the complex. So, for example, the referent of 'Jane and Elaine' has the referents of 'Jane' and 'Elaine' as constituents, and has the referent it does because those expressions have the referents they do. A theory on which the resultant referent of 'Jane and Elaine' is Dewayne—some other individual—would be bizarre. Of course, there are expressions that engender deflection of reference—for example, 'the boss of', which maps individuals onto their bosses, and whose combination with a referring expression yields an expression whose referent does not have the referent of the name as a constituent. But 'the boss of' is a functor, not a referring expression, and the referent of 'the boss of *N*' may be found in the referent of complex expressions it is part of. Intensional contexts present further complications (about which I have nothing useful to say here). But in the case of a simple sentence like 'Jane met Dewayne', if we take the referents of 'Jane,' 'met' and 'Dewayne' to be, respectively, Jane, the meeting relation and Dewayne, it seems reasonable to expect that the referent of the complex would be some kind of structured whole containing those referents. This is just what we get if we assign Russellian propositions the role of sentential referents.[5] Sentences with different constituents can have different referents, and the structure of their referents corresponds to the structures of the sentences.

I want to emphasize that I do not take these Russellian propositions to be sentential *contents*. As argued in Chapter 3, semantic and psychological referentialism (or externalism, or anti-individualism) is unmotivated. I have no special attachment to the term 'content', however, and have no wish to engage in (or even to be suspected of engaging in) boring lexical skirmishes. But I do want to insist that there are no good reasons to think that *meaning*—that is, the semantic feature of an expression that is traditionally distinguished from reference—should be bifurcated into narrow and wide (broad), internal and external, intentional and extensional, *de dicto* and *de re* or primary and secondary (etc.) varieties. This is not to deny that reference is a proper semantic property, or to claim that referential relations have nothing to do with what we think and talk about (in a referential sense).[6]

I just said that properties are *denoted*, not *expressed*, by predicates. This is because I think that predicates express senses, and senses are not properties. Senses, on the view defended in this book, are conceptual phenomenal types whose tokens are occurrent experiences. When one thinks, for example, that snow is cold, one's mind instantiates the relevant conceptual phenomenology— not the property coldness. Moreover, to understand this proposition (to instantiate this propositional-phenomenal type) is not, *per se*, to know what *coldness* is. It is to know what one's *concept of* coldness is. And there is no guarantee that our concept of anything reveals to us the intrinsic nature of its referent. Some do and some do not. But even in the case of those that do, like, say, RECTANGULAR,

---

[5] As apparently Russell himself did: "... we assert the object of the thought, and this is, to my mind, a certain complex (an objective proposition, one might say) in which Mont Blanc is itself a component part. This is why for me the *Bedeutung* of a proposition [sentence] is not the true, but a certain complex which (in the given case) is true" (letter to Frege, 12/12/1904; Gabriel et al. 1980: 169). (Russell wrote to Frege in German.) One need not think of such complexes as *facts*.

[6] Thus, though the distinction between the referent and the meaning of a sentence tracks the two-dimensionalist's distinction between primary and secondary sentential intensions (see, e.g., Chalmers 2010c), it is not the same thing. On my view the only semantic "dimensions" are content (meaning, sense) and reference. It is also worth noting that this approach accommodates a posteriori necessities: If 'Snoop Dogg' and 'Calvin Broadus' refer to the same individual, then the singular proposition denoted by 'Snoop Dogg is Calvin Broadus' is necessarily true. But it is not knowable a priori whether 'Snoop Dogg' and 'Calvin Broadus' refer to the same individual.

grasping the concept (instantiating the conceptual-experiential type) is not instantiating the property it is a concept of.

To return to the issue of nominal identity statements, on my view, a sentence like

(22)   Alban is Alban

is not necessarily true, since it is not necessary that the two 'Alban's refer to the same individual (or that they refer at all). Moreover, even if on a given occasion of use the 'Alban's co-refer, it is possible that *those very utterances* of 'Alban' might have had different referents. And this is consistent with saying that in describing other possible worlds we use our terms with our meanings, since the meaning of 'Alban' does not change with a change of referent. A change in referential interpretation is (on the present view) no more a change of meaning for a name than it is for a definite description. ('the president of the United States' means the same thing now as it did fifty years ago.)

On Kripke's view, if (22) is true, it is necessarily true. I maintain, rather, that if (22) is true, then, necessarily, it refers to a necessarily true proposition. But this is not to say that the *sentence* is necessarily true, or that any *utterance* of it is necessarily true. Since it is not necessary that either (22) (or any utterance of it) is true (even if its terms refer), it is not necessary that it refers to a true proposition at all.

The modal status of (22) is thus similar to the truth-security of (23), where 'a bearer of "Alban"' is predicative:

(23)   Alban is a bearer of 'Alban'

(On the predicative reading, (23) is equivalent to 'Alban is Alban'.) If the name 'Alban' refers, then, necessarily, (23) is true—it refers to a true proposition. (It cannot be the case that if 'Alban' (literally) refers, it does not refer to a bearer of 'Alban'.) However, the true proposition it refers to is not *necessarily* true. On the other hand, if the 'Alban's in (22) refer to the same individual, then, necessarily, (22) is true, and the proposition it refers to *is* necessarily true. (It cannot be the case that if the first and second occurrences of 'Alban' refer to the same thing, the first Alban is not identical to the second Alban.) We can say that while (23) is truth-secured (necessarily, if 'Alban' refers, (23) is true), (22) is *necessary*-truth-secured. If the 'Alban's refer to the same thing, then, necessarily, (22) is true, and the proposition it refers to is necessarily true. But since it is not necessary in either case that the conditions for truth be satisfied, neither *sentence* is necessarily true. It is not necessary that (22) refer to a necessarily true proposition, since it is not necessary that it refer to a true proposition at all—because it is not necessary that its 'Alban's refer to the same Albans.

(23) is like (24a–c):

(24a)　Now is now
(24b)　Here is here
(24c)　You are you

Since indexicals do not have type-referents, there is no guarantee that an utterance of any of these sentences is true. If they are true, it is because the indexicals co-refer. And if the indexicals co-refer, the propositional referents of the sentences are necessarily true. But since there is no semantic guarantee that the indexicals co-refer, it is possible for utterances of these sentences to be false. So the sentences are not necessarily true.

(23) is also like (25):

(25)　The first woman in space was the pilot of Vostok 6

If 'the first woman in space' and 'the pilot of Vostok 6' refer to the same individual, then the sentence refers to a necessarily true Russellian proposition, consisting of an object (or two occurrences of an object) and the identity relation. What is obvious in the case of (25)—that the *sentence* is not necessarily true, since the constituent descriptions do not have to have the same referent—is true of (23) as well, though the tendency to treat proper names like individual logical constants obscures this.

Thus, though referring to a true proposition is sufficient for truth, neither necessarily referring to a true proposition nor referring to a necessarily true proposition is sufficient for necessary truth. What must be the case for a sentence to count as necessarily true is, I submit, that it *necessarily* refer to a necessary proposition. In order for an identity sentence to be necessarily true, it must be the case that its terms cannot fail to refer, and that they cannot fail to refer to the same thing. On this taxonomy, only identity statements with co-referring *strongly* rigid terms are necessarily true.

While the *truth value* of a sentence is determined by the truth value of its propositional referent, the *modality* of a sentence is determined, not by the modality of the proposition it refers to, but by the modality of its referential relation to the proposition it refers to.

An utterance of 'I am here now' cannot, according to Kaplan, fail to refer to a true proposition if its terms refer, though the proposition it refers to is not necessarily true. And the same is true of 'Béla is a bearer of "Béla"'. 'Béla is Béla', on the other hand, *can* fail to refer to a true proposition if its terms refer (but to different things), though if they refer to the same thing the proposition the sentence refers to is necessarily true. Still, none of these sentences are necessarily true—it is not necessary that any of them be true. On the other hand, if a term *a* is logically singular, then the sentence '*a* is *a*' is necessarily true, since it is not possible for its terms not to co-refer in any possible world (though they do not each have to refer to the same thing in every possible world). Such sentences are rare, if not completely absent, in English, since logically singular terms are (though we could introduce them). Perhaps 'the actual world' is such a term. Since 'the actual world' necessarily refers in any world, and necessarily refers to one and only one thing in any world, 'the actual world is the actual world' is necessarily true; and since it is a true identity statement, it refers to a necessarily true proposition. However, since 'the actual world' necessarily refers to different worlds in different worlds, 'the actual world is the actual world' does not refer to the same necessarily true proposition in every possible world. (Indeed, it cannot. This makes 'the actual world' not quite a logically singular term as I defined the notion, since, as I defined them, logically singular terms *can* refer to different things in different interpretations (worlds).)

The identity sentence 'two is the only even prime', in contrast, is (at least on one way of thinking of abstract objects) *rigidly* necessarily true. It cannot be false, since (if) its constituent terms cannot possibly fail to refer (they have necessary existents as referents), and its terms cannot possibly fail to co-refer, since it is necessarily true that two is the *only* even prime.

The modality of a Russellian proposition is, on the other hand, relatively straightforward. If its objects must have the properties the proposition predicates of them, then it is necessarily true. If it cannot have such properties, it is necessarily false. If it may or may not have those properties, it is contingent. And it is unproblematic to talk about such propositions being true or false at all or some possible worlds, since they do not require referential interpretation. The relation between the components of a singular proposition and the objects that make it true or false is not *reference*, but *identity*.

What of (26)?

(26)   A bearer of 'Béla' is a bearer of 'Béla'

There are two ways to read (26). Just as names can function as predicates or referring expressions, so can the indefinite descriptions they are semantically equivalent to. (Compare Bach 1994: 59ff., on two uses of definite descriptions.) In addition to being readable as a predication of the property of being a bearer of 'Béla' to Béla, it can be read as an identity statement, taking 'a bearer of "Béla"' to be a singular term (as in 'a bearer of "Béla" is sitting at the bar'). On the first reading (26) is truth-secured. It is just like (23). On the second reading, it is like (22): if it is true, if the two occurrences of 'a bearer of "Béla"' refer to the same individual, the sentence refers to a necessary proposition.

5.3 Kripke's Puzzles

The metalinguistic description theory developed here provides ready solutions to Kripke's (1979) puzzles about belief ascription. The sense of the name 'Londres' is *a bearer of 'Londres'*, and the sense of the name 'London' is *a bearer of 'London'*. Since quoted expressions do not get translated, Pierre's Parisian belief about London must be rendered in English as 'A bearer of "Londres" is pretty'. But this is not logically inconsistent with the (alleged) belief he expresses in London, which is that a bearer of 'London' is not pretty. An analogous solution is available for cases involving different names in the same language, as in the 'Cicero'/'Tully' case. Finally, the 'Paderewski' case does not lead to paradox because the propositions *a bearer of 'Paderewski' had musical talent* and *a bearer of 'Paderewski' had no musical talent* are not contradictory (cf. 'A book I read was difficult' and 'A book I read was not difficult'). As long as Peter knows that 'Paderewski' can have more than one bearer, and he believes that his assessments of musical ability concern different bearers, he is not being irrational.

That said, I think that these puzzles have a solution independent of the metalinguistic description theory. Given principles that Kripke accepts, they do not even arise.

Kripke claims that all that is needed to generate his puzzles about our practices of ascribing beliefs using names is the following disquotational principle:

(DP) If a normal English speaker, on reflection, sincerely assents to 'p', then he believes that p.[7]

But he notes that this principle cannot apply in cases of linguistic confusion or ignorance. For example, a speaker who assents to 'Jones is a doctor' but not to 'Jones is a physician', Kripke says, either "does not understand one of the sentences normally, or should be able to correct himself 'on reflection'" (1979: 138, n. 23). In either case, the speaker's assent to one and dissent from the other is, in the moment, evidence of linguistic ignorance: he does not know that 'doctor' and 'physician' are different terms for the same profession in English, the language he speaks. In cases of linguistic ignorance, "we *cannot* straightforwardly apply disquotational principles" (1979: 138, n. 23). Presumably this is because it would be unfair to impute explicit irrationality in such cases.

In 'Cicero'/'Tully'-type cases the obvious explanation for the difference in assent is that the speaker does not know that different names name the same person. But if not knowing that two terms are equivalent counts as linguistic

---

[7] A stronger principle, that "[a] normal speaker of English who is not reticent will be disposed to sincere reflective assent to 'p' if and only if he believes that p," (Kripke 1979: 138) generates a contradiction for the ascriber, as well. But it is not required for the puzzles about believers.

ignorance in the 'doctor'/'physician' case, why should it not also count as linguistic ignorance in the 'Cicero'/'Tully' case? Likewise in cases in which a speaker does not know that two uses of the same name ('Paderewski') refer to the same individual, and in cases in which the speaker does not know that 'London' and 'Londres' name the same city. The puzzles do not arise, because the disquotation principle does not apply, because the speaker is linguistically ignorant.

Kripke objects to this move as follows (1979: 146, n. 28):

> It is not possible in this case [Pierre], as it is in the case of the man who assents to "Jones is a doctor" but not to "Jones is a physician," to refuse to apply the disquotational principle on the grounds that the subject must lack proper command of the language or be subject to some linguistic or conceptual confusion. As long as Pierre is unaware that 'London' and '*Londres*' are codesignative, he need not lack appropriate linguistic knowledge, nor need he be subject to any linguistic or conceptual confusion, when he affirms '*Londres est jolie*' but denies 'London is pretty'.

But it is not clear that a bilingual speaker who does not know that terms in the two languages he speaks are codesignative does not lack appropriate linguistic knowledge. A monolingual speaker of English is not expected to know what terms in other languages mean, and which are equivalent to terms in the language he speaks. But unless being bilingual entails *no* requirement that a speaker know equivalences across languages—i.e., have the ability to translate terms and sentences of each language into the other—the fact that a bilingual speaker does not know an equivalence ought to count as an instance of (bilingual) linguistic ignorance. (It would be odd, to say the least, if Pierre were a fluent French speaker and a fluent English speaker, but was unable to match any term in either language with its translation in the other. I do not think Kripke has such a situation in mind.) Pierre's being unaware that 'London' and 'Londres' are codesignative is a case of bilingual linguistic ignorance, and should prevent the application of the disquotation principle.

In any case, the fact that the disquotational principle governs the *ascription* of belief (*What should we say about what someone believes on the basis of their sincere utterances?*), the fact that *we know* that Pierre does not know that 'Londres' and 'London' are names for the same city ought to prevent us from attributing to him the belief that London is not pretty on the basis of his inclination to assent to 'London is not pretty', without further ado. We should at least *hesitate* in our attribution, out of charity, given that it would result in attributing to Pierre contradictory beliefs. And we may withhold the attribution until we inform Pierre of the co-referentiality of 'Londres' and 'London' (to see what he would assent to *on reflection*, given the relevant information—e.g., 'This *part* of London is not pretty'). But the main point here is that the disquotational principle governs, not what Pierre believes, but what we should say he believes. And we should not say that he believes contradictory propositions without good reason. So the puzzles do not arise on Kripke's own principles.

5.4 Determining Nominal Reference

Because metalinguistic descriptions are minimal—they characterize their referents only as bearers of the names they mention—the content of name (or a nominal concept) will not by itself be sufficient to pick out one of its many bearers. How, then, does a user of a name (a speaker or thinker) succeed in referring to just one of them on an occasion of use?

I submit that names function the way some indexicals do. Their contents *constrain* what they can refer to on any given occasion of use (cf. 'she' is constrained to refer to a female), but they do not by themselves *determine* which of their bearers they refer to. This must be done by the user of the name. There must be an intention to refer to some particular bearer of the name, and in order to form such an intention, the user must have some way of singling out the intended referent. Though perception is a way of focusing on a particular individual, if it is *conceptual* reference that is to be determined—reference *in thought*—the intended referent must be distinguished from other bearers of the name conceptually—that is, by description. Mere causal connection to a bearer is not sufficient.

For one thing, while a chain of usage may *maintain* a referential connection between a name and its bearer, it is not what *establishes* the connection. If a chain of usage leads back to an object, it is because it leads back to a descriptive take (conceptual or perceptual) on that object that enabled the namer to name it—to establish a referential connection between the name and its referent. Again, even if perception is involved in relating the namer to a particular object, if we are concerned with the contents of nominal thoughts, application of concepts is essential. The concepts may be minimal, like THIS or THAT, but, as argued in Chapter 4, conceptual contents cannot be percepts or images. Hence, if there were no descriptive identification of the thing to be named, there could have been no cognitive act of naming. In the initial case, that content must be sufficient to single out *one* thing to be a bearer of the name—even if it is only something like THE THING I SEE BEFORE ME.

Thus, though one's present usage of a name may be connected to its bearer by a chain of communication leading to something one is not acquainted with and could not directly describe, one must have *some* sort of descriptive content beyond the meaning of the name in order to insert oneself in this chain of communication. Suppose that someone says "John is a philosopher," and you ask what they mean. If the speaker has *nothing* to say about which John is meant, then even if in fact they picked up on a chain of usage that does lead to a particular John, it does not make sense to say that they have succeeded in referring to that John. If they have no idea at all which bearer of 'John' they mean to be talking about—if when asked they just shrug their shoulders and say "Beats me!"—they have not succeeded in referring to anyone in particular. They must at least be prepared to say something like "The John you were talking about," or "The John I heard people saying insulting things about yesterday." They must be able to form *some* conceptual-descriptive connection to a particular bearer of 'John'—even if it is just a connection to a chain of usage.

Moreover, failing to refer does not prevent a user of a name from thinking or meaning something by the thought or sentence. What is thought is that a bearer of 'John' is a philosopher. This is analogous to thinking HE IS TALL with no one in particular in mind. This thought is true if a male is tall. The thought JOHN IS A PHILOSOPHER is true just in case a bearer of 'John' is a philosopher. But if the user of a name is to refer to some particular bearer of 'John', they must have some descriptive access to it, even if this is indirect.

Nevertheless, there is no reason to think that this extra-nominal descriptive content becomes part of the meaning of the name. When a name is tokened, its user may have some specific bearer of the name in mind, who is the intended referent. Having a specific bearer in mind is more than entertaining the metalinguistic concept *a bearer of 'N'*. The thinker will have some identifying description, or set of descriptions, in mind that are sufficient for singling out, in thought, its intended bearer. These will be substantive descriptions and will function to fix a particular referent of the name in thought. But they are not part of the content of the nominal concept the thinker uses to refer, and they do not *become* part of the concept. Though on a particular occasion of use a speaker or thinker will usually have some one of the bearers of a name in mind, and the communicative intention of the utterance might not be realized if the hearer does not identify which one it is, the description that singles it out is not part of what the sentence (the thought) *means*. The content of neither the nominal sentence nor the nominal thought by itself can select one from among the many bearers of a name. This is done, directly or indirectly, by distinct, supporting descriptive thoughts, whose contents are distinct from that of the nominal thought. A nominal concept has the same content as it does on an occasion of use in which the user has *no* specific bearer in mind. The content of a nominal concept is not sufficient to determine a particular referent.

I thus disagree with Bach (1994) and Katz (1994, 2004), who claim that the meanings of names are *enriched* on given occasions of use, such that the sense of the name in that context is sufficient to determine a unique referent. For example, they claim that the way to solve Kripke's Paderewski puzzle is to enrich the content of tokens of 'Paderewski' so as to avoid the inconsistency in someone's believing both PADEREWSKI HAD MUSICAL TALENT and PADEREWSKI DID NOT HAVE MUSICAL TALENT. They suggest that in the sentence 'Paderewski had musical talent' 'Paderewski' means *the bearer of 'Paderewski' who is a musician,* and in the sentence 'Paderewski did not have musical talent' it means *the bearer of 'Paderewski' who is a politician*. But I do not think any enrichment of the meaning of a name is required.

According to Bach, "When 'N' has many bearers, this description ['the bearer of "N"'] is *incomplete*, so that a full specification of the content of a belief involving 'N' would be of the form ... 'S believes that the bearer of 'N' who/which is F is G'" (1994: 166). It is common to call a description 'incomplete' when it (its meaning) is not sufficient to pick out a referent. I think this is tendentious terminology. If a description is well formed and meaningful, it is complete. It has everything it needs to do what it is supposed to do, viz., in the case of a name, to supply a necessary condition for literal reference (literal use). The reference of a nominal concept is *constrained* but not *determined* by its content. A name N cannot be used literally to refer to something that does not satisfy the description 'a bearer of "*N*"', but this description is not sufficient for picking out just one of them. Names, like indexicals, are not meant to function as uniquely referring expressions. This is what makes it possible for different individuals to have the same name.

If a thinker knows that any name can have more than one bearer, and believes that the bearers of a name deployed in two thoughts are different, there is no inconsistency in their thinking N IS F and N IS NOT F. For this is not to think that something both is and is not F. It is like thinking THE KING IS DEAD, LONG LIVE THE KING (which entails THE KING IS DEAD AND THE KING IS NOT DEAD), which is (though I blush to confess it took me years to figure this out!) a perfectly consistent thought. The thinker is not thinking that some dead king is not dead if the intention is to refer to two different kings.

Likewise, even such a thought as PADEREWSKI IS NOT PADEREWSKI can be consistently entertained. Thoughts of the form N IS NOT N have an antonymous conceptual structure. But antonymy no more entails (necessary) falsehood than analyticity entails (necessary) truth. Truth and falsity depend upon reference. If a sentence is analytic, then, necessarily, it is true if its constituent terms refer. If a sentence is antonymous, then, necessarily, it is false if its constituent terms refer *to the same thing* (and it is not necessary that the sentence is false if the terms refer to different things). Given the possibility of multiple referents, a thinker is only inconsistent in thinking N IS NOT N if the thinker believes that the bearers of the Ns are the same (an unlikely state of mind). Indeed, acceptance of a sentence '*N* is not *N*' is *prima facie* evidence that the thinker does *not* believe that the names have the same referent. (Cf. Katz 1994.)

5.5 The Paratactic Theory of Nominal Concepts

I have argued that some kind of description theory of names is required for the phenomenal intentionality of thought thesis as applied to nominal thought. And

I have defended a version of the metalinguistic description theory as the best account of a number of linguistic and psychological data. On this view nominal senses, and the contents of nominal concepts, are name-involving.

If, however, we suppose a Fregean, *purist* view about senses and conceptual contents, on which complex senses are composed of senses alone, there is a serious *prima facie* problem for such theories: *names are not senses*. And since they are not senses, they cannot be components of senses. Hence, a metalinguistic description cannot, after all, give the sense of a name, and no sentence containing a metalinguistic description can express a (Fregean) proposition.

An analogous problem arises for the phenomenal intentionality of thought thesis. If concepts and thoughts are propositional-phenomenal types, and their tokens propositional-phenomenal tokens, they cannot have constituents that are not cognitive-phenomenal. Since visual and auditory experiences of names are not conceptual experiences, they cannot be parts of nominal concepts or thoughts. (Nor, as per the Principle of Phenomenal Purity, can external name tokens.) There are no concepts with name-experiences as constituents, and no name-containing thoughts expressed by sentences containing metalinguistic descriptions.

Now, it might be suggested that the semantic contribution of "'N'" in 'a bearer of 'N'' is not its referent, the name N, but its sense, and, hence, that the metalinguistic theory poses no threat to the Fregean purist. But what could the sense of "'N'" be? It cannot be the sense of the name N, on pain of regress. And, *pace* Davidson (1979), it is not plausible that quotation marks are singular terms with senses (*the expression a token of which is here*). (A description theory in the style of Tarski (1943) and Geach (1957) only displaces the problem to the referents of quoted letters.) Quotation expressions are directly referential: they simply *present* the expressions quoted.

It might also be suggested that the metalinguistic description theory entails that nominal concepts must be hybrid entities, having both conceptual and auditory or visual experiential components, and that nominal thought contents are singular propositions whose objectual constituents are token name-experiences. But I cannot accept this suggestion, for two reasons. First is my commitment to the idea that thought contents must be *thinkable*. Since auditory and visual images are not thinkable, they cannot be constituents of concepts or thoughts. (Nor, for the same reason, can external name tokens.) Second is my commitment to the Principle of Phenomenal Immiscibility. If thoughts are *sui generis* propositional experiences, they cannot be composed of experiences of any other kinds. I thus have the same reasons for rejecting name-experience-containing metalinguistic concepts as I do for rejecting sensory-experience-containing phenomenal concepts. Whatever the proposed hybrid entities might be, they cannot be *concepts*.

Thoughts must be *conceptually complete*. They cannot have non-conceptual constituents, and they cannot be *gappy*. Hence, the referent of a metalinguistic nominal concept—a name token—cannot be a constituent of it, or the thought it is a constituent of, since a name is not a concept. What is needed for a metalinguistic description theory of nominal concepts is a conceptual constituent that refers to a name, and does so without mentioning any of its phonological or orthographic features. (The concept THE NAME WHOSE FIRST LETTER IS 'T' AND ... AND WHOSE FINAL LETTER IS 'D', for example, has the same problem as the concept THE NAME 'THEOBALD'.) I propose the demonstrative concept THIS NAME.

The concept associated with a name N is the concept A BEARER OF THIS NAME, and the concept comes to be associated with the name by being demonstratively applied to a displayed token of it: A BEARER OF THIS NAME: N. (This why I call this account the "paratactic" theory of nominal concepts. It is, of course, similar to Davidson's descriptive theory of quotation (Davidson 1979). The essential difference is that I am not claiming that quotation marks or their mental equivalents are meaningful singular terms.) For example,

A BEARER OF [THIS NAME]
↓
Theobald

Moreover, the thinker will be thinking of a particular bearer of the name as the intended referent of the concept in virtue of descriptive information associated with the name on an occasion of its use. For example,

⟦A BEARER OF [THIS NAME]⟧
↓
⇓   Theobald
Theobald

Thus, the *thought* one expresses when one says 'Theobald is a painter' is just A BEARER OF THIS NAME IS A PAINTER. But one thinks the thought of (i.e., referring to) a particular name, 'Theobald', and a particular bearer of the name. One may think the very same thought about different names and about different bearers of the name, and in virtue of this come to think of some particular bearer of the name that he is a painter. When we think about something using its name, we think about the name (a token of which is experienced), and about the thing *qua* bearer of the name. Since the name is inwardly heard or seen, the auditory or visual experience of it is part of one's total mental state. But it is no more a part of what one *thinks* than an auditory experience is part of what one *sees*, or a visual experience is part of what one *hears*, when one is in a state of simultaneously hearing and seeing something. As argued above, the idea that a concept must contain content sufficient to establish its reference should be resisted. The reference of a concept on a particular occasion of its tokening may be established by non-conceptual means, for prime example, by perception. In general, conceptual states can rely on non-conceptual states to get us out of our heads.

On this account, nominal concepts, though they do not contain names, are *nominal* for two reasons. First, they have the concepts BEARER and NAME as constituents, which are themselves (non-metalinguistic) nominal concepts; and, second, their referents are names. They are thus analogous to phenomenal concepts, as I understood them in Chapter 4, which are phenomenal not because they contain experiences, but because they have concepts of experiences of various kinds (THIS COLOR, THIS PAIN, THIS DISAPPOINTMENT) as constituents, and their referents are experiences (of color, of pain, of disappointment).

Nominal and phenomenal concepts are also both *indexical*, since they contain demonstrative concepts, and their referents can change depending on their context of use, thinker intention, collateral information, etc. Just as the contents of the concepts THIS and THAT do not change with their referents, neither do the contents of the concepts THIS NAME and THIS DISAPPOINTMENT.

Moreover, all nominal concepts on this account have the *same* content (and all names express the same concept): *a bearer of this name*. Semantic differences between tokens are purely referential, as is the case for indexical concepts in general. There is no difference in content between a token of A BEARER OF THIS NAME that refers to the name 'Theobald' and one that refers to 'Serafina'. Thus, if two thinkers think A BEARER OF THIS NAME WAS A PAINTER, where one demonstrates an inner token of the name 'Theobald' while the other demonstrates an inner token of the name 'Serafina', they have thought the same thought, though they have thought it about different names, and (if their uses are literal and referentially successful) about different individuals. (Likewise if two thinkers think the thought about different bearers of the same name.) The thinkers' total conscious mental states may be different, because, for example, one is hearing the name 'Theobald' and the other is seeing the name 'Serafina'; but what they are *thinking* is the same. This is analogous to the case in which two thinkers who think I AM HUNGRY or I HATE THAT COLOR are thinking the same thought, though since the thoughts must be (in the first case) or in fact are (in the second case) about (refer to) different individuals, they can have different truth values.

An analogous account is available to the Fregean purist about senses. An utterance of a name refers to the name uttered, a particular physical token, but the name is not part of the sense of the name, or the sense of any sentence it appears in. All names have the same sense: *a bearer of this name*.

6
Unconscious Thought

In this chapter I confront what may be the most serious challenge for the thesis that thought content is phenomenally constituted. If it is, as many believe, a conceptual (or otherwise metaphysically necessary) truth that phenomenology requires consciousness, then the thesis entails that there can be no unconscious thought. But there are good reasons to think that there is unconscious thought. Freud showed that rationalizing explanations of human behavior frequently require the attribution of unconscious beliefs, desires, fears, etc.—states whose contents are *thought* contents. Moreover, ordinary experience seems to present us with many instances of thought processes occurring unconsciously—as, for example, when one sleeps on a problem, or otherwise withdraws conscious attention from it, only to find it later solved.

Indeed, resistance to the very idea of a proprietary phenomenology of thought might stem as much from commitment to the existence of unconscious thought and the impossibility of unconscious phenomenology as from the seeming introspective elusiveness of thought experience. Even before one tries (and allegedly fails) to detect such experience, one is on the basis of these commitments predisposed to think that there simply *could not be* such a thing.

The question of unconscious *thought* should be distinguished from the question of unconscious representation generally. There may well be unconscious states that indicate, or represent, or carry information, in the sense appealed to by naturalistic theories of intentional content and computational theories of subpersonal cognitive processing. I am prepared to concede that there are such things, and that they have "intentionality" in some sense. But it is not the sense I will be concerned with. Such states do not have intentionality in the way that thoughts do. They either suffer from well-known problems of indeterminacy of content, or their contents are not thinkable or judgeable. The question I want to address is whether the phenomenal intentionality of thought thesis is compatible with there being unconscious states with determinate, thinkable, judgeable intentional content—i.e., unconscious *thoughts*.

I begin the chapter by considering, and rejecting, compromise positions suggested by Searle, Strawson, Kriegel, Smithies, and Horgan and Graham, which attempt to reconcile the conflict by holding that unconscious thoughts have intentional content that is in one way or another *derived from* or *dependent on* the *original* intentional content of conscious thoughts. I argue that such "derived intentionality" is not intentionality at all, and I conclude that there are only two stable positions one can take on the issue: one must either accept that there can be unconscious phenomenology, or deny that there can be unconscious thought.

I develop both of these positions. With respect to the former, I argue that the phenomena of blindsight and phenomenal sorites can plausibly be understood as implicating unconscious qualitative experience. I will also suggest that there might be states conscious in themselves, but not for the individual whose behavior they explain. If there is unconscious phenomenology in this sense—that is, *in-itself* consciousness that is not *for-me* consciousness—then the connection between consciousness and intentionality is direct, as Descartes held: there can be no thought without consciousness.

With respect to the denial of the existence of unconscious thought, I will argue that unconscious states and processes postulated to provide rationalizing explanations of behavior and thought need not themselves have content in order to do so. Such states and processes can respect the logico-semantic relations we take to be constitutive of rational thought without themselves having any content at all.

In the end I will suggest that, after all, there may be a role for all three kinds of states—unconscious phenomenal, in-themselves-but-not-for-me conscious phenomenal, and unconscious contentless—to play in the constitution of our mentality.

6.1 Searle

Searle is fundamentally committed to the Cartesian thesis that there is no genuine mental activity without consciousness. Yet, he also accepts that there are unconscious states with the kind of intentional content that conscious thoughts, beliefs and desires have: "The explanatory power of the notion of the unconscious is so great that we cannot do without it" (Searle 1992: 151). Searle's position is an attempt at a compromise. He claims that "there are no deep unconscious intentional states" (1992: 162), where a *deep* unconscious state is one that cannot, in principle, be brought to consciousness (because it is not the right *kind of* state), but that an unconscious state may be intentional if it is, in principle, potentially conscious. (There may be reasons why, as a matter of fact, it may never become conscious (repression, etc.), but it is the right *kind of* state to be conscious.) Thus, according to Searle, the property of an unconscious intentional state in virtue of which it is intentional is a property it would not have unless it were potentially conscious. But what property is that?

Searle maintains that "[t]he link...between intentionality and consciousness lies in the notion of an *aspectual shape*" (1991: 52, my emphasis). In my view, Searle nowhere gives a clear account of what aspectual shape is supposed to be, but he makes the following claims about it. It is in virtue of having aspectual shape that a mental state has intentional content: "To be intentional, a state or process must be thinkable or experienceable; and to be thinkable or experienceable, it must have an aspectual shape" (1991: 52). Moreover, aspectual shape is irreducibly *subjective*: "aspectual [shape] must exist from [the thinker's] point of view" (1991: 52, 53). Yet, a state need not be conscious to be subjective: "there is something subjective about mental states even when they are unconscious" (1991: 52, 56).

Aspectual shape properties, therefore, would appear to be the likely candidates for those properties in virtue of which an unconscious intentional state is intentional. For the last two claims of the preceding paragraph together seem to entail that a state need not be conscious in order to have aspectual shape.

Yet, Searle *also* says that "The ontology of mental states, at the time they are unconscious, can only consist in the existence of purely neurophysiological phenomena" (1991: 53). Such "third-person" facts cannot, however, determine an aspectual shape for a mental state: "There isn't any aspectual shape at the level of neurons and synapses" (1991: 59). So it looks like there is a flat-out contradiction here: an unconscious intentional state both has and cannot have aspectual shape. Searle comes closest to stating an explicit contradiction in Searle 1992: 161: "intentional states, conscious or unconscious, have aspectual shapes, and there is not aspectual shape at the level of neurons."

Searle recognizes the problem: "now we seem to have a contradiction: the ontology of unconscious intentionality is entirely describable in third person, objective neurophysiological terms, but all the same the states are irreducibly subjective. How can this be?" (Searle 1991: 57). Of course, it cannot be. Searle attempts a compromise in the following way. He claims that an unconscious state may be intentional—may have aspectual shape—if it is *potentially* conscious: "When we characterize an unconscious intentional state in terms of its aspectual character [by which he must mean *when we characterize an unconscious state as intentional*], we are characterizing a present brain state in terms of its *causal capacity* to produce a conscious thought or experience" (1991: 58; my emphasis). Thus, Searle's official position seems to be that the essential link between consciousness and intentionality lies in the fact that the property that makes an unconscious state intentional is its potential for consciousness—i.e., a causal power.

But this seems to imply an identification of the aspectual shape of an unconscious brain state with its power to cause aspectual shape, since it is the aspectual shape of a conscious state that makes it intentional. If Searle intends a distinction between unconscious aspectual shape and conscious aspectual shape, then he owes us an account of it. But, I will now argue, there is no account of the difference that would meet all of the constraints Searle accepts. He is faced with two dilemmas, one embedded in the other. The main dilemma is this: either unconscious aspectual shape is distinct from conscious aspectual shape, or it is not. If it is not, then Searle is forced into the incoherent position of identifying a property with a disposition to manifest that property. (This problem has been recognized by others. See, e.g., Coleman 2022b.) If unconscious aspectual shape *is* distinct from conscious aspectual shape, then (this is the embedded dilemma) the difference is either sufficient to render it non-intentional, or it is not. If it *is* sufficient, the thesis that there are unconscious intentional states is no longer honored—unconscious states cannot have aspectual shape. But if it is *not* sufficient, Searle loses his thesis of an essential connection between consciousness and intentionality, for it would then be possible for an unconscious state to be fully intentional, independently of any relations it might have to consciousness. (This is, essentially, Armstrong's objection (see Armstrong 1991 and also Coleman 2022b.))

In fact, I do not think it is entirely clear what Searle's position is.[1] It does seem to me, however, that none of the reasonably faithful interpretations of what he says presents him with a position he can accept. His view comes to grief because of his assumption that phenomenal properties must be conscious. Together with his view that phenomenal properties ("aspectual shape") determine intentionality, this implies that intentional states must be conscious. His attempt to avoid this inevitable conclusion was destined to fail.

6.2 Strawson

In *Mental Reality* (Strawson 1994), Strawson claims that "[t]here is a clear and fundamental sense in which *meaning*, and hence *intentionality, exists only in the conscious moment...*" (1994: 209), and, hence, that "true or original or intrinsic intentionality is found only in the case of experiencing beings" (1994: 187). Nonetheless, he maintains that "[o]ne can acknowledge the sense in which meaning exists only in the conscious moment while endorsing a theory that attributes intentionality to some of the nonexperiential [i.e., non-conscious] states of experiencing beings" (1994: 209). So, for Strawson, the connection between consciousness and intentionality obtains not at the level of states, but of creatures: only creatures capable of consciousness ("conscious creatures" for short) can be in intentional states, though not all intentional states need be conscious.

Now, this position immediately raises the question, which Strawson recognizes, of how it is that the capacity for conscious experience could make such a difference. Why is it that unconscious states of conscious creatures can have intentional content while those of non-conscious creatures cannot? *Prima facie* it would seem that unconscious states (physical, neural, dispositional, etc.) of the former could be intrinsically type-identical to those of the latter. So why would

---

[1] Fodor and Lepore (1994) are also at a loss to understand what Searle thinks the connection between intentionality and consciousness is. However, I suspect that their trouble is due more to a basic lack of sympathy with the idea that intentionality is an experiential phenomenon than with any difficulty in interpreting what Searle actually says.

they then not both have intentional content? More specifically, suppose that an unconscious state U of a conscious creature C^+ has the intentional content *that p*. If it is possible for a non-conscious creature C^- to be in an unconscious state U' of a type identical to U, why should not U' have the content *that p*? U and U' are intrinsically identical; why should their occurring in C^+ and C^- make this difference?

A possible answer is suggested by Strawson's discussion (1994: 205) of an objection to the thesis that only conscious creatures can be in intentional states. Perhaps intentionality appears only in conscious creatures because the property P that renders a creature capable of intentionality is a property only a conscious creature could have. And this might be because P has the second-order property P' of being instantiable only in conscious creatures, and the second-order property P'' of being necessary for intentionality, and $P' \neq P''$. Presumably, P would have these distinct second-order properties in virtue of its structure: it is a compound of distinct first-order properties P_1 and P_2, such that P_1 can only be instantiated by conscious creatures, and P_2 is necessary for intentionality.

In these terms, the answer to the question posed above—Why should the state of the unconscious creature not have the same intentional content as the type-identical state of the conscious creature?—is that, contrary to what the question assumes, C^- could *not* be in a state U' type-identical with U, because, given that U has intentional content, and that its having that content is essential to its type identity, C^- would not be capable of being in it, since C^- is not capable of consciousness. Since C^- cannot instantiate P (because it cannot instantiate P_1), it cannot instantiate P_2 (because P_2 comes bundled with P_1), and, hence, none of its states can be intentional.

Strawson rightly rejects this view. Why, he asks, could there not be some property P^* which shares P_2 with P, but not P_1? If P_1 and P_2 are distinct properties, then, unless it is metaphysically necessary that only P has P_1 as a constituent (which cannot be assumed without argument), why could there not be a creature possessing P_2 but not P_1? (This is also essentially Armstrong's objection to Searle.) To insist otherwise—to insist that P_2 could *only* be bundled with P_1—seems simply to be just another way to claim, without explanation, that the capacity for consciousness and the capacity for intentionality are essentially linked. And a similar objection would apply to an account on which the instantiation of P_1 (and, hence, P) is not just *limited to* conscious creatures, but in fact *bestows* the capacity for consciousness on the creatures that instantiate it, as well as to an account on which the relevant properties were properties of *states* rather than *creatures*.

Having rejected this approach, Strawson does not propose a solution to the problem in *Mental Reality*. More recently, he has offered the following:

> We can allow that these unconscious mental occurrences [those attributed in an explanation of behavior] have...determinate intentionality only if we can allow that they possess it in virtue of the causal-historical fact that...determinate

cognitive-experiential taking was involved in the original process of interaction that led to the presence of the dispositions that are now being manifested in the causing of an action by these unconscious mental occurrences.

(Strawson 2010: 357)

On this view, being *caused by* a genuinely intentional conscious state confers intentionality upon an unconscious state. But it is hard to see how this could be—*unless* the causing were to bestow an intrinsic unconscious property sufficient for the possession of real intentional content. If that were the case, however, then the essential connection between consciousness and content would be lost. If content is separable from consciousness, then the connection between them is contingent, and, as above, it is unclear why unconscious states could only receive it from conscious ones.

A more fundamental difficulty, which besets the other views discussed in this chapter as much as Strawson's, is that it is simultaneously committed to the theses that intentionality is phenomenally constituted, that phenomenality requires consciousness, and that unconscious states can have intentionality. These theses are inconsistent. It is of no avail to claim that the intentionality of unconscious states is *derived*. For, unless derived intentionality is *real* intentionality, there are no genuinely intentional unconscious states. But if it is real intentionality, then, by Strawson's lights, it must be phenomenally constituted.

6.3 Horgan and Graham

Terry Horgan and George Graham (Horgan and Graham 2012) consider three responses to the problem. The first denies the possibility of unconscious content-determinate (i.e., genuinely *mental*) states, but maintains that the third-person explanatory purposes for which such states are attributed might be as well served by unconscious content-indeterminate informational/computational states. Such states may then be said to have *as-if* determinate content.

The second response is Searle's. But they object that this response cannot account for the determinate intentionality of states (such as deeply repressed beliefs and desires) that cannot be made conscious.

On the third response, unconscious states can be assigned determinate (personal-level) content on the basis of their causal-dispositional integration into a network of states some of which are conscious. The conscious states constitute "anchor points," and provide the basis for the determinate interpretation of the system as a whole. Unconscious states have the determinate content assigned to them by the unique interpretation on which state-transitions in the network are "systematically content-appropriate" with respect to the anchor points. Horgan and Graham recognize that the need for a *unique* interpretation makes this view problematic.

I have already given reasons for joining Horgan and Graham in rejecting Searle's view. My objection to their other two proposals is, as noted above, that *as-if* intentionality is not intentionality. A state's being *interpretable as having a content* does not change its intrinsic character, and so cannot be content-conferring on the phenomenal-constitution view. Nor can its being causally related to states with determinate content. If intentional content is phenomenally constituted, then nothing without phenomenal properties can have it. Having as-if intentional content is no more having content than having as-if color is having color.

6.4 Kriegel

In his paper "Cognitive Phenomenology as the Basis of Unconscious Content" (Kriegel 2011a), Kriegel maintains that genuine, original intentionality is phenomenally constituted, and thus requires consciousness. An unconscious state, however, can have intentional content if it is *best interpreted as* having it. He writes: "On the account I offer, what makes a phenomenally unconscious item have the intentional content it does, and an intentional content at all, is (very roughly) that it is profitably interpreted to have that content" (Kriegel 2011a: 82).

He refines the rough claim as follows. The relevant interpretations are made on the basis of applications of Dennett's "intentional stance," in which states with intentional content are attributed to a system in order to predict and explain its behavior. Unlike Dennett, however, Kriegel thinks the attributions one makes in this way are literally true. Moreover, Kriegel also maintains that a given act of interpretation need not itself be conscious. However, to prevent vicious regress, he maintains that any unconscious interpretive act, or series of such acts, must be grounded in an originally contentful, conscious interpretive act. Additionally, Kriegel also claims that interpreters should be taken to be *ideal*—i.e., they "exercise the intentional stance perfectly under all conditions" (2011a: 84). Finally, Kriegel holds that there need not be an *actual* interpretation of an unconscious state in order for it to have determinate intentional content. What is required is that the state itself "must have the *disposition* to elicit the right interpretation in the right interpreters, but not that the disposition be *manifested*" (2011a: 87–8).

His view is summarized in his principle (A2):

(A2)   Epistemically necessarily, for any unconscious item x and any intentional content C, x has C iff there are a possible conscious item y, a possible ideal interpreter N, and possible conditions K, such that (i) y has the content <x has C> and (ii) x is such as to elicit y in N under K.

One obvious problem with this is that it entails that a token unconscious state has many, perhaps infinitely many, possible interpretations, and, hence, that it has as many intentional contents. So either an unconscious state's intentional content is (perhaps infinitely) disjunctive, or there is no fact of the matter about which interpretation is correct. Moreover, it seems possible that given the right Ks and Ns, the attributed contents might even be inconsistent.

But I think Kriegel's view shares the fundamental problem of all the compromise positions I am considering. Interpretation does not change the *intrinsic* nature of the interpreted state. So, assuming, as Kriegel does, that intentionality is phenomenally constituted, and that phenomenality and consciousness are intrinsic properties, in spite of the fact that it is *treated as if* it had intentional content, it does not really have it. And if it does not *really* have it, then it just does not have it. Being interpretable as thinking that p is as distinct from thinking that p as being interpretable as being in pain is from being in pain.

6.5 Smithies

In his paper "The Mental Lives of Zombies" (Smithies 2012), Declan Smithies maintains that Searle's view comes to grief on the fact that beliefs are unconscious dispositions to conscious judgments, and, hence, cannot themselves become conscious. (I do not in general agree with this sort of dispositional account of belief; and I do not think this is the central problem with Searle's view.) He argues that the proper way to think about the relation between unconscious intentional states and conscious intentional states is that the *contents* of the former can be *contents* of the latter (not that the unconscious states can themselves become conscious).

His overall view on the relation of consciousness and cognition is the one we encountered in Strawson: a creature incapable of consciousness is incapable of cognition: there can be no "cognitive zombies." His reasons for adopting this thesis are, however, different. He argues that genuinely cognitive processes such as reasoning must be accessible to consciousness. In the absence of accessibility to consciousness there can be no rational assessment and no genuine cognition—no genuinely cognitive states. Cognition is either conscious or accessible to consciousness in the sense that the contents of reasoning either are or can become conscious. And since conscious reflection is a kind of conscious experience, the contents of such states are phenomenally individuated.

Smithies distinguishes genuine cognitive states from the purely informational unconscious intentional states postulated by computational theories of the mind. Such states are not subject to rational assessment (though they are subject to different kinds of normative assessment (Smithies 2012: 360)). Thus they do not have the kinds of contents that conscious cognitive states do. He does allow, however, that there can be genuinely cognitive unconscious states, subject to rational assessment. Such states must have the kinds of contents that conscious cognitive states have. Yet Smithies does not accept that there can be unconscious phenomenology. So he is in the same position as Searle and Strawson.

In place of Searle's connection thesis, Smithies offers what he calls the *rational connection thesis*, according to which

> an intentional state plays a rational role if and only if it is either conscious or individuated in such a way that its content is accessible to consciousness as the content of a conscious state. (Smithies 2012: 358)

The proper way to individuate such states is in terms of their dispositions to cause conscious cognitive states. An unconscious state has a genuine cognitive content C if it has a disposition to cause a conscious judgment with genuine cognitive content C. Unconscious states (beliefs) inherit the content of the conscious states (judgments) they are disposed to cause. To say that its content is accessible to consciousness is just to say that it is the kind of content a conscious state can have.

I think Smithies's proposal comes to grief in the same way as all the others. If genuine cognitive content is phenomenally constituted, but there is no unconscious phenomenology, then no unconscious state can *literally* have *genuine* cognitive content. Relational phenomenal individuation does not suffice for phenomenal *constitution*, and so cannot confer phenomenally constituted content. To say that the cognitive content of a conscious state is phenomenal is to say something about its *intrinsic* properties, since phenomenal properties are intrinsic. So if there is no unconscious phenomenology, the contents of unconscious states can be, at best, *as-if* content. But, again, as-if content is not content.

If intentionality is experiential, then there is no such thing as derived intentionality. Nothing that is not an experience can have meaning—including language. It is only our experience of language that has meaning. This meaning may be *associated* with linguistic expressions, but it cannot be, literally, *conferred upon* them. There is no tenable compromise position for a proponent of the phenomenal intentionality of thought thesis with respect to unconscious states. The only workable resolutions are thus (a) to accept that unconscious phenomenology is possible, and (b) to deny that there is such a thing as unconscious thought. In the next section I consider two ways to understand the notion of unconscious phenomenology.

6.6 Unconscious Phenomenology?

The first way to construe the idea of unconscious phenomenology is, *literally*. To say that there is unconscious phenomenology is to say that there are states that have (intrinsic) phenomenal character but which are not conscious. The second way to understand unconscious phenomenology is to distinguish between a state's being conscious *in itself* and its being conscious *for its possessor*. On this way, to say that there is unconscious phenomenology is to say that there are phenomenal states conscious in themselves but not for a particular individual, but which nonetheless can in some sense be said to be states of that individual.

6.6.1 Intrinsic Unconscious Phenomenology

The claim that there are unconscious states with intrinsic phenomenal properties is not conceptually incoherent. It has, in fact, been entertained by philosophers and psychologists as a possible explanation of various dissociative conditions, such as blindsight, subliminal perception, change blindness, inattentional blindness and hemi-neglect. The hypothesis that these phenomena involve the dissociation of consciousness from qualitative experience is not *nonsense*; it is not conceptually necessary that a state with phenomenal properties is conscious. (Some philosophers, for example Sam Coleman, think the existence of unconscious phenomenology is completely unproblematic. See Coleman 2022a and Forthcoming.)

Further, it is not the case that the property of being phenomenal just *is* the property of being conscious. There are so many *kinds* of phenomenology, so many *ways* of being conscious—many quite radically different from each other—all of which nonetheless are (or can be) conscious *in exactly the same sense*. To say that an experience of pain is conscious and that an experience of bright yellow is conscious is to say the same thing about them. *Qua conscious* there is no difference between them.

Perhaps consciousness can come in *degrees*, so that one state (the pain) might be *more* or *less* conscious than another (the bright yellow) (or vary in consciousness itself over time). But this need not, *per se*, constitute a difference in the intrinsic *pain* and *yellow* phenomenal characters. In which case degrees of consciousness could be safely set aside here. On the other hand, if there are varying degrees of consciousness, and *how* conscious a state is affects its (total) phenomenal character (or, even if there are not, and it does not), perhaps consciousness *itself* is a species of (second-order) phenomenology, alongside all the others. (Perhaps it is something like experiential *illumination*—in contrast to, e.g., experiential *yellow*, experiential *loudness*, etc.). It would then perhaps be easier to see how a state could be phenomenal without being conscious: it is the same sort of thing as being phenomenal without being, say, *painful*. (Though then it might not be easy to see why a state could not be conscious without being phenomenal in some *other* way—i.e., why it cannot be *simply* conscious.) In that case, the relation between consciousness and intentionality would be like that between ice and steam: they are both *forms* of phenomenality, just as ice and steam are both forms of water.

Even if one insists that the forms of phenomenology are *just* forms of consciousness, no more capable of independent existence than, say, the creases in a pair of pants, it is still the case that phenomenality is a different *property* from consciousness. In general, even if it were metaphysically necessary that phenomenality and consciousness are co-instantiated, it would not follow that they are the same property.

Moreover, there are psychological phenomena that can plausibly be interpreted as providing empirical reason for thinking that consciousness and phenomenology are *nomologically* distinct properties. I discuss two such phenomena in the following two sections.[2]

6.6.1.1 Blindsight

It is sometimes claimed that the phenomenon of blindsight provides evidence of the nomological independence of consciousness and phenomenality—viz., the existence of unconscious qualitative experience. I think this interpretation of blindsight cases is plausible, though I think it has not been sufficiently developed or defended. Here I wish to strengthen the case for the unconscious qualia interpretation of the phenomenon of blindsight.

In Weiskrantz's famous experiments (see, e.g., Weiskrantz 1986), subjects with damage to area V1 of the visual cortex experience blind spots ("scotomata") in their field of vision—areas within the visual field in which there is a complete lack of conscious visual experience—nonetheless responded surprisingly accurately (in some cases perfectly) when asked to guess at stimuli presented in their blind field. For example, if asked whether or not a light had been flashed in the blind area, patients guessed correctly at rates far above chance. Even more striking are cases in which patients were able to accurately guess at the completion of an irregular figure, half of which is consciously experienced and half of which is within the blind field.

Some philosophers have wanted to claim that this shows there can be unconscious sensations—i.e., unconscious experiences with qualitative character. There is, however, an obvious alternative explanation of blindsight patients' capacities that does not posit unconscious qualia—viz., that non-phenomenal *information* about the properties of the stimulus can in these patients still get through to a central processor (or whatever). Thus, though there might be some problem with a blindsighter's visual cortex, his rods, cones, retinas, optic nerves, and all manner of other apparatus up to the visual cortex are in normal working order. And whatever connections there may be between lower-level differential activity in

---

[2] Some have suggested that distinct "dorsal" and "ventral" stream processing in the brain separately subserve consciousness and qualitative experience—in which case it would seem nomologically possible for one to occur without the other. (See Block 2001 and references therein.) As far as I am aware, however, there is no consensus on this. Nor am I competent to evaluate the evidence. So I will set this phenomenon aside.

one's visual system and what gets tokened in one's "belief box" are intact in these patients, though the connections to mechanisms that generate conscious, phenomenal experience are disrupted.

Is there anything that can be said in response to this? I think there is. But one needs a clear idea of what phenomenology *does* for us—that is, of what someone lacking a certain kind of qualitative experience could not do that someone possessing it could. For if we had a clear idea of that, then we might be able to say something about what blindsighters can do that those completely lacking phenomenology cannot do, and sidestep the whole question of consciousness.

In general, if phenomenology does anything at all for us, it appears to be to enable us to make certain kinds of perceptual distinctions. We can distinguish things purely on the basis of the way they *appear* to us—i.e., purely on the basis of the qualities of the experiences they cause us to have. Perhaps something else *could* do what phenomenality does for us. It is not difficult to imagine creatures who could make all the perceptual discriminations we do, who are as adept at navigating their environments as we are, and who are as attuned to their inner states as we are, but who have no phenomenal states at all. But it does not seem at all plausible that in ordinary conscious perception something else does it *for us*. If you deprive *us* of phenomenality we suffer drastic reductions, if not extinctions, in these functions of our conscious experience. It is therefore not unreasonable to think that it is *phenomenology* that enables us to do these things, and not the non-phenomenal, unconscious neural processing that remains when phenomenality (and, hence, consciousness) is removed. Those non-phenomenal creatures who are as competent as we are would have to have much more sophisticated non-phenomenal mechanisms than we do. It may be that evolving phenomenality is easier (or maybe just easier on Earth), or that it is a historical accident that these various functions are subserved by phenomenology in us; but I do not think it can reasonably be denied that phenomenology does what it does for us. And if we can still do some of what conscious phenomenology allows us to do when consciousness is removed, then it is not unreasonable to conjecture that it is still phenomenology that explains the residual abilities.

Consider those who lack, not consciousness, but phenomenology of a certain kind—for example, people with *achromatopsia*. Achromats lack, to varying degrees, color vision; *complete* achromats see only in black and white and shades of gray. Their visual experiences of things are thus, phenomenologically, very different from those of the normally sighted. They may be incapable of, or have great difficulty in, identifying or distinguishing things on the basis of their colors. Red things and black things, for example, may look the same to them; whereas to those who are not achromats the experience of seeing a red thing is quite different, phenomenologically, from the experience of seeing a black thing. (See Nordby 1990 for a fascinating first-hand report of such phenomena.) What is the significance of the difference? Just this: normally sighted individuals can *visually* distinguish red and black things on the basis of their color, and achromats cannot. That is, it seems that it is the *phenomenology* that makes the difference here, for, we may assume, achromats are otherwise phenomenologically and cognitively just like the normally sighted—including being equally conscious.

Now, if blindsighters could make distinctions on the basis of color that the achromat cannot, I think we would have a stronger (though not, of course, conclusive) reason for thinking that the phenomenon of blindsight, or at least some cases of it, do show that there can be unconscious phenomenology. But it seems that they can. Dennett (1991), for example, cites an experiment, reported in Stoerig and Cowey 1990, that, he says, provides evidence that it is possible for blindsighters to discriminate colors in their blind field. But if this is an ability that in normal perceivers depends on there being phenomenological differences between the experiences of the stimuli, then there is reason to suspect that blindsighters nonetheless experience phenomenology, though unconsciously.

Compare the conscious and fully sighted to the conscious though achromatopsic to blindsighters to those who are completely unconscious. Blindsighters can do things the completely unconscious cannot; conscious achromats can (one assumes) do things the blindsighted cannot; and, of course, the fully sighted and fully conscious can do still more. But notice that this progression presents a building up of capacity, and suggests that the capacity for consciousness and the capacity for phenomenology are distinct. The achromats compare to the "chromats" with respect to phenomenological capacity; the blindsighted compare to the fully sighted chromats with respect to capacity for consciousness, but not with respect to capacity for phenomenology; and the fully unconscious compare (rather unfavorably) in all respects to all of the others.

But why not offer the same explanation for the blindsighters' ability as before? Why not say, that is, that what gets through is non-phenomenal information, and go on to claim that it is just *that* that is missing from the achromats?

I think there are reasons, offered by Diana Raffman (1995), to think that this could not be true in the general case. And if it could not be true in the general case, then perhaps the very examples that Raffman discusses could be implicated in blindsight cases.

Raffman argues that we are able to make phenomenal distinctions that outstrip our capacity for making conceptual distinctions, and that, therefore, there is a distinctively phenomenal sort of information that we are capable of possessing. (Christopher Peacocke (1983) has made similar claims, though I think he has since revised his view.) If there is such information, and blindsighters can make distinctions made by the normally sighted on the basis of it, *and* if we have no other way to represent the color differences, then it would seem to follow that in at least some cases blindsighters discriminate perceptual stimuli on the basis of phenomenology alone.

Unfortunately, it is still open to the opponent of unconscious qualia to argue that there *are* other ways of representing the relevant information. He can claim that the processes that deliver the relevant information and make accurate conscious judgment possible do not work with *concepts* of the discriminated shades. Raffman may have shown that there is *conscious* phenomenal information; but it does not follow that there is *unconscious* phenomenal information. The argument from blindsight, though suggestive, is not conclusive.

6.6.1.2 Phenomenal Sorites

There are series of objectively different color samples which are such that normal perceivers cannot distinguish the colors of adjacent members, but can distinguish those of non-adjacent members. This is commonly taken to engender a paradox. In a progression from a yellow chip to a red chip in which adjacent chips cannot be colorwise distinguished, for example, it seems we are committed to saying that the first (yellow) chip and the last (red) chip are colorwise indistinguishable, which is clearly false. Yet the transitivity of indistinguishability is hard to deny.

Thus, suppose we have three color chips, a, b and c, such that a is colorwise indistinguishable from b, and b is colorwise indistinguishable from c, but a is colorwise distinguishable from c. (It may be that more than three chips are needed in order for the first and last to be distinguishable. This would complicate the argument but change nothing relevant to the use I wish to make of the phenomenon. It would still be the case that two chips with different colors are indistinguishable.) Now, if the color of a were identical to the color of b, then a would be indistinguishable from c, since b is. But, by hypothesis, a is distinguishable from c. Therefore, the color of a is not the same as the color of b. Yet we cannot see—cannot consciously visually experience—the difference. This shows that there can be differences in objective color that escape conscious detection, and, hence, that there are colors that are, in certain circumstances, not consciously seen. If a and b look to have the same color, but they do not, then it must be the case that the color of (at least) one of them is not seen. It cannot be the case that both colors are seen, but one is misperceived. It may be possible to misperceive an *object* without failing to perceive the object. But to misperceive a *property* of an object is to experience it as having some *other* property, and, hence, not to perceive that property at all.

Let us suppose that the color a looks to have is the color it in fact has. Then, since a and b look the same, but the color b has is not the color that a has, b has a color that is (in the circumstances) not seen. We might suppose that *neither a nor b* has the color it looks to have in a particular case. But, assuming as I am for the moment that colors are intrinsic properties of objective surfaces, unless we *never* see the colors things actually have, there will be sorites series in which the color a chip looks to have *is* the color it has. And surely any chip in the series would have the color it looks to have at least in some circumstances—e.g., if it were the *only* thing being perceived. (It does not matter if perceived colors are not intrinsic properties of objective surfaces, since soritical examples can be constructed for objective intrinsic properties like shape and size. So there is no harm in pretending that colors are Edenic (Chalmers 2006). Moreover, all phenomenal properties of *experiences* are intrinsic properties of them, which is all I will need for the argument.)

I do not think it is correct to say, as Timothy Williamson (1990) and Farkas (2008a) do, that indistinguishability can be explained in terms of inability to form beliefs or activate (propositional) knowledge of difference. There is a purely *experiential* sense in which two chips may look the same or different. We visually focus on the chips, and we can *see* no difference between them—they *look* the same. The seeing, the visual experience, does not involve the application of concepts or the formation of judgments—though of course it can provide the justificatory foundation for such cognitive activities as conceptualization and judgment. (It is easy to imagine how perceptual indistinguishability could be established for non-verbal, non-conceptual creatures. And see Raffman 1995 for an argument that experience outstrips conceptual capacity in our own case.) Moreover, given that the chips are simultaneously in view and the focus of close attention, it seems highly unlikely that their looking the same, or their being judged to look the same, is some sort of mistake occasioned by limitations of attention or memory. As far as conscious experience goes, the colors of the chips are the same. But the colors of the chips are not the same; hence, in certain circumstances colors can elude conscious perception.

Now suppose we have a series of *internal* samples—experiences e, f and g—for which this phenomenon arises. We may take them to be perceptual experiences of the chips, or artificially induced experiences, or dream images (you are dreaming you are comparing color chips), or afterimages. When speaking of e, f and g, I will use 'color' to refer to their subjectively experienced intrinsic chromatic properties. By parity with the above reasoning, if the color of f were the *same* as the color of e, then f ought to be colorwise distinguishable from g, since e is. But, by hypothesis, f is not distinguishable from g. Hence, the phenomenal characters of e and f must differ. But their difference is consciously undetectable: as far as consciousness goes, the colors of e and f are the same. But their colors are not the same; hence, there are (subjective) colors that in certain circumstances elude conscious perception. Hence, there are differences in *phenomenology* that do not register in consciousness. Hence, in general, phenomenal reality is independent of consciousness.[3]

More specifically, if we suppose that it is the color of f that is not consciously experienced, then that phenomenal property, that quale, is experientially

---

[3] Michael Lockwood (1989: 163–4) presents an argument like this. (It occurred to me independently.) See also Edward Feser's (1998) critique of the argument, and Lockwood's (1998) response.

instantiated but not conscious. We thus have a case of an unconsciously instantiated phenomenal property.

It may be objected that an experience could not possibly fail to appear to have a phenomenal property it has, or appear to have a phenomenal property it does not have. The very idea seems incoherent. Indistinguishability in spite of difference, while possible in the case of perception of external objects and their properties, is not possible in the case of experiences themselves. Subjective indistinguishability in spite of *objective* difference is possible because objective colors (whatever they are) are distinct from subjective colors (the phenomenal properties they cause us to consciously experience). But subjective indistinguishability in spite of *subjective* difference is not possible, since we can make no sense of a distinction between the properties experiences have and the properties they appear to have. And this is because experiences *are* appearances: the way they appear is the way they are. For an experience *not* to appear the way it is would therefore be for it not to appear. But this is impossible. We cannot consciously *mis*-experience a conscious state.

So, the objection continues, f has whatever color we are conscious of it having—whatever color it consciously appears to us to have. Hence, it is *not* the case that f can appear to have a color it does not have, or not appear to have a color it has. The color it appears to have is the color it has, because it is an appearance. The way it appears is the way it is. There can therefore be no subjective sorites cases, and my argument does not show that there can be unconsciously instantiated phenomenal properties.

But if this were the case, then we could not explain the fact that e and f appear to have the same color consistently with the fact that e and g appear not to have the same color. If f must have the color it appears to have, and it appears to have both the color of e and the color of g, and the colors of e and g are not the same, then f must have two different colors at the same time, which is impossible. To avoid this, we must hold that the colors of e and f are not the same, regardless of how they consciously appear to us. That is, we must make an appearance–reality distinction for appearances themselves. But this is only possible if appearances can be unconscious.

For an external object to appear is for it to cause mental states with phenomenal properties. For an experience to appear, in contrast, is simply for it to *occur*: appearance is the mode of existence of phenomenal tokens. The occurrence of an experience entails the instantiation of one or more phenomenal properties. And since, necessarily, nothing can have a property it does not have, no experience can appear—can *be*—otherwise than it is. (Change of appearance is change of experience.) But this does not entail that appearance must be *conscious*, since (or so I have argued) it is not a *logical* truth that all experience is conscious. And if appearance—experiential occurrence—need not be conscious, then one can make a coherent distinction between appearance and reality for experiences. Experiences cannot consciously appear otherwise than they consciously are; and they cannot unconsciously appear otherwise than they unconsciously are. But they may consciously appear otherwise than they unconsciously are. An unconscious phenomenal state may be insufficiently "illuminated" by consciousness—just as an objective color sample may appear otherwise than it is because it is insufficiently illuminated. And this provides a way of understanding what is going on in the phenomenal sorites case: an unconscious experience is consciously *mis*-experienced. *f* consciously appears differently than it unconsciously is.

How exactly should conscious misperception of unconscious phenomenal states be understood?

One way to is suppose that for an unconscious phenomenal state to become conscious is for it to be *represented by* (or to *cause*) a distinct conscious phenomenal state. We could thus recognize two distinct levels of experiential states, the unconscious and the conscious. And if we do this the possibility of error is introduced. When the states have matching phenomenal character, we are conscious of the phenomenal character of the unconscious state. It, and its phenomenal properties, become conscious by being consciously represented. When its properties are accurately represented, the properties we are conscious of are its actual properties. When it is not accurately represented, we are not conscious of its actual properties, which remain unconscious.

But one may well worry that the conscious phenomenal properties of the representing states may be subject to soritical effects as well, which would engender an infinite regress. (The regress might not be vicious; but it would make a mess.) It also seems implausible (*pace* David Rosenthal (e.g., 2006)) that a state is conscious because it is the object of some *other* state. (And there is a threat of a different regress here.) Finally, our access to our conscious states is *direct*. We do not become aware of our conscious states by becoming aware of distinct states that represent them.

So let us consider another possibility. We could say that there are unconscious states with phenomenal properties, and that what it is for one of these to become conscious is for *it* to come to have the property of being conscious. On the first proposal we have two levels of experiential reality by having two distinct systems of states. On this proposal we have two levels of experiential reality by having experiences that can be conscious or not, where consciousness is an intrinsic property of the experience. Then the soritical effect would be explained as occurring, not when there is a higher-order state misrepresenting a first-order state, but when the first-order state has properties which cannot, or do not, for whatever reason, become conscious. (Objective analogy: the chips have different colors; but shining a flashlight on them does not differentially illuminate them, because of the limited resolving power of the light. (Better: illuminating them *from within* does not reveal the difference in their colors.))

There would be no threat of infinite regress on this account, since there are no distinct states for which soritical phenomena could arise. There is just the state unconsciously instantiating a phenomenal color property, which is "mis-revealed" by consciousness. The inner chips can appear in consciousness to have colors they do not intrinsically have.

This account also offers a way out of the paradox in the subjective case that is exactly analogous to Howard Robinson's solution to the objective paradox. When we look at b, it is not as though it looks to have no color at all. So what color do we experience b as having? The color of a? This cannot be right, since a is colorwise distinguishable from c, whereas b is not. But it also cannot be that we experience a as having the color of b, since b is colorwise indistinguishable from c, whereas a is not. Yet a and b look the same. Robinson (1972) argues that the way out of the paradox is to maintain that b *does not have a constant appearance*. (A less developed version of this proposal can be found in Jackson and Pinkerton 1973.) When we compare it with a, we experience it as having the color of a; but when we compare b with c, we experience it as having the color of c. The color we experience b as having *changes*, so there is no constant middle term, 'the color b appears to have'. Rather, we have 'the color b appears to have when viewed next to a' and 'the color b appears to have when viewed next to c', and these colors are different. In this way the transitivity of 'looks the same as' can be maintained without contradiction.

And if the color b appears to have when viewed next to a is not the color it appears to have when viewed next to c, then the intrinsic color of b (the color it would appear to have if it were the only thing being perceived) must not be at least one of the colors it appears to have when compared to a and g (it cannot be both). So in at least one case, and possibly in both cases, the color b appears to have is not the color it has.

Likewise, in the subjective case, one may claim that the conscious appearance of f is different when it is compared to e than when it is compared to g. At least one of these appearances must be a *mis*appearance, which both secures the existence of unconscious phenomenal character and allows for the elimination of the constant middle term 'the conscious appearance of f' (and the resolution of the paradox).

It might be objected that what subjective sorites cases show is not that there can be unconscious qualia, but, rather, that there can be phenomenal differences in conscious experience that one is not consciously aware of.[4] If this means that there can be differences in consciousness that do not register consciously, I deny it as contradictory. A more charitable interpretation would be that the differences are there in consciousness, but that they cannot be detected by the experiencer. I can think of two reasons this might be the case, neither of which I find persuasive. One might argue that the failure to detect the difference is

---

[4] David Chalmers and Andrew Lee have independently suggested this possibility to me, in conversation.

due to limited resources or resolving power of attention, or that one cannot form concepts of the undetectable shades.

I think it is sufficiently clear that it is not necessary that one have a concept of an experience in order to have it or to be able to distinguish it from others. And I am skeptical of the claim that closely attentive experience of a conscious state could fail to reveal all of its conscious properties. Introspection is not inner *perception*: it does not, like introspective *belief* or *judgment*, involve forming a representation of one's experience. Simple (non-epistemic) introspection is (*pace* a previous Pitt time slice (2004: 10)) simply conscious occurrence: a subject's experience cannot be conscious without being conscious to that subject—i.e., without the subject being aware of it. And awareness of one's own experience is just what introspection *is*. Since no appearance–reality distinction can be made *within* consciousness, phenomenal properties cannot be properties of conscious experience without being conscious. And if they are conscious they are, *eo ipso*, introspected—the subject is aware of them. Hence, for a conscious experiential difference to be introspectively undetectable would be for it not to be conscious. But, again, this is contradictory. If experiential differences cannot be detected, they cannot be conscious.

If there is a difference between attentive and inattentive conscious experience, it is not that the former involves the formation of a (possibly non-veridical) representation of the experience while the latter does not. I am not sure I know what it is; but if attending to a conscious experience makes a *phenomenal* difference, then the experience has changed, and, like the unattended experience, must consciously be exactly as it consciously appears.

Edward Feser (1998: 409) offers a similar objection in response to Lockwood (1989). He faults Lockwood for neglecting the possibility that the difference between subjectively indistinguishable color patches is a non-phenomenal property of phenomenal properties, and, hence, that failure to perceive it is not failure to perceive a phenomenal property. So, for example, it may be the case that e and f have different colors, but that failing to be aware of the difference is not failure to be aware of one of their colors. It is, however, hard to see how one could fail to be aware of a second-order difference property without also failing to be aware of the first-order phenomenal properties it supervenes on. One is unaware of the difference because the patches look the same.

Finally, it might be argued that it is an open empirical question whether or not subjective soritical phenomena are possible, and, hence, that one cannot simply help oneself to the supposition that they are. To this one may reply that since it is not impossible that Berkeleyan idealism is true, it is not impossible that what we think of as the objective phenomenal sorites is already itself subjective. So it is at least metaphysically possible that there are subjective phenomenal continua. But this is not an effective response to the challenge that they never *in fact* occur (perhaps by physical or psychological necessity), and so not an effective response to the challenge that there are never in fact unconscious qualia. Only psychologists, not philosophers, can tell us whether or not there are.

I am not sure there is a philosophical response to this challenge.

6.6.1.3 The Mark of the Mental

The phenomena discussed in this section, blindsight and phenomenal sorites, are suggestive, but not conclusive. But the possibility of unconscious qualia remains coherent and interesting, and has important consequences.

For example, if there is unconscious phenomenology, then the intimate connection many see between consciousness and intentionality is indirect, via phenomenality. This would be an interesting alternative to the three major types of account of the essential nature of mentality that take experience seriously, the *Cartesian*, the *Brentanian* and the *Humean*. On a Cartesian view, *consciousness* is the defining feature of the mental: creatures not capable of consciousness are not capable of mentality. But (arguably) not all mental states are conscious, and not all creatures incapable of consciousness are incapable of mentality. So the Cartesian view does not adequately characterize what is distinctive of mentality. On a Brentanian view (e.g., Dretske's, Lycan's or Tye's reductive representationalism; see also Crane 1998, Dretske 1995, Lycan 1996, Tye 2000), *intentionality* is seen as the defining property of the mental: a state is mental if and only if it is *about* something, and a creature not capable of such states is not capable of mentality. But (arguably) not all mental states are intentional (e.g., simple sensations), and it seems at least possible for there to be individuals (e.g. Davidsonian swamp creatures, lifelong brains-in-vats, perhaps "Ganzfelders" (a made-up term for creatures capable only of homogeneous visual experience, one color at a time)) capable of experience but not of intentionality. But even if all such states are intentional, it is at least arguable that they are intentional *in virtue of* their phenomenal properties. So the Brentanian view does not provide an adequate characterization of the nature of mentality either. On a Humean view, *sensationality* is the defining feature of mentality: the contents of the mind can be divided into sensations (sensory and introspective experiences) and copies of sensations (images), and a creature incapable of inner or outer experience would not be capable of mentality. But (arguably) not all mental states are sensational (e.g., cognitive states are not), and it seems possible for there to be *purely* cognitive beings (God?). So the Humean view also fails to capture what is distinctive of the mental.

On the assumption that there is a distinctive sort of conceptual phenomenology, together with the possibility that phenomenology in general need not be conscious, and the assumption that sensational and conceptual states are all the mental states there are, there is another way to characterize what distinguishes the mental from everything else. What thoughts, conscious and unconscious, and sensations, conscious and unconscious (and any other states, e.g., emotions or perceptions, that might be constructible out of them) all have in common is that they are *phenomenal*. I think Strawson is right when he says (1994: xi) that "the only distinctively mental phenomena are the phenomena of conscious experience," but that the implication that the phenomena of consciousness are *essentially* conscious can be questioned. What makes the phenomena of conscious experience—sensations, perceptions, thoughts, emotions, moods, etc.—*mental* is their having phenomenal properties, not their being conscious. The phenomena of consciousness are, *qua* mental, essentially phenomenal. *Phenomenality* is the mark of the mental.

Or it would be, if there were unconscious phenomenology. Given that it has not been conclusively established that there is, it is worth exploring other options.

6.6.2 Unconscious Consciousness

In this section I sketch a version of the Cartesian view that there can be no unconscious intentional states (because there can be no unconscious phenomenology), on which unconsciousness need not be an *intrinsic* property (or privation) of a mental state. I argue that there could be conscious states correctly attributable to an individual of which that individual is nonetheless unaware. That is, there could be states conscious *in themselves* that are not conscious *for* the individual whose states they are.

Clearly there exist conscious states that one is not directly aware of—viz., everyone *else's*. But is there any sense in which a conscious state that I am not directly aware of could nonetheless be *mine*? Is a conscious state *mine* if and only if it is conscious *for me*? To ask this is not to ask if a state is conscious if and only if it is conscious for *someone*. Maybe this is true (maybe consciousness presupposes a *self*). The question is whether when a conscious state is *mine* the someone *for* whom it is conscious has to be *me*. I think the answer is no. There is a sense of a conscious state's being *mine*—of being correctly attributable to me—that does not entail that I am directly aware of it.

Consider your own consciousness, your own direct awareness, in relation to the conscious states of another individual. Call her Penelope. You are not conscious, not directly aware, of Penelope's conscious thoughts: they are not part of your conscious experience. Why not? Presumably, at least in part, because you are physically distinct. Your brain and central nervous system produce your conscious experience, her brain and central nervous system produce hers, and the two are distinct systems.

But suppose they could be interconnected in such a way that Penelope's conscious thoughts begin to figure in the etiology of your behavior. Sometimes you do things because of what you consciously believe and desire; sometimes you do things because of what Penelope consciously believes and desires. In such a case the explanation of your behavior would occasionally have to advert to Penelope's conscious states. Though Penelope's thoughts are hers in the sense that they originate in her brain and not yours, and in the sense that she is directly aware of them and you are not, they must occasionally be cited in the course of rationalizing your behavior.

Now suppose that we transplant Penelope's brain, hooked up to yours in the same way as in the previous paragraph, into your skull. Given that Penelope's brain is now housed in your skull, I think there is reason to say that you now have two brains—just as we might say that you have two hearts if someone else's heart were transplanted into your chest alongside your original one. You are now a *double-brain* patient. You have (we may suppose) two distinct streams of consciousness flowing in your head, both of which have an influence on your behavior, but only one of which *you* are directly aware of.

Now suppose that only half of Penelope's brain is transplanted into your head, replacing the corresponding half of your brain, while remaining connected to the other half in such a way that her conscious states affect your behavior without your being directly aware of them. In this case you would be in significant ways like a *split-brain* patient. Such individuals also appear to host two distinct centers of consciousness in their skulls; yet we say these consciousnesses are both *theirs*. Moreover, we also say of them that their behaviors are theirs, though there is a detectable split in their etiologies: some behaviors are controlled by the right hemisphere and some are controlled by the left. If these are indeed two distinct centers of consciousness and control, the fact that they coexist in the same skull and exercise control over the same body nonetheless prompts us to attribute the conscious thoughts that figure in the etiology of the individual's behavior to the *same* individual. In these ways, your brain and Penelope's brain have become just like the two hemispheres of a split-brain patient—though instead of resulting from a fission, they result from a kind of fusion. Hence, if Penelope's brain is now your brain, then her conscious thoughts would be your thoughts in the additional sense that they arise from your brain.

Of course the split-brain patient's separate consciousnesses were once one (whatever exactly that might mean), and the separated hemispheres have a common history, whereas yours and Penelope's consciousnesses need never have been shared, and your brains have separate histories. And this might be taken to be (though I doubt that it is) sufficient reason to resist accepting that Penelope's brain is now yours (or a part of yours). But even if we concede that Penelope's brain has not become (part of) your brain, there is still a substantive sense in which Penelope's conscious thoughts are *yours*: they still have a direct effect on your behavior. We would have to refer to conscious states of the second brain in order to explain some of what you do. And this is after all just what the Freudian does in adverting to states of your brain that you are not aware of—because they are intrinsically unconscious—in order to explain your behavior. The difference is that these Penelope-brain states are not *intrinsically* unconscious, though they are unconscious *for you*—*you* are not directly aware of them. But there is the same reason to attribute them to you in the imagined case as there is to attribute unconscious states of your own brain in the Freudian case.

The moral of this thought experiment is this. It does not seem impossible that there could be, in my head, conscious thoughts that have direct effects on my behavior, but of which I am not directly aware. These would be thoughts conscious in themselves, but not conscious for me, yet still mine. They would be simultaneously conscious and unconscious, though in different ways. They would be conscious in the sense that they have phenomenal character (where this is thought of as *entailing* consciousness); but they would be unconscious in the sense that I am not directly aware of them.

The Penelope-brain could produce such thoughts, as could a split-brainer's hemispheres. In the latter case, the conscious thoughts of each hemisphere are, to the other, unconscious, though all are thoughts of the same individual. But then it also seems possible that some part(s) of a single, intact brain could do it too. Perhaps, assuming that consciousness requires a self, we all have a Penelope—or a multitude of perhaps permanent, perhaps momentary, Penelopes—in our heads, all of them capable of exerting some influence over our behavior, though none experienced as part of *us*. If consciousness does not require a self, a view of the sort sketched here would not have to populate our heads with any *others*, but merely with ownerless intrinsically conscious states. If this is possible, then what we call our unconscious states, because we are not conscious *of* them, may nonetheless be intrinsically conscious, and, hence, phenomenal; and they may be states of the individual in whose brain they arise in the functional sense of figuring in the etiology of the individual's behavior, and, hence, in rationalizing explanations of it.

6.7 Unconsciousness Contentlessness

I have argued that the only tenable options for phenomenal intentionalists in dealing with the question of unconscious thought are affirming that there is unconscious phenomenology and denying that there is unconscious thought. In previous sections I tried to motivate the affirmation. In this section I explore the feasibility of the denial—the view that genuine thought, exists, as Strawson puts it, *only* "in the conscious moment." Can we do without unconscious thought (or unconscious mentality in general)? The challenge is to offer satisfying accounts of apparent cases of unconscious thinking.

Consider the following question. Are there photographs on your computer's hard drive? It might seem that the answer is obviously *yes*—for one's photographs are *stored on* such things, are they not? And it seems straightforwardly true to say that if the drive is erased the photographs on it are erased, that one can copy one's photographs from the hard drive to a thumb drive, and so on.

On reflection, however, it ought to be clear that it is not *literally true* that there are photographs on your computer's hard drive. If you open it up and inspect the disk you will not find any photographs (little tiny images) there. Storing photographs on your hard drive is not like storing photographs in your photo album. What *is* on your hard drive are *encodings* of photographs, from which, given the proper sorts of programs and devices, the photographs can be *recreated* in an appropriate medium (your computer screen, a piece of paper). (This point is made in Strawson 1994, but Strawson does not draw the conclusion that unconscious states do not have intentional content.) The encodings are like *recipes* for making photographs. Obviously, instructions for making something are not the things that can be made from them. No one would confuse a cake recipe with a cake, or think that a cookbook has cakes in it. The spots on the disk where your pictures are "stored" are not pictures. They have no intrinsic photographic *content*. Given different interpreting programs and devices, they could be used to produce virtually anything—music, speech, cake recipes (another point made by Strawson). The content they can be used to produce is not content they *have*—either originally or derivatively.

I want to suggest that we can say something analogous about unconscious (non-phenomenal) neural states. Some of them code for (conscious) content, but do not possess content, either originally or derivatively. And I want to suggest, further, that sequences of these contentless states can link conscious episodes in such a way that they are appropriately related with respect to their contents.

Consider a computer program that alters photographs by processing non-photographic encodings of them, such that, for example, when a certain photograph is input (e.g., scanned and encoded), certain operations defined purely in terms of the code produce a new encoding of whatever kind of photograph one wants to end up with. For example, a program might govern the "colorizing" of a black-and-white photograph, *not by controlling the application of pigment to it*, but by altering its coding so that, in the context of the program/CPU/screen environment, a new screen image with the desired colorization is produced. No colors are involved in the *process*: there is no literal *coloring* going on in the computational process that produces the encoding of the colorized photograph. (Though of course there might be, if, say, a program controlled the application of colored ink to a printed photograph. But this is not what is going on *inside the computer*.) The processes the hardware and operating system make available can be *exploited* in such a way that desired results are achieved; but the processes themselves are neutral with respect to the photographic content they are used to produce. The same hardware and operating system can be programmed to do lots of other things, such as word processing or musical composition or arithmetical calculations.

Or, more relevantly, consider a computer program that yields, e.g., encodings of consequents of conditionals given encodings of the conditionals and their antecedents. *Pace* Turing, we are not constrained to treat the processes themselves as logical inferences, even if they produce logically entailed outputs. If they are non-conscious, and there is no unconscious content (because there is no unconscious experience), then such processes are not *inferences*, since inferences are transitions between contentful things (states, sentences, propositions,...). We can design programs to give results we recognize as logically entailed. And we do this in such a way that the program produces appropriate output for *arbitrary* input. But it does not follow that the computer (or the program) is *thinking*. We can insist that the computer (program) is not *deducing* consequents from conditionals and their antecedents, even if it is reliably *producing* representations of consequents from representations of conditionals and their antecedents. I would insist that it is not thinking because thinking is a kind of experience, and (by hypothesis because it is not conscious) it is not experiencing anything. (Affinities with Searle's views on computation and cognition should be obvious here.)

We can avail ourselves of all of the resources of computational theories of mind (whether "classical" or connectionist) in explaining how unconscious, meaningless, non-mental processes can reliably and logically subserve conscious thinking.

On naturalistic theories of intentionality (such as Dretske's or Fodor's or Millikan's), content is not an intrinsic property of states that have it. Content is *acquired* through the evolution or learning of *indication* relations (or *functions*). Thus, on such views, computation and content are metaphysically distinct. Even if our brains evolved their programs and acquired their contents concurrently, an unevolved physical duplicate of an evolved brain could still run the relevant formal programs. Its computational states would be meaningless; but so are the computational states of our evolved brains. Content accrues by virtue of the establishment of *relations* to objects and properties, and such states do not, *per se*, have the relevant relational properties.

On the view defended in this book, in contrast, content comes on the scene with a specific kind of *experience*. And while indication relations/functions can accrue to unconscious states as well as conscious ones, on the view I am exploring here the appearance of content—of *mind*—must leave unconscious states contentless, because experiential features are necessarily conscious, and *intrinsic* to the states that have them. On both views, however, the computational *brain* is metaphysically independent of the contentful *mind*, though the former can be programmed to subserve the latter.

So who programmed our brains?

Presumably, they got to be the way they are through evolutionary processes. So if they are programmed, evolutionary processes determine (or at least are involved in) their programming. Here's a (ridiculously simplistic) account of how it could have happened. Since the (macro) world is itself a logical place—there are no instantiated contradictory (macro) states of affairs, states of affairs in which p and if p then q are true are states of affairs in which q is true, etc.—the logical creatures survived and the illogical ones did not. That is, the ones whose representations of the facts that p and *if p then q* led them to act as if q were true fared better than those whose representations of the facts that q and *if p then q* led them to act as if p were true. Their brain processes are "designed" by evolution to "follow" rules of valid inference, much as systems of syntactic rules of deduction in formal systems (whether computationally implemented or not) are designed by us to be truth-preserving. So Nature programmed our brains.

However, *non-conscious* Nature cannot produce states with the kind of maximally fine-grained contents that our conscious thoughts have, and so cannot program the unconscious brain to subserve conscious states with such contents. There are distinctions we can make in conscious thought that non-conscious Nature cannot make. For example, consider the properties of triangularity and trilaterality. Since it is metaphysically necessary that anything that is triangular is trilateral, and vice versa, we cannot have encountered instances of triangularity that were not instances of trilaterality. So we cannot have acquired a brain mechanism whose function is to indicate triangularity whose function is not also to indicate trilaterality on the basis of our causal interactions with the world. Yet we can distinguish these properties in (conscious) thought. (This is, of course, the problem of the indeterminacy of causally individuated content discussed in Chapter 1.) And the same is true for *nomologically* necessarily co-instantiated properties, as well.

Thus, non-conscious Nature cannot produce brain states that encode for conscious states with such fine-grained contents, or program brain processes to respect the semantic relations among such conscious states. But *we* can do these things. So *consciousness* itself must have an important role in programming the brain. (That is, conscious *Nature* must have had a role in programming the brain. I do not want to suggest that consciousness is non-natural. I have no idea what it is. No one does.) Evolutionarily speaking, conscious creatures capable of finer-grained distinctions in content could evolve unconscious states encoding for such fine-grained conscious states, as well as unconscious processes that respect the content relations of the conscious states. But the pressure comes from above. The fine-grained distinctions available to consciousness are not available to unconscious Nature nor, therefore, to the unconscious brain. The unconscious brain must be molded by the conscious mind to subserve its fine-grained representational system. And this can also be a quite deliberate process, as when one *trains oneself* to think reflexively in accordance with certain rules of inference. What is laboriously grasped consciously can become unconsciously encoded and automatically processed. (Dretske's distinction between evolved and learned functions is echoed here.) The conscious mind programs the unconscious brain.

Thus, what happens when you get stuck on a philosophical problem, sleep on it, and wake up to its solution is that unconscious processes that have been "trained up" (by your conscious philosophical studies) to respect contents their constituent states cannot instantiate chug away while you are sleeping and eventually produce an encoding of a solution, which becomes conscious when you do.

And what happens when you repress hideous desires directed at your parents is that you (somehow) force them out of consciousness. However, (somehow) unconscious encodings of them persist (perhaps because they are very strong). And these encodings can be processed into encodings of things like intentions to do away with one parent and marry the other. When these in turn threaten or begin to produce the conscious states they encode, you become extremely nervous and feel compelled to wash your hands every five minutes. (Or something.)

But how can there be unconscious encodings of fine-grained conscious contents, if such contents are unconsciously unavailable?

The idea is that since the unconscious system cannot represent such contents, it cannot encode them—it, so to speak, does not know what needs to be encoded, and so cannot produce a structure that encodes it. (A computer cannot, from scratch, program itself to colorize correctly.) But the conscious mind *does* know what needs to be encoded, and so can marshal unconscious encoding processes to produce appropriate structures. Less fancifully, the relevant fine-grained meanings are explicitly present in consciousness. Hence, they are available to whatever the process is by which we consciously train our unconscious brain processes. (E.g., learning to play the piano.) Do not ask how the unconscious brain could produce conscious states with fine-grained contents in the first place. Explaining it would require a solution to the mind-body problem, which nobody has.

But if unconscious brain activity can *produce* such fine-grained contents, why cannot it *instantiate* them? How can the unconscious brain lack properties the conscious mind has if it has the capacity to produce them? Why can it not secure them for itself?

Mind-body problem again (bottom-up). If unconscious processes can produce states that are *conscious* (we *know* they can) without themselves being conscious, then why should they not be able to produce states with *other* properties they do not have?

6.7.1 The Causal Role of Content

It is worth noting that this view also makes available a solution to a causation-in-virtue-of-content problem. This is the problem of making content relevant to the causal explanation of behavior, and it arises wherever content is construed in such a way that it is neither constituted by those very causal relations (functionalist and conceptual role theories) nor an intrinsic property of the states that have it.

On a naturalistic view like Fodor's, the problem takes the form of an inconsistent tetrad of principles, all of which we see reason to accept. The first is that states such as beliefs and desires are causes of behavior. The second is that beliefs and desires have the causal powers they do with respect to behavior because they have the contents they do. The third is that states have their causal powers in virtue of their intrinsic properties. The fourth is that content properties are not intrinsic properties.

If phenomenal properties are intrinsic causal-power-conferring properties, then the phenomenal content thesis does not face the problem faced by theories like Fodor's and Dretske's. (See Taylor 2017a, b.) Assuming, however, that we cannot understand how phenomenal properties could be physical, and so supposing that they are not, the problem is that even if they are intrinsic, we cannot understand how they could confer causal powers. So we cannot understand how beliefs and desires could cause actions because of what they are beliefs in and desires for.

The solution I propose is a lot like Dretske's solution to the problem for naturalistic theories. Dretske (1988, 1989, 1993) argues that it can be the case that one state causes another *because* it has the externally constituted content it does, if its having that content is a *structuring cause* of its effect. That is, the fact that the state represents what it does is a reason for its causing what it causes because it was "recruited," by evolution or through learning, to perform a certain function in a system because it represents what it does. To use Dretske's analogy, it is like a bimetallic strip being assigned the function of controlling the operation of a furnace because its states co-vary in a lawful way with ambient temperature.

Similarly, we can say that the properties that are doing the causing are the intrinsic properties of the encoding brain states. *Those* properties are, of course, not content properties; but the *causal structure* of the system of encoding states—which states cause which—is controlled by a program that is "written" by the conscious mind.

So, suppose you consciously teach yourself that a material conditional with a false antecedent is true. That is, when you consciously think of a conditional that it has a false antecedent, you consciously apply this rule and consciously infer that (think that) the conditional is true. Because this is counterintuitive (no one speaks First Order), you have to keep reminding yourself of the rule, and explicitly making the inference. But eventually it becomes automatic: when you encounter a conditional with a false antecedent, the conscious thought that it is true immediately occurs to you. The "inference" itself has become unconscious. The state encoding the content of the thought that a particular conditional has a false antecedent—call it ES_1—hooks up with the encoding of the rule that conditionals with false antecedents are true—call it ES_2. Together (because of their intrinsic causal powers) ES_1 and ES_2 cause the encoding of the thought that the conditional in question is true—ES_3, which forthwith gets decoded into consciousness. This little unconscious mechanism was set up by the conscious rehearsal of the inference. And it was given the causal structure it has *because of* what ES_1, ES_2 and ES_3 code for—that is, *because* the conscious states have the content they do. Meanwhile, at the level of causation there's no competition between mental (content) properties and physical properties; the former do not occur there, so the latter are completely in charge. But conscious content properties are not epiphenomenal, since it is because of them that the contentless encoding states have the causal relations they do.

Conscious thought is a structuring cause of unconscious, contentless processes. As such it could be, both phylogenetically and ontogenetically, a significant contributor to the evolving circuitry of the brain. Dretske cautions that we should not take the thermostat/furnace analogy too seriously, since its construction requires an engineer, and so presupposes intentionality, whereas we cannot presuppose intentionality in telling the story of how the engineer got engineered. But he does recognize that, through learning, we can to an extent engineer ourselves. And I am suggesting that consciousness plays an important role in this self-engineering. It can grasp and encode contents that unconscious Nature cannot; and it can structure unconscious processes in accordance with these contents in such a way that the processes respect fine-grained content relations and can also be said to be as they are because they encode what they do.

This leaves untouched the problem of "downward" causation in virtue of content—i.e., the problem of how conscious states with fine-grained content can bring about the relevant unconscious encoding states. I am content to pair it with the "upward" problem of how the unconscious brain produces conscious states with fine-grained content, and to declare that I have nothing to say about it. We know it happens, but we do not understand how it is possible. (Mind-body metaphysics is a mug's game.)

6.8 Concluding Remarks

I have suggested three ways to respond to the unconscious thought challenge to the phenomenal intentionality of thought thesis. The first argues for unconscious states with intrinsic phenomenal properties; the second denies that there can be such states, and postulates intrinsically conscious states not conscious for their possessor. The third denies that there are unconscious thoughts, but shows how unconscious states lacking content could encode conscious content and be processed in ways that respect fine-grained content relations.

Though of course it could not be the case that there is and is not unconscious phenomenology, or that there is and is not unconscious thought, it could nonetheless be that there are unconscious intrinsically phenomenal states, intrinsically conscious states unconscious for their possessor, *and* contentless encoding states faithfully subserving conscious states with fine-grained content. That is, it is possible that we host all three of these kinds of states. And each kind might have its own sort of function. But if I had to choose, I would go with the third option.

7
Conceptual Reference

The focus of this book has been what we can call "intensional intentionality"—i.e., the kind of meaningfulness or contentfulness that a concept that lacks an extension (e.g., PHLOGISTON, THE LARGEST NATURAL NUMBER) can have.[1] The thesis I have defended is that intensional intentional content is phenomenally constituted. Some might complain that this addresses only part of the phenomenon of intentionality, or even that it does not address it at all. The notion of intentionality and its cohorts (e.g., aboutness, ofness) are also standardly applied to relations between intentional states and the things they represent. Thoughts of or about things in this sense are susceptible to evaluation with respect to relational properties such as reference, extension, truth conditions and truth values. Such extensional intentionality has been seen as either all there is to intentionality, the foundation of it, its most important kind, or at least an aspect of it that must be accounted for by any satisfactory theory of it. (Cf. Fodor and Pylyshyn (2015: 158): "...reference and truth are the only semantic properties of mental or linguistic representations"; Lewis (1970: 18): "Semantics with no treatment of truth conditions is not semantics.") After all, what are thoughts for, if not for thinking about things? At best, the complaint might continue, what I have defended is a phenomenal theory of *narrow* intentionality or content, and left half the job of accounting for intentionality undone.

If by a narrow/wide distinction is meant simply the good old-fashioned distinction between sense and reference (intension and extension, connotation and denotation), I have no problem with it. But if what is meant is the distinction introduced (by Putnam) and developed (by Fodor and others) to mark a distinction with respect to *content*—i.e., what is expressed by 'that'-clauses (Loar 1988); *what* one is thinking—I reject it. I do not deny that reference, extension, truth conditions and truth value are genuine semantic properties. Nor do I claim that the phenomenal intentionalist can blithely ignore them and their relations to internally determined semantic properties. But I do think that extensional individuation of conceptual content is unmotivated, and, consequently, that a bifurcated notion of content is otiose. The classic externalist thought experiments do not support it; and the psychosemantics of indexical and nominal concepts does not need it.

---

[1] I mean this term to get at what is characterized as "narrow" content, but without the implication of the narrow–wide distinction.

And I cannot have it, since it is strictly prohibited by the phenomenal intentionality of thought thesis: extensional relata and relations cannot in general be constitutive or determinative of conceptual content if content is an intrinsic phenomenal property of the states that have it.[2]

If, however, the complaint is that the phenomenalist owes an account of how conceptual phenomenology determines or mediates reference and extension, especially such relations to external objects and properties, then it is both worthy of reply and addressable.

For a phenomenal intentionality of thought theorist such as myself, extensional semantic properties, while not quite second-class citizens, are yet dependent upon intrinsic intensional semantic properties to provide them useful work. When it comes to thoughts and concepts, cognitive-phenomenal content comes first. We cannot think about things, or know what is the case with them, unless we have materials to think and know with: we cannot entertain concepts that have extensions, or thoughts that have truth values, until we have concepts and thoughts to entertain. Moreover, we can think thoughts that are not, in the referential sense, about anything. (Indeed, an active mind in an empty universe would have nothing at all to think about, in this sense.)

An externalist (or empiricist) might say that our conceptual repertoire is bestowed upon us by our causal congress with the world, and so external semantic relations come first: we cannot think or know anything about the world we inhabit until we have interacted with it. But if conceptual contents are phenomenally constituted and individuated, then, since phenomenology is internally determined and instantiated, conceptual contents cannot be installed from the outside. Even if it is true that (some) concepts are *activated by* relations to our external environment, it is not the case that such relations create their contents.

Still, there is an elegance and efficiency in the way externalist theories bring content and extension together, which it may seem a shame to give up. Causal-informational approaches have the virtue of establishing general conceptual content and extension simultaneously[3]: the properties instances of which reliably cause tokenings of conceptual representations (in the proper circumstances) are their contents, and the extensions of those properties are the extensions of the concepts. Moreover, the extensions of concepts acquired in this way are guaranteed to be non-empty (at least at the time of acquisition), since they are acquired on the basis of interactions with instances of the properties. And it may seem that

---

[2] An exception with respect to relata is thoughts that contain thoughts or concepts they are about. My thought I HAVE HAD OCCASION TO REVISIT MY OPINION THAT MOZART IS BORING, for example, contains and is therefore partially constituted by the thought MOZART IS BORING, which is also the referent of the concept MY OPINION THAT MOZART IS BORING (or its that-clause). Note, however, that that concept is not the concept it is *because it refers to* that thought. Its identity is determined by its intrinsic phenomenal properties.

[3] Direct reference theories do the same for particular (nominal, indexical definite-descriptive) concepts.

phenomenal intentionalism cannot do this. And if it does not (or cannot) offer an alternative account, it may appear to be theoretically hobbled in comparison with externalist views, or at least relatively inelegant. Fortunately, however, there are familiar non-externalist ways to connect content and extension, which can be straightforwardly adapted by the phenomenal intentionalist.

Perceptual experience acquaints us with external objects and properties, and thereby provides opportunities to refer to and characterize them in thought and language through the application of concepts. But I think there is also a substantive sense in which perceptual experiences themselves, unconceptualized, *refer to* such things. (Cf. Chastain 1975; Burge 2022: 16: "Perceptual states function to refer to—to pick out—particular entities in the environment"; and Loar 2003 (the "paint that purports to point").) The things we perceive are the objects of our perceptual experience (what we perceive), analogously to the way in which the things we conceive of are the objects of our thought (what we think about). For something to be a perceptual object for us is for it to be singled out and presented as distinct from yet present to the subject—as out there, in the mind-independent world, yet at the same time spatially related to us in specific ways, and capable of being acted upon and acting upon us.[4] Perceptual experience is thus a kind of *passive* reference—it refers us to objects. (Conceptual reference, in contrast, is (often enough) something a subject does, even in cases in which perception provides referents. Whereas in perception objects are *given*, in thought they are *pursued*.)

This sort of reference is not simply causal relation to objects, but experiential presentation of objects to the subject. A pure causal theory says that a perceptual state refers to a thing if that thing causes the state. But more is required for what I have in mind. An experience of an elephant caused by a refrigerator does not perceptually refer one to the refrigerator. Causal relations are necessary for perceptual experiences to be veridical (for them to be of existing external objects); but such relations, and, hence, veridicality, are not given in perceptual experience. (Nor is the identity of particulars, as discussed below.) Perceptual referentiality, on the other hand, is phenomenally present in perceptual experience. Only certain kinds of experiences refer us to refrigerators.

Perceptual reference enables particular conceptual reference, including indexical and nominal reference, as well as the reference of other concepts whose contents are necessary but not sufficient to determine a referent or extension. One might, for example, use the concept SHE demonstratively to single out a particular female presented in perception, in the course of thinking the thought SHE IS A PHILOSOPHER of her. Or use the concept A BEARER OF THIS NAME, with

---

[4] I think it is arguable that this combination of distinctness from yet presence to the self is the essence of intentionality—of what it is for something to be an object of thought or perception for us. (Cf. Frey 2013.)

accompanying display of the name 'Kati', to refer to a particular bearer of that name, in the course of thinking the thought KATI IS A PHILOSOPHER of her. Or use the concept THE MAN AT THE BAR DRINKING A LOUIS JADOT MONTRACHET to single out a particular man one sees drinking a Louis Jadot Montrachet at a bar. Perceptual experience can provide a context in which the application of such concepts can pick out particular individuals, and allow us to think thoughts about them. So phenomenalist accounts of singular perceptual reference and conceptual reference based on perceptual experience are available.

In the case of things not present in perception, additional thoughts or concepts can play the same role for singular thought. For example, I might think the thought SHE IS A PHILOSOPHER of the person I saw yesterday by also deploying the concept THE WOMAN I SAW YESTERDAY ON OKTOBER 6 UTCA, or think the thought KATI IS A PHILOSOPHER of that same person by also entertaining the concept THE KATI WHO IS MARRIED TO TIM. (Imagery can also provide or supplement context for conceptual reference.) As I argued in Chapters 4 and 5, however, such additional identifying conceptual (or imagistic) content need not (cannot) be crammed into indexical, nominal and definite-descriptive concepts. It may be seen, like perceptual experience, as presenting a context in which the tokening of a general concept refers to a particular individual. Such concepts are not "incomplete" because they do not determine particular reference on their own.

On the view defended in this book, conceptual contents are one and all descriptive, and, hence, one and all general. There are no coherent concepts that are not by nature potentially true of different things in different contexts. This includes indexical, nominal and definite-descriptive concepts, as well as highly specific (even maximal) concepts that designate one and only one individual in the actual world—for example, COMPOSER WHO WAS BORN IN BAYONNE, NEW JERSEY ON MAY 6, 1915 TO RUSSIAN IMMIGRANTS, GREW UP ON FARMS IN WISCONSIN AND INDIANA, SERVED IN THE US ARMY FROM 1943 TO 1946, PUBLISHED HIS FIFTH STRING QUARTET IN 1960 AND DIED ON JANUARY 23, 2009. (It also includes *de facto* rigid definite-descriptive concepts, which are yet intrinsically suited to have different referents in different possible worlds, even if objective facts conspire to prevent them from doing so.)

There are no singular concepts (or thoughts) as these are understood by direct reference theorists. Getting a thing into a thought (to use Bach's phrase (Bach 2010)) is, I have argued, in general not possible. Thoughts are *sui generis* cognitive experiences, while most of the things we think about are not. (The exceptions being, again, thoughts and concepts themselves.) The Principle of Phenomenal Purity forbids non-phenomenal objects from being constituents of phenomenal states (both cognitive and perceptual). A "singular concept," in my parlance, is a concept apt for singular *reference*, not one having singular *content*; and "singular reference" is reference to one thing. The kind of singularity the direct reference theorist wants for thoughts is not available experientially. Whereas causal relations can make it the case that one is thinking of (or perceiving) a particular object *o*, as opposed to a distinct but qualitatively identical object *o**, this fact is neither determined by representational properties of concepts (or percepts) nor present in the experience of thinkers (or perceivers). Neither perception nor conception can register the *haecceity* of individual concrete objects. (Which is not to say that haecceity itself cannot be conceptually represented.) They can only give us *individuality* and *distinctness*.

We can have perceptual experiences of an individual thing (a ripe persimmon on a gray table), and of several distinct, qualitatively indistinguishable things (three ripe persimmons on a gray table). And one and the same singular concept can be used to think of an individual or of distinct individuals. One could think THAT PERSIMMON LOOKS DELICIOUS of one or more of three qualitatively identical persimmons one sees. But we cannot *see* whether or not three qualitatively identical persimmons presented to us individually are two or more different persimmons or the same persimmon three times. And even a concept like THE OBJECT I AM PERCEIVING RIGHT HERE AND NOW, WHICH IS NOT IDENTICAL TO ANY OTHER INDISTINGUISHABLE OBJECT I MIGHT HAVE BEEN PERCEIVING RIGHT HERE AND NOW cannot on its own give us an object in its uniqueness. Causal relations can connect us to one among the many indistinguishable things we could be perceiving or thinking of. But such relations are experientially inaccessible. The twin veils of perception and conception cannot be penetrated by either perception or conception.[5]

All concepts are general. So, the fundamental question facing the phenomenal intentionalist is how such concepts acquire their type-extensions. The extensions of complex concepts can be derived from the extensions of their ultimate constituents and their structural relations. So the focus is really on the extensions of simple concepts.[6] Since I am not sure I know what those are, however, I use complex concepts as examples.

Causal (and other) accounts of content typically take conceptual contents to be objectual properties. Their story about how concepts get their contents is the story of how they latch on to the properties whose extensions they inherit, which properties are their contents. For example, the content of the (adjectival) concept LIQUID is the property *liquidity* (*being liquid*)—the property that things in its extension instantiate. On the phenomenalist view, however, as noted above, conceptual contents are phenomenal types tokened in experience: minds *instantiate* rather than *represent* (or *express*) conceptual contents. So the content of the concept LIQUID, for example, cannot be the property *liquidity*, since this would

---

[5] Obviously, I am not a direct realist. I find direct realism about as plausible as the claim that an empty frame held up to a landscape is a painting of it. (See also Section 3.3.)
[6] I distinguish *simple* concepts from *primitive* concepts, as follows. Simple concepts have no conceptual constituents. Primitive concepts are (like simple concepts) not definable, but may nonetheless have conceptual constituents. I think color concepts are like this (see Pitt 1999).

entail that minds liquefy (instantiate liquidity; become liquid) when they entertain the concept LIQUID. This would be unfortunate (if it is even possible).

So, for the phenomenalist, conceptual contents can be neither the properties they pick out nor the extensions of those properties. They must be a third kind of thing, and their relations to those properties and extensions must be a relation other than identity. They must be something like Fregean senses, only psychologized.

Frege held that concept words refer to (*bedeuten*) functions from objects to truth values—what he called "concepts" (what I am calling "properties")—which have objects "falling under" them (values of the functions; instantiators of the properties) in their extensions. The concept-word thereby has the extension of the property. Moreover, a concept-word refers to the property it does in virtue of its sense (Frege 1891: 149). Since, for Frege, senses are descriptive, and it is in virtue of their senses that referring expressions have their extensions, it follows that concept-word senses denote properties by describing them. (I should note that when I say Fregean senses are *descriptive*, I do not mean that they are one and all expressible by complex linguistic expressions. Surely some are simple. What I mean is that they are identity conditions for their extensions.)

The phenomenal intentionalist can say something analogous about conceptual contents. They are conceptual-phenomenal types: *phenomenalized* senses. More precisely, on the phenomenalist view, concepts *are* contents—conceptual type-phenomenologies; and concept tokens are tokens of those phenomenal types (contents), not content-expressing syntactically individuated representational "vehicles." There are no mental analogs of Frege's concept-words. However, like Fregean senses, conceptual experience types denote properties, and thereby inherit their extensions. Whereas Frege thought that senses are *sui generis* non-mental abstract particulars, I think (perhaps along with Husserl; but who can tell?) they are *sui generis* abstract mental (experiential) types. My view, as detailed in my 2009 paper "Intentional Psychologism" (which might just as well have been entitled "Intensional Psychologism"), is a kind of *type* psychologism.[7]

But how is it that conceptual phenomenology has descriptive power? In virtue of what is it that such phenomenology establishes a representational link between a purely mental, experiential state and the property that provides its extension? This problem is especially acute in the case of objective, non-mental properties

---

[7] Mendelovici (2018: ch. 9, app. G) argues that phenomenal contents must be taken to be concrete tokens, not abstract types, since one is never directly acquainted with abstract types, as one is with the contents of one's occurrent conscious thoughts. However, insofar as thoughts are repeatable and shareable, there is good reason to identify them (i.e., propositional contents) with types. And there is, furthermore, no special reason not to. Types are *generalizations* of what we are aware of in our particular experiences of tokens. They are theoretical entities. I see no difficulty in the idea that in general we are indirectly acquainted with the natures of types in virtue of being directly acquainted with their tokens (cf. Pitt 2018). (Shall we say that *pain* is not a feeling-type because we cannot feel abstract objects?)

(how, for example, could the mind latch on to *liquidity* or *electronegativity*, *a priori*?). But it also besets non-conceptual mental properties (*painfulness, loudness*). If the world does not reach into the mind via causal relations, creating world-facing contents and securing their extensions, but, instead, the mind reaches out to the world, how does it do it?

I would assume that Frege thought that his senses in general are intrinsically, primitively descriptive-intentional. (If in fact he did not think this, I think he should have. Burge (1979b: 425; my emphasis) seems to interpret him in this way: "Frege required that senses be sufficiently complete to determine their associated referents *by their very nature.*") Senses do not inherit their intentional contents from anything else; they *are* intentional contents.

And the same is true for conceptual phenomenology. It is intrinsically, primitively, inexplicably, descriptively intentional. It is *of its nature* to be *about* things—to point beyond itself; to *describe*. To ask how it is that conceptual phenomenology can describe is like asking how it is that pain can hurt. These are basic facts.

When we reflect on our conscious thoughts, we are directly aware of their contents, as well as the fact that those contents point beyond themselves—that they are *of* things (in the non-referential sense). We do not need to seek out and become aware of external relations in order to determine what they are and what they are about. We do not need to ask ourselves "How is it that this concept is about what it is about?" or "How is it that this concept is C and not some other concept C*?"—any more than we need to ask ourselves "How is it that this sensation is itchy?" or "How is it that this smell is musty and not fruity?" It is revealed through introspection that this is what they are, intrinsically, by nature. Such is the way of phenomenology in general. Our awareness of our thoughts is awareness of their intentional contents, because our thoughts *are* intentional contents. And in becoming aware of their contents we become aware of their intentionality—their sheer *aboutness*. (Just as we become aware of the *visuality* of visual experiences in having them, and of *phenomenality* in having any conscious experience at all.) Our primal encounter with intentionality is our encounter with the contents of our own minds, and is the basis for the notion of intentionality itself.

So it turns out that phenomenal intentionalism establishes type extension and contents simultaneously, after all—though the order of determination is reversed. It is not that a concept is the concept it is because it has the extension it does: a concept has the (type) extension it does because it is the concept it is. What has not been recovered, however, is a general automatic connection between conceptual content and worldly properties. There is no assurance that the way we conceive of the world, the things in it, and their properties, is the way it is—that the property a concept denotes is the property characteristic of things we use the concept to refer to, or that there even is such a property.

If the content of a concept is a particular property because instantiations of the property are what cause its tokenings, then it cannot fail to be the case that things in the extension of the concept are things in the extension of the property. What we think things in the extension of such a concept are must be what they are, since the contents of our thinking are in pre-established harmony with the properties things have. But if content is internally, non-causally, internally determined, there is no such guarantee.[8] We encounter things and form concepts of them and their properties, but we cannot in general be certain that the concepts we form denote those properties. We may get things badly wrong. We may get properties like shape, size and number right most of the time (since, arguably, they appear to us as they are). But our concepts of properties like *solidity*, *temperature*, *magnetism*, *equinity*, *life* are often shots in the dark that miss their intended targets. A concept of properties like this formed in response to causal interaction with objects need not be properties the objects actually have. If we happen to get it right without further ado, it is a matter of luck.

But this is no special cause for alarm, and it is not a fault that can be laid at the phenomenal intentionalist's doorstep. It is the human condition. Indeed, I think it is very implausible that we should, simply by virtue of our causal interaction with the world, come to know its nature, as causal-informational-teleological psychosemantics would seem to have it. This strikes me as of a piece with the overreaching ambition of defeating traditional philosophical skepticism with linguistic and psychological externalism. It is simply too good to be true (and a bit hubristic). We form concepts in response to our interactions with worldly things that exist independently of us, and whose nature we are not directly and certainly acquainted with. Typically, it takes time and effort to attune our concepts to the properties that are in fact instantiated by the things we encounter and wish to understand the nature of, and there is always the chance we have gotten things wrong. Such is the lot of science.

With this phenomenalist account of conceptual extension, I have done all I think I need to do to address the complaint this chapter began with. Some will be disappointed (or annoyed) that my answer to the question "How does conceptual phenomenology determine extension?" is, essentially, *It just does*. But given the nature of phenomenology in general, I think this kind of answer is to be expected. It is the nature of conceptual experiences to describe, just as it is the nature of sounds to sound and smells to smell. These are facts that have no further explanation. They are fundamental, like facts about properties and relations of

---

[8] Except of course in the case of *a priori* concepts, such as those of theoretical, fictional or abstract objects, where we would rather say that their extensions are empty, not that we got the natures of the things in their extensions wrong. (We do not say we got the nature of caloric wrong because heat phenomena are not fluid-based, or that we got the nature of witches wrong because no women have magical powers derived from satanic sources. Nor do we say that we have misconstrued the nature of squares because square things are not two-dimensional.)

elementary particles. This is just the way the world is. It is not a failing of physics that it declares basic facts to be inexplicable. Likewise, it is not a failing of the phenomenal intentionality of thought thesis that, having placed thought in the general category of experience, it declares the thoughtiness of thought to be a primitive feature of it. This is just the way experience is.

Bibliography

Adams, F. R., and Aizawa, K. 1997. "Fodor's Asymmetric Causal Dependency Theory and Proximal Projections," *Southern Journal of Philosophy* 35: 433–7.
Antony, L., and Levine, J. 1991. "The Nomic and the Robust," in B. Loewer and G. Rey, eds., *Meaning in Mind: Fodor and His Critics*, Oxford: Blackwell: 1–16.
Armstrong, D. M. 1981. *The Nature of Mind and Other Essays*, Brisbane: University of Queensland Press.
Armstrong, D. M. 1991. "Searle's Neo-Cartesian Theory of Consciousness," in Villanueva 1991: 67–71.
Bach, K. 1981. "What's in a Name," *Australasian Journal of Philosophy* 59: 371–86.
Bach, K. 1994. *Thought and Reference* (revised version), Oxford: Clarendon Press.
Bach, K. 1988. "Burge's New Thought Experiment: Back to the Drawing Room," *Journal of Philosophy* 85: 88–97.
Bach, K. 2002. "Georgione Was So-called Because of His Name," *Philosophical Perspectives: Language and Mind* 16, Atascadero, CA: Ridgeview Publishing Co.: 73–103.
Bach, K. 2010. "Getting a Thing into a Thought," in R. Jeshion, ed., *New Essays on Singular Thought*, Oxford: Oxford University Press: 39–63.
Balog, K. 1999. "Conceivability, Possibility, and the Mind-Body Problem," *Philosophical Review* 108: 497–528.
Balog, K. 2012. "In Defense of the Phenomenal Concept Strategy," *Philosophy and Phenomenological Research* 84: 1–23.
Bayne, T., and McClelland, T. 2016. "'Finding the Feel': The Matching Content Challenge to Cognitive Phenomenology," *Phenomenology and Mind* 10: 26–43.
Bayne, T., and Montague, M., eds., 2011a. *Cognitive Phenomenology*, Oxford: Oxford University Press.
Bayne, T., and Montague, M. 2011b. "Cognitive Phenomenology: An Introduction," in Bayne and Montague 2011a: 1–34.
Bilgrami, A. 1992. *Belief and Meaning*, Oxford: Blackwell.
Block, N. 1986. "Advertisement for a Semantics for Psychology," *Midwest Studies in Philosophy* 10, Minneapolis: University of Minnesota Press: 615–78.
Block, N. 2001. "Paradox and Cross Purposes in Recent Work on Consciousness," *Cognition* 79, 197–219.
Block, N. 2007. "Max Black's Objection to Mind-Body Identity," in T. Alter and S. Walter, eds., *Phenomenal Concepts and Phenomenal Knowledge: New Essays on Consciousness and Physicalism*, Oxford: Oxford University Press: 249–306.
Block, N. 2023. *The Border Between Seeing and Thinking*, New York: Oxford University Press.
Brentano, F. (1874/1973). *Psychology from an Empirical Standpoint*, London: Routledge & Kegan Paul.
Brewer, B. 2008. "How to Account for Illusion," in Macpherson and Haddock 2008: 168–80.
Broad, C. D. 1925. *The Mind and Its Place in Nature*, London: Routledge & Kegan Paul.
Burge, T. 1973. "Reference and Proper Names," *Journal of Philosophy* 70: 425–39.

Burge, T. 1978. "Belief and Synonymy," *Journal of Philosophy* 75: 119-38.
Burge, T. 1979a. "Individualism and the Mental," in P. A. French, T. E. Uehling, and H. K. Wettstein, eds., *Midwest Studies in Philosophy, Vol. IV*, Minnesota: University of Minnesota Press: 73-121.
Burge, T. 1979b. "Sinning Against Frege," *The Philosophical Review* 88: 398-432.
Burge, T. 1982a. "Two Thought Experiments Reviewed," *Notre Dame Journal of Formal Logic* 23: 284-95.
Burge, T. 1982b. "Other Bodies," in Woodfield 1982: 97-120.
Burge, T. 1986. "Intellectual Norms and Foundations of Mind," *Journal of Philosophy* 83: 697-720.
Burge, T. 1989. "Individuation and Causation in Psychology," *Pacific Philosophical Quarterly* 70: 303-22.
Burge, T. 2007. "Postscript to 'Individualism and the Mental," in *Foundations of Mind: Philosophical Essays, Volume 2*, Oxford: Oxford University Press: 151-81.
Burge, T. 2010. *Origins of Objectivity*, Oxford: Oxford University Press.
Burge, T. 2022. *Perception: First Form of Mind*, Oxford: Oxford University Press.
Byrne, A. 2005. "Introspection," *Philosophical Topics* 33: 79-104.
Byrne, A. 2008. "Knowing That I Am Thinking," in A. E. Hatzimoysis, ed., *Self-Knowledge*, Oxford: Oxford University Press: 105-24.
Byrne, A. 2011. "Transparency, Belief, Intention," *Aristotelian Society Supplementary Volume* 85: 201-21.
Byrne, A. 2018. *Transparency and Self-Knowledge*, Oxford: Oxford University Press.
Byrne, A., and Tye, M. 2006. "Qualia Ain't in the Head," *Noûs* 40: 241-55.
Carruthers, P., and Veillet, B. 2011. "The Case Against Cognitive Phenomenology," in Bayne and Montague 2011a: 35-56.
Carruthers, P., and Veillet, B. 2017. "Consciousness Operationalized, a Debate Realigned," *Consciousness and Cognition* 55: 79-90.
Chalmers, D. J. 1996. *The Conscious Mind: In Search of a Fundamental Theory*, New York, Oxford University Press.
Chalmers, D. J. 2003. "The Content and Epistemology of Phenomenal Belief," in Q. Smith and A. Jokic, eds., *Consciousness: New Philosophical Perspectives*, Oxford: Oxford University Press: 220-72.
Chalmers, D. J. 2004. "The Representational Character of Experience," in B. Leiter, ed., *The Future for Philosophy*, Oxford: Oxford University Press: 153-81.
Chalmers, D. J. 2006. "Perception and the Fall from Eden," in T. Szabó Gendler and J. Hawthorne, eds., *Perceptual Experience*, Oxford: Clarendon Press: 49-125.
Chalmers, D. J. 2007. "Phenomenal Concepts and the Explanatory Gap," in T. Alter and S. Walter, eds., *Phenomenal Concepts and Phenomenal Knowledge: New Essays on Consciousness and Physicalism*, Oxford: Oxford University Press: 167-94.
Chalmers, D. J. 2010a. *The Character of Consciousness*, New York: Oxford University Press.
Chalmers, D. J. 2010b. "Perception and the Fall from Eden," in Chalmers 2010: 381-454.
Chalmers, D. J. 2010c. "Appendix: Two-Dimensional Semantics," in Chalmers 2010a: 541-68.
Chalmers, D. J. 2017. "Naturalistic Dualism," in M. Velmans and S. Schneider, eds., *The Blackwell Companion to Consciousness*, 2nd edition, Hoboken, NJ: Wiley & Sons: 363-73.
Chastain, C. 1975. "Reference and Context," in K. Gunderson, ed., *Minnesota studies in the philosophy of science 7: Language, Mind, and Knowledge*, Minneapolis: University of Minnesota Press: 194-269.

Chudnoff, E. 2015a. "Phenomenal Contrast Arguments for Cognitive Phenomenology," *Philosophy and Phenomenological Research* 90: 82–104.
Chudnoff, E. 2015b. *Cognitive Phenomenology*, London: Routledge.
Chudnoff, E. 2021. *Forming Impressions: Expertise in Perception and Intuition*, New York: Oxford University Press.
Coleman, S. 2022a. "Intentionality, Qualia, and the Stream of Unconsciousness," *Phenomenology and Mind* 22: 42–53.
Coleman, S. 2022b. "The Ins and Outs of Conscious Belief," *Philosophical Studies* 179: 517–48.
Coleman, S. Forthcoming. "An Argument for Unconscious Mental Qualities," *Australasian Journal of Philosophy*.
Conee, E. 1994. "Phenomenal Knowledge," *Australasian Journal of Philosophy* 72: 136–50.
Crane, T. 1991. "All the Difference in the World," *Philosophical Quarterly* 41: 1–25.
Crane, T. 1998. "Intentionality as the mark of the mental," in A. O'Hear, ed., *Contemporary Issues in the Philosophy of Mind*, Cambridge: Cambridge University Press.
Crane, T. 2009. "Is Perception a Propositional Attitude?", *Philosophical Quarterly* 59: 452–69.
Crane, T. 2014. *Aspects of Psychologism*, Cambridge, MA: Harvard University Press.
Crane, T. and Mellor, D. H. 1990. "There Is No Question of Physicalism," *Mind* 99: 185–206.
Davidson, D. 1979. "Quotation," *Theory and Decision* 11: 27–40.
Donnellan, K. 1978. "Speaker Reference, Descriptions, and Anaphora," in P. Cole, ed., *Syntax and Semantics 9: Pragmatics*, New York: Academic Press: 47–68.
Dretske, F. 1981. *Knowledge and the Flow of Information*, Cambridge, MA: MIT Press.
Dretske, F. 1986. "Misrepresentation," in R. Bogdan, ed., *Belief: Form, Content, and Function*, Oxford: Oxford University Press: 17–36.
Dretske, F. 1988. *Explaining Behavior*, Cambridge, MA: MIT Press.
Dretske, F. 1989. "Reasons and Causes," *Philosophical Perspectives 3: Philosophy of Mind and Action Theory*, Atascadero, CA: Ridgeview Publishing Co.: 1–15.
Dretske, F. 1995. *Naturalizing the Mind*, Cambridge, MA: MIT Press.
Dretske, F. 1996. "Phenomenal Externalism, or if Meanings Ain't in the Head, Where Are Qualia?," *Philosophical Issues* 7: 143–58.
Dretske, F. 1999. "The Mind's Awareness of Itself," *Philosophical Studies* 95: 103–24.
Dummett, M. 1973. *Frege: Philosophy of Language*, London: Duckworth.
Elbourne, P. D. 2005. *Situations and Individuals*, Cambridge, MA: MIT Press.
Enç, B. 1982. "Intentional States of Mechanical Devices," *Mind* 91: 161–83.
Evans, G. 1982. *The Varieties of Reference*, Oxford: Oxford University Press.
Fara, D. G. 2015a. "Names Are Predicates," *Philosophical Review* 124: 59–117.
Fara, D. G. 2015b. "'Literal' Uses of Proper Names," in A. Bianchi, ed. *On Reference*, Oxford: Oxford University Press: 251–79.
Farkas, K. 2003. "What Is Externalism?" *Philosophical Studies* 112: 187–208.
Farkas, K. 2008a. *The Subject's Point of View*, Oxford: Oxford University Press.
Farkas, K. 2008b. "Phenomenal Intentionality Without Compromise," *The Monist* 91: 273–93.
Feser, E. 1998. "Can Phenomenal Qualities Exist Unperceived?" *Journal of Consciousness Studies* 5: 405–14.
Field, H. 1977. "Logic, Meaning and Conceptual Role," *Journal of Philosophy* 69: 379–409.
Fish, B. 2008. "Disjunctivism, Indistinguishability, and the Nature of Hallucination," in Macpherson and Haddock 2008: 144–67.

Fodor, J. A. 1982. "Cognitive Science and the Twin-Earth Problem," *Notre Dame Journal of Formal Logic* 23: 98–118.
Fodor, J. A. 1984. "Semantics, Wisconsin Style," *Synthese* 59: 231–50.
Fodor, J. A. 1987. *Psychosemantics*, Cambridge, MA: MIT Press.
Fodor, J. A. 1990a. *A Theory of Content and Other Essays*, Cambridge, MA: MIT Press.
Fodor, J. A. 1990b. "A Theory of Content, I: The Problem," in Fodor 1990a: 51–87.
Fodor, J. A. 1990c. "A Theory of Content, II: The Theory," in Fodor 1990a: 89–136.
Fodor, J. A. 1994. *The Elm and the Expert*, Cambridge, MA: MIT Press.
Fodor, J. A. 1998. *Concepts: Where Cognitive Science Went Wrong*, New York: Oxford University Press.
Fodor, J. A., and Lepore, E. 1992. *Holism: A Shopper's Guide*, Oxford: Blackwell.
Fodor, J. A., and Lepore, E. 1994. "What *Is* the Connection Principle?" *Philosophy and Phenomenological Research* 54: 837–45.
Fodor, J. A., and Pylyshyn, Z. W. 2015. *Minds without Meanings: An Essay in the Content of Concepts*, Cambridge, MA: MIT Press.
Frege, G. 1884. *The Foundations of Arithmetic*, trans. J. L. Austin, Oxford: Blackwell, 1950.
Frege, G. 1891. "Letter to Husserl," in M. Beany, ed., *The Frege Reader*, Oxford: Blackwell Publishers, 1997: 149–50.
Frege, G. 1918. "Thoughts," in P. T. Geach, ed. and trans., and R. H. Stoothoff, trans., *Logical Investigations*, Oxford: Blackwell, 1977: 1–30.
Frey, C. 2013. "Phenomenal Presence," in Kriegel 2013: 71–92.
Gabriel, G., Hermes, H., Kambartel, F., Thiel, C., and Veraart, A., eds. (trans. H. Kaal). 1980. *Gottlob Frege: Philosophical and Mathematical Correspondence*, Chicago: University of Chicago Press.
Geach, P. T. 1957. *Mental Acts*, London: Routledge & Kegan Paul.
Gertler, B. 2015. "Self-Knowledge," *Stanford Encyclopedia of Philosophy*, ed. Edward N. Zalta, https://plato.stanford.edu/archives/spr2020/entries/self-knowledge/.
Geurts, B. 1997. "Good News about the Description Theory of Names," *Journal of Semantics* 14: 319–48.
Goff, P. 2012. "Does Mary Know I Experience Plus Rather Than Quus? A New Hard Problem," *Philosophical Studies* 160: 223–35.
Goff, P. 2017. *Consciousness and Fundamental Reality*, New York: Oxford University Press.
Goldman, A. 1993. "The Psychology of Folk Psychology," *Behavioral and Brain Sciences* 16: 15–28.
Gottlieb, J., and Rezaei, A. 2020. "When Nothing Looks Blue," *Synthese* 199: 2553–61.
Graham, G, Horgan, T. and Tienson, J. 2007. "Consciousness and Intentionality," in M. Velmans and S. Schneider, eds., *The Blackwell Companion to Consciousness*, Oxford: Blackwell: 468–84.
Graham, G., Horgan, T. and Tienson, J. 2009. "Phenomenology, Intentionality, and the Unity of the Mind," in *The Oxford Handbook of Philosophy of Mind*, B. McLaughlin, A. Beckermann and S. Walter, eds., Oxford: Clarendon Press: 512–538.
Gray, A. 2014. "Name-Bearing, Reference, and Circularity," *Philosophical Studies* 171: 207–31.
Grice, P. 1957. "Meaning," *Philosophical Review* 66 (3): 377–88.
Harman, G. 1973. *Thought*, Princeton: Princeton University Press.
Harman, G. 1987. "Nonsolipsistic Conceptual Role Semantics," in E. Lepore, ed., *New Directions in Semantics*, London: Academic Press: 55–81.
Harman, G. 1990. "The Intrinsic Quality of Experience," *Philosophical Perspectives 4: Action Theory and Philosophy of Mind*, Atascadero, CA: Ridgeview Publishing Co.: 31–52.

Heck, R. 2000. "Nonconceptual Content and the 'Space of Reasons'," *Philosophical Review* 109: 483–523.
Horgan, T. 1993. "From Supervenience to Superdupervenience: Meeting the Demands of a Material World," *Mind* 102: 555–86.
Horgan, T. 2011. "From Agentive Phenomenology to Cognitive Phenomenology: A Guide for the Perplexed," in Bayne and Montague 2011a: 57–78.
Horgan, T., and Graham, G. 2012. "Phenomenal Intentionality and Content Determinacy," in R. Schantz, ed. *Prospects for Meaning*, Berlin: de Gruyter: 321–44.
Horgan, T., and Kriegel, U. 2008. "Phenomenal Intentionality Meets the Extended Mind," *The Monist* 91: 347–73.
Horgan, T., and Tienson, J. 2002. "The Intentionality of Phenomenology and the Phenomenology of Intentionality," in D. Chalmers, ed. *Philosophy of Mind: Classical and Contemporary Readings*, Oxford: Oxford University Press: 520–33.
Jackendoff, R. 1996. "How Language Helps Us Think," *Pragmatics and Cognition* 4: 1–34.
Jackson, F., and Pinkerton, R. J. 1973. "On an Argument Against Sensory Items," *Mind* 82: 269–72.
Jacob, P. 1997. *What Minds Can Do: Intentionality in a Non-Intentional World*, Cambridge: Cambridge University Press.
Johnston, M. 2004. "The Obscure Object of Hallucination," *Philosophical Studies* 103: 113–83.
Jorba, M., and Vicente, A. 2020. "Phenomenal Contrast Arguments: What They Achieve," *Mind and Language* 35: 350–67.
Kant, I. 1781. *Critique of Pure Reason*, trans. N. K. Smith, New York: St. Martin's Press, 1965.
Kaplan, D. 1989. "Demonstratives," in J. Almog, J. Perry, and H. Wettstein, eds., *Themes from Kaplan*, Oxford: Oxford University Press: 481–614.
Katz, J. J. 1990. "Has the Description Theory of Names Been Refuted?", in G. Boolos, ed., *Meaning and Method: Essays in Honor of Hilary Putnam*, Cambridge: Cambridge University Press: 31–61.
Katz, J. J. 1992. "The New Intensionalism," *Mind* 101: 689–719.
Katz, J. J. 1994. "Names Without Bearers," *Philosophical Review* 103: 1–40.
Katz, J. J. 2001. "The End of Millianism: Multiple Bearers, Improper Names, and Compositional Meaning," *Journal of Philosophy* 98: 137–66.
Katz, J. J. 2004. *Sense, Reference, and Philosophy*, Oxford: Oxford University Press.
Kneale, W. C. 1962. *The Development of Logic*, Oxford: Oxford University Press.
Koksvik, O. 2015. "Phenomenal Contrast: A Critique," *American Philosophical Quarterly* 52: 321–34.
Kriegel, U. 2007. "The Phenomenologically Manifest," *Phenomenology and the Cognitive Sciences* 6 (1): 115–36.
Kriegel, U. 2011a. "Cognitive Phenomenology as the Basis of Unconscious Content," in Bayne and Montage 2011a: 79–102.
Kriegel, U. 2011b. *The Sources of Intentionality*, New York: Oxford University Press.
Kriegel, U., ed. 2013. *Phenomenal Intentionality: New Essays*, Oxford: Oxford University Press.
Kriegel, U. 2015. *The Varieties of Consciousness*, Oxford: Oxford University Press.
Kriegel, U. 2020. "Beyond the Neural Correlates of Consciousness," in Kriegel, ed., *The Oxford Handbook of the Philosophy of Consciousness*, Oxford: Oxford University Press: 261–76.
Kripke, S. 1979. "A Puzzle About Belief," in A. Margalit, ed., *Meaning and Use*, Dordrecht: Springer: 239–83, reprinted in S. Kripke, *Philosophical Troubles: Collected Papers Volume 1*, Oxford: Oxford University Press, 2011: 125–61.

Kripke, S. 1980. *Naming and Necessity*, Cambridge, MA: Harvard University Press.
Kripke, S. 1982. *Wittgenstein on Rules and Private Language*, Cambridge, MA: Harvard University Press.
Langendoen, D. T., and Postal, P. 1984. *The Vastness of Natural Languages*, Oxford: Blackwell.
Leckie, G. 2013. "The Double Life of Names," *Philosophical Studies* 165: 1139-60.
Levine, J. 1983. "Materialism and Qualia: The Explanatory Gap," *Pacific Philosophical Quarterly* 64: 354-61.
Levine, J. 2011. "On the Phenomenology of Thought," in Bayne and Montague 2011a: 103-20.
Lewis, D. 1970. "General Semantics," *Synthese* 22: 18-67.
Lewis, D. 1986. *On the Plurality of Worlds*, Oxford: Blackwell.
Lewis, D. 1998. "Index, Context, and Content," in *Papers in Philosophical Logic*, Cambridge: Cambridge University Press: 21-44.
Loar, B. 1976. "The Semantics of Singular Terms," *Philosophical Studies* 30: 353-77.
Loar, B. 1981. *Mind and Meaning*, Cambridge: Cambridge University Press.
Loar, B. 1987. "Subjective Intentionality," *Philosophical Topics* 15: 89-124.
Loar, B. 1988. "Social Content and Psychological Content," in R. H. Grimm and D. D. Merrill, eds., *Contents of Thought: Proceedings of the 1985 Oberlin Colloquium in Philosophy*, Tucson, AZ: University of Arizona Press: 99-110.
Loar, B. 1997. "Phenomenal States," in N. Block, O. Flanagan, and G. Güzeldere, eds., *The Nature of Consciousness*, Cambridge, MA: MIT Press: 597-616.
Loar, B. 2003. "Phenomenal Intentionality as the Basis of Mental Content," in M. Hahn and B. Ramberg, eds., *Reflections and Replies: Essays on the Philosophy of Tyler Burge*, Cambridge, MA: MIT Press: 229-58.
Lockwood, M. 1989. *Mind, Brain and the Quantum*, Oxford: Blackwell Publishers.
Lockwood, M. 1998. "Unsensed Phenomenal Qualities: A Defence," *Journal of Consciousness Studies* 5: 415-18.
Lormand, E. 1996. "Nonphenomenal Consciousness," *Noûs* 30: 242-61.
Lycan, W. G. 1987. *Consciousness*, Cambridge, MA: MIT Press.
Lycan, W. G. 1996. *Consciousness and Experience*, Cambridge, MA: MIT Press.
Lycan, W. G. 2001. "The Case for Phenomenal Externalism," *Philosophical Perspectives* 15: *Metaphysics*, Atascadero, CA: Ridgeview Publishing Co.: 17-35.
Lycan, W. G. 2008. "Phenomenal Intentionalities," *American Philosophical Quarterly* 45: 233-52.
MacFarlane, J. 2007. "Nonindexical Contextualism," *Synthese* 166: 231-50.
MacFarlane, J. 2014. *Assessment Sensitivity: Relative Truth and its Applications*, Oxford: Oxford University Press.
Macpherson, F., and Haddock, A., eds. 2008. *Disjunctivism: Perception, Action, Knowledge*, Oxford: Oxford University Press.
Marcus, R. B. 1983. "Rationality and Believing the Impossible," *Journal of Philosophy* 80: 321-38.
Marcus, R. B. 1990. "Some Revisionary Proposals about Belief and Believing," *Philosophy and Phenomenological Research*, L Supplement: 133-53.
Martin, C. B. 2008. *The Mind in Nature*, Oxford: Clarendon Press.
Martin, M. G. F. 2000. "An Eye Directed Outward," in Crispin Wright, Barry C. Smith, and Cynthia Macdonald, eds., *Knowing Our Own Minds*, Oxford: Oxford University Press: 99-122.

Martin, M.G.F. 2002, "The Transparency of Experience", *Mind and Language* 17: 376–425.
Matushansky, O. 2005. "Call me Ishmael," *Proceedings of Sinn und Bedeutung* 9: 226–40.
Matushansky, O. 2008. "On the Linguistic Complexity of Proper Names," *Linguistics and Philosophy* 21: 573–627.
McClelland, T. 2016. "Gappiness and the Case for Liberalism About Phenomenal Properties," *Philosophical Quarterly* 264: 536–58.
McDowell, J. 1984. "*De Re* Senses," *Philosophical Quarterly* 34: 283–94.
McGinn, C. 1977. "Charity, Interpretation, and Belief," *Journal of Philosophy* 74: 521–35.
McGinn, C. 1982. "The Structure of Content," in Woodfield 1982: 207–59.
McGinn, C. 1989. "Can We Solve the Mind-Body Problem?" *Mind* 98: 349–66.
McGinn, C. 1999. "The Appearance of Colour," in *Knowledge and Reality: Selected Essays*, Oxford: Clarendon Press: 314–25.
Mendelovici, A. 2018. *The Phenomenal Basis of Intentionality*, Oxford: Oxford University Press.
Metzinger, T., ed. 1995. *Conscious Experience*. Paderborn: Schöningh/Imprint Academic.
Millikan, R. 1984. *Language, Thought and Other Biological Categories*, Cambridge, MA: MIT Press.
Millikan, R. 1989. "Biosemantics," *Journal of Philosophy* 86: 281–97.
Millikan, R. 2000. *On Clear and Confused Ideas*, Cambridge: Cambridge University Press.
Millikan, R. 2017. *Beyond Concepts: Unicepts, Language, and Natural Information*, Oxford: Oxford University Press.
Montague, M. 2016. *The Given*, Oxford: Oxford University Press.
Moore, G. E. 1962. "Propositions," in *Some Main Problems of Philosophy*, New York: Collier Books: 66–87.
Moran, R. 2001. *Authority and Estrangement*, Princeton: Princeton University Press.
Nagel, T. 1974. "What Is It Like to Be a Bat?" *Philosophical Review* 83(4): 435–50.
Neander, K. 1995. "Misrepresenting and Malfunctioning," *Philosophical Studies* 79: 109–14.
Neander, K, 2012. "Toward an Informational Teleosemantics," in D. Ryder, J. Kingsbury and K, Williford, eds., *Millikan and Her Critics*, Malden: Wiley-Blackwell: 21–40.
Neander, K. 2017. *A Mark of the Mental: A Defense of Informational Teleosemantics*, Cambridge, MA: MIT Press.
Nelson, M. 2002. "Descriptivism Defended," *Noûs* 36: 408–35.
Nida-Rümelin, M. 1995. "What Mary Couldn't Know: Beliefs About Phenomenal States," in Metzinger 1995: 219–41.
Nordby, K. 1990. "Vision in a Complete Achromat: A Personal Account," in R. F. Hess, L. T. Sharpe, and K. Nordby, eds., *Night Vision: Basic, Clinical and Applied Aspects*, Cambridge: Cambridge University Press: 290–315.
Papineau, D. 1998. "Teleosemantics and Indeterminacy," *Australasian Journal of Philosophy* 76: 1–14.
Papineau, D. 2002. *Thinking About Consciousness*, Oxford: Clarendon Press.
Pautz, A. 2013. "Does Phenomenology Ground Mental Content?" in Kriegel 2013: 194–234.
Peacocke, C. 1983. *Sense and Content: Experience, Thought and Their Relations*, Oxford: Oxford University Press.
Peacocke, C. 1998. "Conscious Attitudes, Attention, and Self-Knowledge," in C. Wright, B. C. Smith, and C. Macdonald, eds., *Knowing Our Own Minds*, Oxford: Oxford University Press: 63–98.
Perry, J. 1979. "The Problem of the Essential Indexical," *Noûs* 13: 3–21.
Pitt, D. 1999. "In Defense of Definitions," *Philosophical Psychology* 12: 139–56.

Pitt, D. 2004. "The Phenomenology of Cognition, Or, *What Is It Like to Think That P?*" *Philosophy and Phenomenological Research* 69: 1–36.

Pitt, D. 2009. "Intentional Psychologism," *Philosophical Studies* 146: 117–38.

Pitt, D. 2011. "Introspection, Phenomenality and the Availability of Intentional Content," in Bayne and Montague 2011a: 141–73.

Pitt, D. 2013. "Indexical Thought," in Kriegel 2013: 49–70.

Pitt, D. 2016. "Conscious Belief," Symposium on Tim Crane's *Aspects of Psychologism*, *Rivista Internazionale di Filosofia e Pscologia* 7: 121–6.

Pitt, D. 2017. "The Paraphenomenal Hypothesis," *Analysis* 77: 735–41.

Pitt, D. 2018. "What Kind of Science is Linguistics?" in C. Behme and M. Neef, eds., *Essays on Linguistic Realism*, Amsterdam: John Benjamins Publishing: 7–20.

Place, U. T. 1956. "Is Consciousness a Brain Process?" *British Journal of Psychology* 47: 44–50.

Putnam, H. 1973. "Meaning and Reference," *The Journal of Philosophy* 70: 699–711.

Putnam, H. 1975. "The Meaning of 'Meaning'," *Minnesota Studies in the Philosophy of Science* 7: 131–193.

Prinz, J. 2011. "The Sensory Basis of Cognitive Phenomenology," in Bayne and Montague 2011a: 174–96.

Quine, W. V. O. 1960. *Word and Object*, Cambridge, MA: MIT Press.

Raffman, D. 1995. "On the Persistence of Phenomenology," in Metzinger 1995: 293–308.

Rami, D. 2014. "The Use-Conditional Indexical Conception of Proper Names," *Philosophical Studies* 168: 119–50.

Robinson, H. 1972. "Professor Armstrong On 'Non-Physical Sensory Items," *Mind* 81: 84–6.

Rosenthal, D. 2006. *Consciousness and Mind*, Oxford: Oxford University Press.

Russell, B. 1911. "Knowledge by Acquaintance and Knowledge by Description," *Proceedings of the Aristotelian Society* 11: 108–28.

Russell, B. 1912. *The Problems of Philosophy*, London: Thornton Butterworth Ltd: 46–59.

Russell, B. 1918–19, "The Philosophy of Logical Atomism", *The Monist* 28: 495–527; 29: 32–63, 190–222, 345–80.

Sacchi, E. 2016. "On the Relationship Between Cognitive and Sensory Phenomenology," *Phenomenology and Mind* 10: 122–39.

Sawyer, S. 2010. "The Modified Predicate Theory of Proper Names," in S. Sawyer, ed., *New Waves in Philosophy of Language*, London: Palgrave Macmillan: 206–26.

Schoubye, A. J. 2017. "Type-Ambiguous Names," *Mind* 126: 715–67.

Schwitzgebel, E. 2011. "The Unreliability of Naïve Introspection," in *Perplexities of Consciousness*, Cambridge, MA: MIT Press: 117–37.

Searle, J. 1980. "Minds, Brains, and Programs," *Behavioral and Brain Sciences* 3: 417–57.

Searle, J. 1987. "Indeterminacy, Empiricism, and the First Person," *Journal of Philosophy* 84: 123–46.

Searle, J. 1991. "Consciousness, Unconsciousness and Intentionality," *Philosophical Issues* 1: 45–66.

Searle, J. 1992. *The Rediscovery of the Mind*, Cambridge, MA: MIT Press.

Segal, G. 2000. *A Slim Book about Narrow Content*, Cambridge, MA: MIT Press.

Shea, N. 2018. *Representation in Cognitive Science*, Oxford: Oxford University Press.

Siewert, C. 1998. *The Significance of Consciousness*, Princeton: Princeton University Press.

Siewert, C. 2011. "Phenomenal Thought," in Bayne and Montague 2011a: 236–67.

Siewert, C. 2016. "For Analytic Phenomenology," in Harald A. Wiltsche and Sonja Rinofner-Kreidl, eds., *Analytic and Continental Philosophy: Methods and Perspectives*.

Proceedings of the 37th International Wittgenstein Symposium, Berlin: De Gruyter: 95–110.
Smithies, D. 2012. "The Mental Lives of Zombies," *Philosophical Perspectives 26: Philosophy of Mind*, Atascadero, CA: Ridgeview Publishing Co.: 343–72.
Soames, S. 1998. "The Modal Argument: Wide Scope and Rigidified Descriptions," *Noûs* 32: 1–22.
Soames, S. 2002. *Beyond Rigidity: The Unfinished Semantic Agenda of Naming and Necessity*, Oxford: Oxford University Press.
Soteriou, M. 2007. "Content and the Stream of Consciousness," *Philosophical Perspectives 21: Philosophy of Mind*, Atascadero, CA: Ridgeview Publishing Co.: 543–68.
Soteriou, M. 2009. "Mental Agency, Conscious Thinking, and Phenomenal Character," in L. O'Brien and M. Soteriou, eds., *Mental Actions*, Oxford: Oxford University Press: 231–52.
Stampe, D. 1977. "Towards a Causal Theory of Linguistic Representation," *Midwest Studies in Philosophy* 2: 42–63.
Sterelny, K. 1990. *The Representational Theory of Mind*, Oxford: Blackwell.
Stoerig, P., and Cowey, A. 1990. "Wavelength Sensitivity in Blindsight," *Nature* 342: 916–18.
Strawson, G. 1986. *Freedom and Belief*, Oxford: Oxford University Press.
Strawson, G. 1994. *Mental Reality*, Cambridge, MA: MIT Press.
Strawson, G. 2004. "Real intentionality," *Phenomenology and the Cognitive Sciences* 3: 287–313.
Strawson, G. 2008. "Real Intentionality 3: Why Intentionality Entails Consciousness," in *Real Materialism and Other Essays*, Oxford: Oxford University Press: 281–306.
Strawson, G. 2010. *Mental Reality* (2nd edition), Cambridge, MA: MIT Press.
Strawson, G. 2015. "Real Materialism" (revised with new postscript), in T. Alter and Y. Nagasawa, eds., *Consciousness in the Physical World: Perspectives on Russellian Monism*, Oxford: Oxford University Press: 161–208.
Strawson, G. 2019. "A Hundred Years of Consciousness: 'a Long Training in Absurdity'," *Estudios de Filosofia* 59: 9–43.
Strawson, P. F. 1974. *Subject and Predicate in Logic and Grammar*, Farnham: Ashgate Publishing.
Tarski, A. 1943. "The Semantic Conception of Truth and the Foundations of Semantics," *Philosophy and Phenomenological Research* 4: 341–76.
Taylor, H. 2017a. "Powerful Qualities and Pure Powers," *Philosophical Studies* 175: 1423–40.
Taylor, H. 2017b. "Powerful Qualities, Phenomenal Concepts and the New Challenge to Physicalism," *Australasian Journal of Philosophy* 96: 53–66.
Thomas, N., "Mental Imagery," *Stanford Encyclopedia of Philosophy*, ed. Edward N. Zalta, https://plato.stanford.edu/archives/fall2021/entries/mental-imagery/.
Thompson, B. 2008. "Representationalism and the Argument from Hallucination," *Pacific Philosophical Quarterly* 89: 384–412.
Tye, M. 2000. *Consciousness, Color and Content*, Cambridge, MA: MIT Press.
Tye, M. 2011. "Knowing What It Is Like," in J. Bengson and M. Moffett, eds., *Knowing How: Essays on Knowledge, Mind, and Action*, Oxford: Oxford University Press: 300–13.
Tye, M. 2015. "Yes, Phenomenal Character Really Is Out There in the World," *Philosophy and Phenomenological Research* 91: 483–8.
Tye, M., and Sainsbury, M. 2011. "An Originalist Theory of Concepts," *Proceedings of the Aristotelian Society* 85: 101–24.
Tye, M., and Wright, B. 2011. "Is There a Phenomenology of Thought?" in Bayne and Montague 2011a: 326–44.

Villanueva, E., ed., 1991. *Philosophical Issues 1: Consciousness*, Atascadero, CA: Ridgeview Publishing Co.

Weiskrantz, L. 1986. *Blindsight: A Case Study and Implications*, Oxford: Oxford University Press.

Wikforss, A. 2001. "Social Externalism and Conceptual Errors," *Philosophical Quarterly* 51: 217–31.

Williamson, T. 1990. *Identity and Discrimination*, Oxford: Blackwell.

Wilson, G. 1978. "On Definite and Indefinite Descriptions," *Philosophical Review* 87: 48–76.

Woodfield, A., ed. 1982. *Thought and Object: Essays on Intentionality*. Oxford: Clarendon Press.

Woodworth, R. S. 1906. "Imageless Thought," *Journal of Philosophy, Psychology and Scientific Methods* 3: 701–8.

Yli-Vakkuri, J. 2018. "Semantic Externalism without Thought Experiments," *Analysis* 78: 81–9.

Index

Achromatopsia 184
Acquaintance 14–15, 42–8, 54–5, 57–8, 60, 122, 132, 146
  knowledge 14–15, 43, 45, 55, 58, 142
Analyticity 135–6, 151–2, 154–5, 169
Anti-individualism 87, 92–6, 98, 99–100, 103–4, 106–7, 109, 161
  perceptual 109
Agnosticism, about mind-body problem 2, 7, 11–12
Antonymy 135–6, 169
Armstrong, David 19, 176
Aspectual shape 1, 24, 174–6
Attitude reports 132

Bach, Kent 144, 151, 154–6, 168–9, 206
Bayne, Tim 76–8
Bilgrami, Akeel 100
Blindsight 16, 174, 182–3, 185–6, 192
Block, Ned 5, 7
Brentano, Franz 24
Burge, Tyler 6, 15, 30–1, 87, 90–110, 144, 146, 209
Byrne, Alex 49–53

Carruthers, Peter 69–74
Causal-informational theory
  of conceptual content 20, 29
  of perceptual content 109
Chalmers, David 4, 11, 133
Coleman, Sam 182
Conceptual-role theory of content 23, 55, 199
Connection principle 24
Connee, Earl 43–4
Consciousness 2, 4–7, 10–12, 24, 26, 38–9, 48–9, 56–63, 70, 73–4, 76, 83–86, 127, 173–85, 189–95, 199–201
  access 7, 60
  degrees of 182
  hard problem of 70
  self- 127
  stream of 15, 75–6
  unconscious 17, 193
Content 1, 14–22, 24, 30, 32–6, 39, 41, 48–50, 53, 58–60, 66, 68, 72, 76, 80, 85, 118, 123, 153, 160, 170, 205

  causal role of 199–201, 209–10
  conceptual 14, 16–17, 19, 22, 25–7, 31, 34, 36–8, 57, 69–70, 74, 78, 81–4, 87, 107, 120, 136, 139–42, 167, 203–4, 206–7
  externalism (*see also* Externalism) 26, 29, 87–105, 107, 200
  extrinsic 55–6
  indexical 125–38
  internalism (*see also* Internalism) 14, 29, 31, 36–8
  intrinsic 56, 204
  metalinguistic 146, 155
  narrow 23, 26, 33, 78, 111, 121, 203
  nominal 143–4, 147, 167–72
  perceptual 28–9, 33, 73–4, 77, 109–10
  phenomenal 25, 42, 56–8, 64, 69, 79, 82–4, 86, 120, 122, 138, 140, 143, 173, 178, 181, 198, 200, 203–4, 207
  propositional 40, 42, 64, 76–7, 86, 122, 143, 161
  singular 143, 157, 206
  unconscious 173–4, 176–81, 197, 202
  wide 23, 26, 33, 38, 78, 121
Crane, Tim 77, 88

Davidson, Donald 170–1
Demonstrative concepts 122, 125, 171–2
  phenomenal 138, 141
  quotational 140
Descartes, Rene 2, 9, 11, 17, 112, 174
Dennett, Daniel 179, 185
Direct realism 115, 207
Direct reference 31, 143, 155, 204–6
Disjunction problem 20–1, 25, 27
Disjunctivism about perception 33, 116–7
Dretske, Fred 13–14, 19, 21–2, 29, 58, 114, 192, 197–8, 200–1
Dreyfus, Hubert 2
Dummett, Michael 151

Elbourne, Paul 146
Eliminativism 7
Emergentism 3, 7
Enç, Berent 19

224 INDEX

Evans, Gareth 49, 50, 120, 125, 141
Externalism 15, 26, 29–31, 55, 87–91, 110, 112, 122, 161, 210
Extrospection 49–50, 53–4

Fara, Delia Graff 146–50
Farkas, Katalin 37, 87, 187
Feser, Edward 187, 191
Fish, William 116
Fodor, Jerry 1, 4, 19–24, 100–3, 176, 197, 200
Føllesdol, Dagfinn 2
Fregean senses 208
Frege, Gottlob 16, 41, 82, 151–2, 155, 160–1, 208–9
Freud, Sigmund 173

Geach, Peter 75–6, 170
General thoughts 128, 136
Geurts 146
Gila monster 67
Gottlieb, Joseph 115
Graham, George 16, 173, 178–9
Gray, Aidan 146
Grice, Paul 118

Heck, Richard 77
Heidegger, Martin 2
Horgan, Terry 16, 73, 173, 178–9
Husserl, Edmund 2–3, 24, 208

Indexical thought 15, 118–26, 128, 131–5
Intentionality (*see also* Phenomenal intentionality) 14, 17, 19, 24–6, 112, 118, 173–82, 192, 197, 201, 203, 205, 209
  conceptual 1, 13–14, 23–4, 26, 37, 109
  derived 118, 173, 178, 182
  extensional 203
  intensional 203
  linguistic 118
  of perceptual experience 29
  of thought thesis 14, 16
  unconscious 175, 178
Internalism 14–15, 29, 31, 119
Introspection 3, 5–7, 10, 14–15, 25, 58–9, 64–5, 74–5, 83, 85, 112, 191, 209

Jacob, Pierre 21
Jackson, Frank 15, 44, 71 138
Johnston, Mark 114

Kant, Immanuel 2, 151–2
Kaplan, David 15, 30, 119–20, 127, 129–30, 136–7, 153, 163
Katz, Jerrold 144, 151–2, 154, 168
Kneale, William 144, 153–4
Knowledge argument 138

Kriegel, Uriah 16, 38, 173, 179–80
Kripke, Saul 15, 16, 25, 30, 143–4, 150–9, 162, 165–8

Language of thought hypothesis 79
Leckie, Gail 146
Levine, Joseph 39, 54–60
Lewis, David 120, 135, 203
Loar, Brian 13, 30, 141
Lockwood, Michael 187, 191
Lormand, Eric 62–3
Lycan, William 114–6, 192

MacFarlane, John 90, 123
Martin, C. B. 19
Martin, Michael 50
Materialism (*see also* Physicalism) 10–11
Matushansky, Ora 146
McClelland, Tom 71, 76–8
McDowell, John 120, 125, 141
McGinn, Colin 30, 114
Mendelovici, Angela 24–5, 83–6, 208
Mentalese 55, 57–9
Mental representation 20–3, 26, 35–6, 48, 56, 58, 109
Merleau-Ponty, Maurice 2
Millikan, Ruth 13, 197
Montague, Michelle 26–27, 29, 110
Moore, G. E. 64
Moran, Richard 49–50
Mysterianism 12

Nagel, Thomas 7
Naturalism 1, 5, 10
Neander, Karen 13, 22
Necessary truths 63, 128, 136–7, 151–2, 162–3, 169, 173
Nida-Rümelin, Martine 44

Panpsychism 10–11
Papineau, David 3
Paraphenomenal hypothesis 112, 114, 116
Peacocke, Christopher 64, 185
Phenomenal compositionality 15, 79, 81
Phenomenal contrast arguments 64–5, 67
Phenomenal demonstratives 138
Phenomenal externalism 15, 31, 112
Phenomenal intentionalism 205, 209
Phenomenal intentionality 13–14, 19, 26, 29–30, 76
  of perception 26
  of thought thesis 1, 14–17, 24, 26, 30–1, 70, 74, 76, 82, 84–5, 119, 121, 140–1, 143–4, 169–70, 173, 181, 201, 204, 211
  research program 1, 13–14, 29

Phenomenality principle 7, 38, 61
Phenomenal sorites 16, 174, 186, 189, 191–2
Phenomenology
  analytic 2–3, 5–7, 10, 13–14, 24
  cognitive 1, 65, 74, 179
  conceptual (*see also* Phenomenology, cognitive) 1, 13–15, 17, 25, 37, 63–70, 72, 74–81, 121, 161, 192, 204, 208–210
  Husserlian 2, 30
  perceptual 6, 74, 109
  propositional (*see also* Phenomenology, cognitive) 1, 36–8, 40, 57, 59, 60, 64, 67, 122
  unconscious 16, 83, 85, 173–4, 181–2, 185, 192–3, 195, 201
Physicalism 3–4, 15
Principle of phenomenal difference 7, 61
Principle of phenomenal immiscibility 7, 15–16, 78, 140, 170
Principle of phenomenal individuation 7, 62
Principle of phenomenal purity 7, 16, 122, 170, 206
Proliferation problem 20
Proper names 15, 143, 147, 155, 163
  description theory of 150
Propositional hallucination 14, 31, 33, 36
Propositional illusion 14, 31, 34–6
Psychologism 41, 42, 77
Putnam, Hilary 15, 30–1, 87–91, 100, 203

Qualia externalism (*see also* phenomenal externalism) 30
Quine, Willard Van Orman 20–1, 25, 27, 151

Raffman, Diana 185–7
Rami, Dolf 146
Reductive representationalism 115, 117, 192
Rezaei, Ali 115
Rigid designator 15, 136, 155, 159
Robinson, Howard 190
Rosenthal, David 189
Russell, Bertrand 10, 43, 144, 146, 152, 159, 161
Russellian propositions 160–1, 163–4
Ryle, Gilbert 112

Sacchi, Elisabetta 65–6
Sainsbury, Mark 15, 141
Sartre, Jean-Paul 2

Sawyer, Sarah 146
Schoubye, Anders 146, 150
Searle, John 1, 16, 24–5, 173–81, 197
Self-knowledge 14, 48–59
Siewert, Charles 2, 24, 64, 67
Smithies, Declan 16, 63, 173, 180–1
Soteriou, Matthew 76
Split-brain 194–5
Stalnaker, Robert 120
Stampe, Dennis 20
Stopping problem 20–1, 25, 27–8, 30
Strawson, Galen 1, 10–11, 16–17, 21, 24–5, 37, 40, 67, 173, 176–8, 180–1, 193, 195–6

Tarski, Alfred 170
Thompson, Brad 115
Turing, Alan 19, 24, 197
Twin Earth 88
Tye, Michael 14–15, 31, 46, 74–6, 114–6, 141, 192

Unconscious contentlessness 195–99, 201–2
Unconscious qualia (*see also* Phenomenology, unconscious) 17, 183, 186, 190, 192
Unconscious thought 16, 73, 173–4, 181, 195, 201
Understanding 24, 40, 44, 55, 65–6, 73, 88, 92–8, 107, 120, 131, 146
  experience 1
  hallucination 69

Veillet, Bénédicte 69–74
Vicente, Agustin 65–6

Weiskrantz, Lawrence 183
Wikforss, Åsa 100
Williamson, Timothy 187
Wittgenstein, Ludwig 49
Woodruff-Smith, David 2
Woodworth, R. S. 37, 140
Wright, Briggs 74–6

Yli-Vakkuri, Juhani 110–11

Zahavi, Dan 2
Zombie 70–3, 141
  cognitive 180
  conceptual 72–3